Expressing Identities
in the Basque Arena

World Anthropology

Series Editors Wendy James & N. J. Allen

* Forthcoming

Expressing Identities in the Basque Arena

Jeremy MacClancy

Professor of Social Anthropology
Oxford Brookes University

James Currey
OXFORD

School for Advanced Research Press
SANTA FE

James Currey
73 Botley Road
Oxford OX2 OBS
www.jamescurrey.co.uk

School for Advanced Research Press
Post Office Box 2188
Santa Fe, New Mexico 87504-2188
www.sarpress.sarweb.edu

British Library Cataloguing in Publication Data
MacClancy, Jeremy
Expressing identities in the Basque arena. - (World
anthropology)
1. Nationalism - Spain - Pays Vasco 2. National
characteristics, Basque
I. Title
320.5'49'0944716

ISBN 978-0-85255-994-9 (James Currey cloth)
ISBN 978-0-85255-989-5 (James Currey paper)

Library of Congress Cataloging-in-Publication Data
MacClancy, Jeremy.
Expressing identities in the Basque arena / Jeremy MacClancy.
    p. cm. -- (World anthropology series)
Includes bibliographical references and index.
ISBN 978-1-930618-99-2 (cl : alk. paper) --
ISBN 978-1-934691-00-7 (pa : alk. paper)
1. National characteristics, Basque. 2. País Vasco (Spain)--Civilization.
3. Nationalism--Spain--País Vasco. I. Title.

DP302.B467M33 2007
320.540946'6--dc22

2007028759

Typeset in 10/12 pt Monotype Photina
by Long House Publishing Services, Cumbria, UK
Printed and bound in Malaysia

Contents

Illustrations

Acknowledgements

Finishing this book has taken me much longer than I expected. My debts have accumulated accordingly. I am sincerely grateful to all those who helped me, whether knowingly or not. But I have not space, nor desire for a list almost as long as the electoral roll. I have to choose and here apologise to anyone who thought they should be on my list of acknowledgements but are not.

First must come my Cirauqui landlords, Francisco Arraiza, his (since deceased) parents Luis and Jesusa, his daughter Pili, her husband Gustavo, and especially his wife María Jesus Goldaráz, who spent such time teaching me about Cirauqui and its inhabitants. Milu, his brother Chuchin, and our friend Javier, were a constant source of support, friendship, and information. Their *cuadrilla*, 'Los Tajudos' (Navarran dialect, 'The Badgers'), accepted me as a full participant in their weekly dinners and in their collective entry to the fancy-dress competition in the village's annual fiestas. (We usually won.) I am also particularly grateful for their help to: María José Dallo, Belen Gurrucharri, Josefina and Txus Laita. All the above, and almost all the other villagers, extended to me a degree of hospitality which I had only ever previously experienced among my Irish kin.

In Pamplona I shared the flat of the long-suffering Juan Luis Ainciburu, who patiently put up with my frustrating Castilian, and who introduced me to his circle of friends. The Navarran historians Angel Pascual and Angel García-Sanz assisted me constantly with my academic enquiries and suggested avenues of enquiry I had not thought of travelling down. In Bilbao Joseba Aguirreazkuenaga and Concepción de la Rua were exemplars of academic fraternity, sharing ideas, providing assistance and ever ready to offer hospitality. For assistance with my work on particular chapters, I thank Oscar Alonso, Borja Bilbao, Francisco Chacón, Javier González de Durana, Vicky Hayward, Ruiz Olabuenaga, and Patxo Unzueta. I am particularly grateful to the Basque anthropologists Kepa Fernández de Larrinoa and Josetxu Martínez Montoya for their aid and friendship.

The funds which enabled me to do fieldwork were generously provided by the ESRC Postdoctoral Research Fellowship Committee, Wolfson College, University of Oxford, the Ministerios de Asuntos Exteriores and de Cultura of the Spanish Government, the Nuffield Foundation, the School of Social Sciences, Oxford Brookes University, and the Arts and Humanities Research Board. Versions of certain chapters were given as seminars at St Andrews

University, the University of Surrey, the University of Oxford, Oxford Brookes University, the University of the Basque Country, the Public University of Navarre, and the Instituto de Gerónimo de Ustáriz, Pamplona. I am grateful to all of the above.

Rodney Needham was an unwavering friend throughout the years I was researching and writing this book. Though he died while it was in press, his memory continues to be an intellectual lodestar.

Sections of some of these chapters have appeared before, usually in a radically different form: a version of Chapter Two appeared in Sharon Macdonald (ed.) *Inside European identities*, Oxford: Berg, 1993, pp. 84–97; some of Chapter Three was first published in Jeremy MacClancy (ed.) *Sport, identity and ethnicity*, Oxford: Berg, 1996, pp. 181–200, a Spanish translation of it is included in F. Xavier Medina and Ricardo Sánchez (eds) *Culturas en juego: ensayos de antropología del deporte en España*, Barcelona: Icaria, 2003, pp. 137–58; extracts from Chapter Four were published, in Castilian, in *Euskonews & Media* (www.euskonews.com) in 2007; fragments of Chapter Five were published in 'Biological Basques, Sociologically Speaking' in Malcolm Chapman (ed.) *Social and biological aspects of ethnicity*, Oxford: Oxford University Press, 1993, pp. 92–129; an earlier version of Chapter Six was in Jeremy MacClancy (ed.) *Contesting art: art, politics and identity in the modern world*, Oxford: Berg, 1997, pp. 183–214; paragraphs in Chapter Seven were first printed in *Focaal*, no. 29, 1997, pp. 91–100. I thank Berg Publishers, the editors of *Focaal* and Oxford University Press for permission to reproduce this material.

In 2003, an earlier version of Chapter Three won the 'First Award' of the Sophie Coe Essay Prize in Food History.

Note on Terminology

I recognize that any characterization of the people(s) who call themselves and/or are called by others 'Basques' is unremittingly political in consequence. In such a highly mobilized society, no definition of 'the Basques' is innocent: all are constructions serving one set of interests or another. To be pedantically correct, I should therefore place every single use of the term in this book in a pair of inverted commas. But that would weary the reader and disrupt the text. I thus recommend that readers imagine the existence of these unprinted pairs every single time they encounter the phrase in this text. And if, as I suppose, that exacting strategy proves too tiring, may I suggest that readers please accept my recognition of this problem and that I do not yet know a suitably readable solution to it?

For similar reasons and in the hope that my Basque colleagues will forgive me, I have given all place-names in their most common (i.e. Castilian) versions. However in order not to pepper the text with accents, all place-names are shorn of their accents. In recent decades, some Basque authors have 'Basquized' their first and surnames, e.g. changing 'ch' to 'tx', 'v' to 'b'. So as not to confuse readers interested in chasing up references, I have in each case used the particular spelling of the author's name which he or she has employed in each particular article. Unless otherwise stated, all translations are my own. Following Iberian academic practice, endnotes provide the first surname of the author(s); references provide both his or her surnames, where they are given.

Acronyms & Glossary

ACRONYMS

ETA	Euskadi ta Askatasuna ('The Basque Country and Freedom')
HB	Herri Batasuna ('Popular Unity')
PNV	Partido Nacionlista Vasco ('The Basque Nationalist Party')
PSOE	Partido Socialista Obrero Español ('The Spanish Socialist Worker Party')
UPN	Unión del Pueblo Navarro ('The Union of the Navarran People')

GLOSSARY

abertzale	Basque nationalist
etarra	ETA combatant
Euskera	The Basque language
ikastola	School where Euskera is the medium of communication
maketos	Non-Basque immigrants to the Basque area (a pejorative term)
vasquista	Promoter or supporter of Basque culture

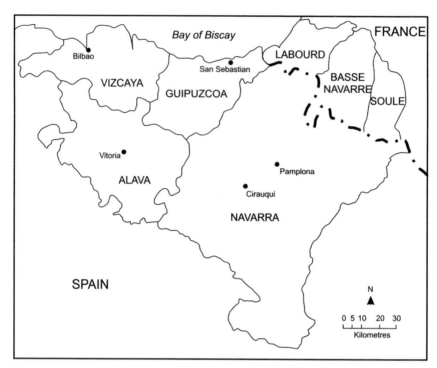

The Basque provinces and sites of fieldwork

1
Of Important General Matters

My father was Irish. In 1946 he accompanied his eldest brother on his first trip over to Britain. On landing at Liverpool, they went to the toilets. While both were standing at the urinals, my uncle looked at the porcelain, then at my father. 'No Shanks here John', he said, smiling.

Over the decades my father told me this anecdote several times. It amused him so much because, I think, it demonstrated in a familial, deeply unpretentious way the nature of national difference. In postwar Britain, my uncle had learnt, even something as everyday as urinals were made by different companies. Shanks and Co. had cornered the Irish trade; other firms dominated the British market. Politicians, poets and other governors of the tongue might propound grand theories about the substance of a nation but, to people like my middle-class Irish forebears, nationality had almost as much to do to with Shanks and that ilk as it did with Finn MacCool and other mythic heroes of the Celtic Renaissance.

My father's delight in telling this vignette may well also lie in the way it gently subverts or implicitly criticizes the bombast of nationalist politicians who liked to tell people what nation they needed. Though a fluent speaker of Gaelic himself, he had had enough of stern schoolmasters forcing the language onto native speakers of Hibernian English. In contrast to the would-be stirring vision of nationalist prophets, he maintained a profoundly unassuming Irishness: one where a love of Joyce, an appreciation of the place of Shanks, and a distanced scepticism of jingoistic historicizing all easily blended together. In short, he upheld what I like to call an unofficial nationalism.

In this book I wish to investigate the diversity of ways by which group identities can be expressed in such a highly politicized arena as the Basque one, where at times it can seem as though nationalism can pervade everything, no matter how apparently small or trivial. In particular, I wish to pay attention to the tensions and dovetailings between everyday kinds of nationalism and the more official versions promoted by ideologues and party leaders. I wish, in other words, to report a sense of what nationalism means, not just to prominent politicians, but to all those who live within its ambience, whether they be teenage activists, football fanatics, gastronomes, anti-racists, painters or museum visitors. In this way I wish to draw out the (usually neglected) cultural dimensions of nationalism. Of course these sorts of phenomena, whether remarkably lasting or relatively ephemeral, need to be placed in their appropriate contexts, however broad they may be: the dynamic configurations of the social, political and economic forces in play at the time, how they shape and are shaped by the cultural field within which and with which they interact.

Cultural accounts of nationalism in Europe have been strangely neglected in the academic literature. For years now there has a plethora of studies of the roles of ideology, the intrigue of political parties, the clash of social classes, and the conflicts between centres and peripheries with respect to nationalisms in Europe. But there has been very little on cultural aspects of these political phenomena, which are generally (however grudgingly) acknowledged as key to our contemporary socio-political order.

This study attempts to redress this surprising imbalance. I say 'surprising' because I do not understand how we can try to comprehend nationalist action unless we take into account the culture of a nationalism, unless we strive to know the leading concepts maintained by nationalists and how they both influence and are influenced by action in the world. Perhaps one reason the cultural dimension has been neglected is that non-anthropologist social scientists misconceive the power of ethnography. In 1994 I was interviewed for a research position in nationalist studies. When I stated my intellectual concerns, the political scientists on the panel quickly raised worries about what they called the 'particularity' of ethnography. They thought it was insufficiently general to tell us anything interesting. I immediately countered that, with the greatest of respect, their vision was too narrow. Without ethnographic understanding of nationalisms, I argued, we run very real risks of misrepresenting them badly. For detailed ethnographies, grounded on long-term intensive fieldwork, offer us the possibility of a nuanced comprehension of the lived reality of people in areas where nationalism is a significant force. If we wish to have a broader understanding of nationalism than just what nationalist leaders write and how many votes they poll when, from which social groups, then we need open-minded fieldworkers prepared to trace the variant ways in which nationalist ideas influence or fail to influence people's conceptions of whom they are, where they come from, where they are going, how they should act, and with (or against) whom they should act, in which context. Fieldworkers need to be open-minded because the ways in which nationalist ideas are enacted may well be unforeseen and unexpected, even to participants. When I, for instance, started work on Basque nationalism, I had no inkling I would eventually be led to study some of the topics examined in this book. I also told my interviewers that while the details of each ethnography may be particular in time and place, the ways in which nationalist ideas are played out in each case might well prove suggestive for fieldworkers studying nationalism elsewhere. Also, by scrutiny of different ethnographic cases, anthropologists of nationalism uphold the real possibility of generating comparative generalizations which by definition transcend particularity. Thus the primarily anthropological approach that I am promoting here may indeed enable us to come to make broad, albeit provisional statements about the role(s), say, of football and cuisine in nationalisms throughout Europe. But, before getting down to the ethnographic nitty-gritty, there are some general issues I need to broach.

Identities, practices

In May 2004 Juan José Ibarretxe, the *lehendakari* (President of the Basque Country), urged Juan Luis Zapatero, the President of the Spanish Government, to come to a satisfactory agreement about the nature of relations between the Basque Country and the Spanish state. For, as he declared, 'We Basques will never form part of a project which does not take into account our identity.' A few months later Zapatero, talking publicly, drew a portrait of a pacific Spain in which, he said, 'the Basque Country could feel itself completely confirmed in its own identity.'[1]

'Identity', whether local, ethnic, national or supernational, is now an established central term in modern politics, especially in areas where one or more local residential groups define themselves in terms of ethnicity. Yet the more social scientists discussed 'identity' and its uses the more problematic a term it came to seem. One difficulty for some was that the term, being a noun, seemed to imply reference to an entity. They were scared of colleagues reifying a non-thing. The Lebanese expatriate writer Amin Maalouf, who has spent his adult life in France, has dealt with this concern magisterially. He notes it is commonly supposed that everyone has 'deep down inside' one affiliation which really matters; it is treated as a 'fundamental truth' about each individual, as an unchangeable 'essence' determined for ever at birth. And when our contemporaries are exhorted to 'assert their identity', it is this fundamental allegiance they are meant to uncover and then flaunt. In contrast to this model, where identity is focused on one single affiliation, Maalouf argues that every individual is the meeting-ground of many different allegiances. Though they are not equally strong, their particular combination in any particular individual is what makes each person unique and irreplaceable:

> Am I half French and half Lebanese? Of course not. Identity can't be compartmentalised. You can't divide it up into halves or thirds or any other separate segments. I haven't got several identities: I've got just one, made up of many different components combined together in a mixture that is unique to every individual.[2]

There will be a hierarchy of these allegiances, but that hierarchy is not immutable. One's identity may well change over time. Further, even though one's identity is made up of a number of affiliations, an individual experiences them as a complete whole. While Maalouf's individualist, dynamic approach greatly downplays the structural constraints people may experience, his argument is a powerful call for caution to those who do not

[1] *Información* 5 v 2004, p. 32; *El País* 13 ix 2004, p.18
[2] Maalouf 2000: 3

recognize 'identity' as a 'false friend', one of those words which seem clearest yet 'are often the most treacherous'.[3]

In reaction to the worry that identity seemed to imply reference to an entity, some academics, who frequently went under the banner of post-structuralists or postmodernists, argue that 'identity' should be qualified by words such as 'multilayered', 'destabilized', or 'fractured'.[4] This is not enough for some, who are worried that even this 'soft' version of the term still implies, however residually, an underlying essence to identity. Anthias, for instance, complains that 'however many "multi" or "layered" prefixes we use, it remains the case that what is retained must have some singular meaning in and of itself, otherwise the term "identity" would be a rhetorical flourish more than anything else.'[5] In its place, she suggests use of the phrase 'translocational positionality', because it highlights the importance of context, especially in complex and shifting locales, and because it recognizes that any agent is already placed within a set of relations and practices which implicate identification and action. Brubaker and Cooper prefer to take the more radical step of forcibly propounding that we do without the concept of 'identity' completely.[6]

I disagree with both these arguments. As Anthias, Brubaker and Cooper all recognize, the diverse meanings given to 'identity' in both academia and the extra-mural world overlap greatly. Yet just because the term is made to bear so many meanings should be no reason for us academics to reject it. Quite the opposite, it is a call for us to investigate it, in its myriad, frequently overlapping forms. For if others, especially politicians and their listeners, choose to use the term in a multiple, slippery fashion surely it behoves us to take their actions seriously? And if such people continue to employ the word, often as implying something unitary while simultaneously recognizing the diverse natures of different identities, then we cannot abandon its use, even if we are only retaining it not as a primarily analytical category but as an academic category which frames an object of study: the use of 'identity' as a classificatory and explanatory category in contemporary social life. In this sense the academic study of 'identity' is no mere 'rhetorical flourish', but a required signpost to the social scientific investigation of the diverse ways it is employed in the vernacular. For in many ways, of course, it is precisely its untidy, sprawling diversity which makes it such a powerful term in political and everyday discourse. Here, it is only on the narrowest of academic terms that any scholastic endeavour to characterize or explain the word and its uses is doomed to failure. These attempts, though bound by limitations, still serve to sharpen our sense of what it is, exactly, that politicians and voters are up to when they make impassioned pleas on behalf of their 'identity'. What Anthias, Brubaker and Cooper are railing against are the attempts by some social scientists to

---

[3] Ibid: 9
[4] See, for example, Jenkins 2002
[5] Anthias 2002: 495
[6] Brubaker and Cooper 2000

provide unitary explanations of *universal* application to the common uses of identity. That criticism may be valid; but it is not an argument against the utility of proposing somewhat narrower explanations of uses of the term.

I do not wish to engage any further in the academic debate about the value of 'identity studies'. I am not interested in winning any of its diminishing returns. Instead I simply observe (1) that the utility of 'identity' as a comparative concept within the social sciences remains problematic, (2) that that difficulty is no excuse for brushing the topic away, and (3) that the value of partial explanations should not be under-emphasized. I have other priorities and, like most field-centred anthropologists, they are ones which have emerged from my attempt to construct even a limited degree of ethnographic coherence. I say 'a limited degree' for indigenous notions of identity in the geographical area I study are not static but dynamic, processual, strategic, shifting, contested, negotiable, exaggerated, where the social encompasses the economic, and the tension between the social and the individual remains forever creatively unresolved.

As an anthropologist, my study of nationalism strives to investigate who is using what ideas when, how, for what reasons and to what end. This is not to focus exclusively on discourse but to recognize its integration within socio-economic life, to acknowledge the pervasive interactions between rhetoric and material factors. At the same time, it is to reintegrate studies of nationalism with the thoroughly political, one dimension of social life which many theorists of nationalism are inclined to neglect. Moreover, since we are not dealing with states but with processes, I do not talk just of 'identities' but of processes of identification as well. This is no mere semantic sleight of hand, rather a further way to acknowledge (1) the role of humans as actors, not as automata thoughtlessly running their lives along the lines of their social rules, and (2) that the ideas which structure their thoughts are not abstract entities coasting in an ethnographic present but evolving concepts deployed for different reasons in different contexts. As such, my deployment of an idea such as 'modes of identification' can be viewed as a particular example of the more general shift in our discipline from the examination of structure to that of agency.

Nationalisms

The best way to argue the case for an anthropological approach to nationalism is to demonstrate the limitations and blind-spots of approaches to the topic from other, related disciplines. I will only deal with the most well-known, well-established of examples.

One of the most-quoted postwar approaches to nationalism was that of Karl Deutsch, a distinguished political scientist who strongly promoted a cybernetic study of society. He deployed what he called a 'functional definition of nationality', which 'consists in the ability to communicate effectively, and over a wider range of subjects, with members of one large group more than with outsiders'.[7] Deutsch lauded quantitative analyses, based on statistical data, and argued that this ability could be surveyed, tested and measured. Concentrating on the historical period encompassing the rise of industrialism and the modern market economy, he claimed that it could be evaluated by delimiting the 'mobilized population', the people integrated into denser networks of communication than those found in traditional societies. This 'social mobilization' could be derived from several yardsticks of measurement, such as the rate of urbanization, the proportion of workers in the secondary and tertiary sectors, the numbers of newspaper-readers, secondary school graduates, conscripts, letter-writers, literate adults, movie-goers, and radio listeners. As is patent, his analysis hinges on a clear dichotomy between the traditional and the modern, and the transition from one to the other.[8]

Deutsch pitched his own criteria too high. As one sympathetic to this approach stated, 'useful time series for *all these* variables are obviously very hard to come by even for a *single* country ... His model is essentially heuristic: it suggests a priority in comparative data collection and then simply exhorts us to develop generalizations inductively through the processing of such materials.'[9] Worse, Deutsch's model does not square with the facts when it comes to ethnic minorities. He argued that members of these minorities would assimilate into the dominant group, shedding much of their ethnic difference for the sake of better jobs and social mobilization. But, as Connor demonstrated in a devastating critique, members of many minorities did not easily shed their cultural particularities:

> Improvements in the quality and quantity of communication and transportation media progressively curtail the cultural isolation in which an ethnic group could formerly cloak its cultural chasteness from the perverting influences of other cultures within the same state ... [These improvements] tend also to increase the cultural awareness of the minorities by making their members more aware of the distinctions between themselves and others. The impact is twofold. Not only does the individual become more aware of alien ethnic groups; he also becomes more aware of those who share his identity.[10]

Thus the accompaniments of economic development – increased social mobilization and communication – tend not to diffuse ethnic tensions. Rather, in many cases, they have exacerbated them and fanned separatist demands.

The influential historian Elie Kedourie took an idealist approach to the study of nationalism. For him nationalism is, over and above everything else, a political philosophy grounded on self-determination, i.e. the rights and duties of the individual. He saw this philosophy as based on Immanuel Kant's doctrine which made the individual 'the very centre ... the sovereign of the universe'. For Kant, 'the good will, which is also the free will, is also the autonomous will.'[11] Thus, 'a good man is an autonomous man, and for

---

[7] Deutsch 1953: 97
[8] Ibid. ch. 6, pp. 122–52
[9] Rokkan 1970: 51, 67, quoted in Jaffrelot 2005: 14.
[10] Connor 1972: 329. See also Smith 1991: 125.
[11] Kedourie 1960: 16, 17

him to realize his autonomy, he must be free'.[12] Thanks to Kant's disciples, especially Johann Gottlieb Fichte, his doctrine was spread, adapted, and then given a nationalist dimension by the German Youth movement, whose example was later imitated by similar groups elsewhere in Europe. On Kedourie's reading, nationalism becomes a child of the Enlightenment and Romanticism, and nationalist movements 'children's crusades'.[13] In other words, they are the organized political response of younger generations to the social upheavals of the late eighteenth and nineteenth centuries which caused 'a breakdown in the transmission of political habits and religious beliefs'.[14] Kedourie thus regards nationalism in functionalist terms: national movements, he says,

> Are seen to satisfy a need, to fulfil a want. Put at its simplest, the need is to belong together in a coherent and stable community. Such a need is normally satisfied by the family, the neighbourhood, the religious community. In the last century and a half such institutions all over the world have had to bear the brunt of violent social and intellectual change, and it is no accident that nationalism was at its most intense where and when such institutions had little resilience and were ill-prepared to withstand the powerful attacks to which they became exposed.[15]

Functionalist approaches are usually hobbled, because they fail to specify the supposed function in anything like a rigorous manner. Kedourie is no exception. We might ask, what we are meant to make of his 'need to belong', which he presents without empirical justification, as though it were an intuitively acceptable, explanatory concept? The anthropologist Bronislaw Malinowski deployed the same strategy in the 1930s, associating different aspects of society with supposedly universal functions discerned by himself, only to be roundly criticized by his own students. Further, why should this supposed need isolated by Kedourie be regarded as similar, and above all as functionally similar, when applied to a family or to a nation? If we were to take this language of 'needs' seriously for a moment, we might state that we were in fact dealing with needs of different orders, ones which are not necessarily complementary, let alone substitutable for one another.

The strength of Kedourie's analysis is his provocative tracing of an intellectual genealogy, that of nationalism. In the eyes of some, it is also his major weakness, for he remained antipathetic to social scientific approaches. Regarding evidence as primary to all theory, he eschewed sociological explanation, which he thought a form of reductionist economism.[16] Here Kedourie was openly criticizing his colleague at the London School of Economics, Ernest Gellner, who had proposed a very different, and still influential theory of nationalism.[17]

[12] Ibid: 22
[13] Ibid: 96
[14] Ibid: 94
[15] Ibid: 96
[16] Kedourie 1993: 142–44
[17] Gellner's theory of nationalism 'has received enormous attention, with *Nations and Nationalism* becoming an influential, much translated bestseller' (Hall 1998a: 1). To Gellner, Kedourie's theory characterized nationalism as 'an artificial consequence of ideas which did not ever need to be formulated, and appeared by a regrettable incident' (Gellner 1983: 129).

Baldly, Gellner's theory is that nationalism is a consequence of the shift from an agrarian society to an industrial one. In an agrarian society a literate class, the clerisy, enables cultural and cognitive storage and centralization while the state, composed of the military and administrative classes, is concerned with political centralization. This ruling stratum constitutes a small minority of the population, and for both this stratum as a whole and for each sub-stratum within it cultural differentiation rather than homogeneity is stressed. The rest of the population is divided into petty communities, whose members live inward-turned lives, strongly tied to locality. Each group differentiates itself from others and, though each may be internally homogeneous, it is most unlikely to use its own particular culture to legitimate a political principle: 'the self-enclosed community tends to communicate in terms whose meaning can only be identified *in context*, in contrast to the relatively context-free scholasticism of the scribes.'[18] A clerisy might try to propagate certain shared cultural norms but these agents of the state have not the means to make literacy near-universal. For these reasons, 'almost everything in agro-literate societies militates against the definition of political units in terms of cultural boundaries.'[19]

Agro-literate societies might tend to be stable, but industrialized societies rely on sustained economic growth, which is allied to 'cognitive growth'. An agro-literate society organizes knowledge according to a purposive, hierarchical cosmos, composed loosely of sub-fields, each with its own idiom and logic. In contrast, industrialized society organizes knowledge into a singular, rational scheme. Morally inert and universally applicable, it undergoes continual innovation and expansion. Here, communication, to be broadly effective, needs to be context-free and precise. Thus education for literacy, no longer a clerical privilege, becomes a universal right provided by the state, whose agents dutifully transmit it to, and so socialize, its younger generations. In the process the agro-literate ideology of hierarchy and stability is replaced by one of egalitarianism and mobility. These new sorts of societies, generally larger than city-states and smaller than empires, require new kinds of political structures, which nationalist movements can claim to provide. For Gellner, these 'well-defined educationally sanctioned and unified cultures constitute very nearly the only kind of unit with which men willingly and often ardently identify.'[20] Thus nationalists strive to make culture and polity congruent and the reason some of them are so successful is that their efforts benefit modern society, fulfilling both socio-economic requirements and something akin to psychological needs.

Gellner's powerful and significant theory is so wide-ranging it is open to a variety of criticisms: his model of agrarian communities is over-simplistic; his account of the transition to industrialization can be questioned on historical grounds; his approach overall is essentially functionalist.[21] His

---

[18] Gellner 1983: 12
[19] Ibid: 11
[20] Ibid: 55
[21] Gellner leaves aside many important features of agrarian societies, he fails to mention the much more complex relations which may exist between their constituent groups, and he

concern with the functions of nationalism mirrors his lack of interest in meaning. A materialist with a reductive approach to human nature (at least in *Nations and Nationalism*), Gellner shows no interest whatsoever in the meanings and significance that nationalist ideas held for nationalist ideologues, leaders and their supporters. Indeed, he openly derides them:

> It is not so much that the prophets of nationalism were not anywhere near the First Division, when it came to the business of thinking: that in itself would not prevent a thinker from having an enormous, genuine and crucial influence on history. Numerous examples prove that. It is rather that these thinkers did not really make much difference. If one of them had fallen, others would have stepped into his place . . . No one was indispensable. The quality of nationalist thought would hardly have been affected much by such substitutions.
>
> Their precise doctrines are hardly worth analysing . . .
>
> What is actually said matters little.[22]

Gellner here ignores the existence of nationalist discourse as an integral phenomenon within the social field. To a good materialist like himself, nationalists' ways of understanding the world are but epiphenomena, super-structural, floss. Yet, as even a half-aware anthropologist knows, any explanation of social behaviour which does not take into account agents' own explanations is inadequate. Already by the 1920s Malinowski was able to define anthropology as the study of what people do, what they say they do, and the ways they justify the gap between the two. Or, to put it differently, the ways people regard and interpret the world affects the way they act in this world. Indeed they are crucial components in the creation and continued development of the world within which they live. To disregard this fundamental condition of social agents is to deny them an essential aspect of their humanity. It is to treat them as pawns in a chess-game 'played' by socio-economic forces. Changing the metaphor, it is to portray people as two-dimensional stick figures in a picture of Gellner's own making. As an academic prepared to tell his readers 'what *really* happens', he leaves aside the all-important subjectivities for the sake of a supposed objectivism.[23]

In reply to his critics, Gellner did modify his position somewhat. He turned his typologies of nationalism into a more historicized set of stages, he

[21] (cont.) ignores other important kinds of societies which also made the transition to indus-trialization, such as autonomous peasant communities and city-states. On factual aspects: most of the nationalist movements in Europe emerged well before the arrival of modern industry (Hroch 1996: 85); it is difficult to accept a direct link between the establishment of a system of mass education and the requirements of industrialized societies for a minimally qualified labour force, because there were so many other reasons for its establishment, such as a desire for discipline, humanitarianism, and concern with a new youth problem (Breuilly 1996: 161). Perry Anderson complains of Gellner's 'single-minded economic functionalism', (as evidenced in Gellner 1983: 140), while Llobera notes that his explanation of nationalists' behaviour as motivated by socio-economic mobility smacks strongly of vulgar materialism (Anderson 1992: 207, quoted in O'Leary 1998: 83; Llobera 1994: 100). Gutiérrez claims he underestimates the power of ethnic movements because they do not constitute the primary social mechanism by which a nation-state is formed (Gutiérrez 1997: 166).

[22] Gellner 1983: 124; 127, orig. italics

[23] Ibid: 57, orig. italics

accepted that some nations 'have navels' (i.e. that they are not complete inventions *ab nihilo*), and he acknowledged the influential role of factors besides industrialization in the genesis of nationalism, though he maintained the functional link between industrialization and nationalism. Heeding their charge of reductionism, he claimed he was able to appreciate the feelings nationalism engenders:

> I *am* deeply sensitive to the spell of nationalism. I can play about thirty Bohemian folk songs (or songs represented as such in youth) on my mouth-organ. My oldest friend, whom I have known since the age of three or four and who is Czech and a patriot, cannot bear to hear me play them because he says I do it in such a schmaltzy way, 'crying into the mouth-organ'. I do not think I could have written the book on nationalism which I did write were I not capable of crying, with the help of a little alcohol, over folk songs, which happen to be my favorite form of music.[24]

Gellner's endearing reply might acknowledge psychological dimensions of nationalism but it makes little concession to the power and role of nationalist discourse within social life. His belated recognition of the power of nationalist subjectivities is only a limited one. In the preface to his father's *Nationalism*, David Gellner tries to defend him by citing the above passage and stating, 'The point is not merely to represent nationalist feelings, but to *explain* them.'[25] But this, of course, only reinforces Gellner's original stance: a reductionist approach which fails to recognize the significance of nationalists' interpretation of the world within the very process they help engender.

Benedict Anderson's *Imagined Communities* was published the same year as Gellner's *Nations and Nationalism* and has been equally, if not more widely, acclaimed. The title comes from Anderson's emphasis that every nation is an 'imagined community', a group so large that no individuals can ever come to know all its other members but are taught instead to imagine that, despite actual inequality and prevailing exploitation, they still share a 'deep, horizontal comradeship'.[26] Like Gellner he sites the emergence of nationalism in a revolutionary period. The key changes he concentrates on are: the decline of Latin as a language enabling access to the Truth, the waning of the concept that societies are naturally centred on sovereigns with pretensions to the divine, the fading of a concept of time which integrated cosmology and the history of humankind. Hand in hand with these changes went the development of publishing techniques and the penetration of capitalism into publishing. Rates of literacy rose, enabling the growth of an expanding market for novels and newspapers. These newly popular forms of literary production enabled the spread of a non-fatalistic, chronological sense of time and the establishment of standardized, national languages, which in turn facilitated the creation of an imagined community. According to this logic, reading a newspaper thus could become a quotidian ritual in which members of these new social units might daily participate:

---

[24] Gellner 1996: 624–5, orig. italics
[25] D. Gellner 1997: ix, orig. italics
[26] Anderson 1983: 7

[Readers] gradually became aware of the hundreds of thousands, even millions, of people in their particular language-field, and at the same time that *only those* hundreds of thousands, or millions, so belonged. These fellow-readers, to whom they were connected through print, formed, in their secular, particular, visible invisibility, the embryo of the nationally imagined community.[27]

Dovetailing with these developments went 'human interchangeability',[28] a central strategy of the modern state. By this Anderson means the centralized education of the intelligentsia and bureaucrats-to-be, who might come from any region within its borders and who, after graduating, might be posted to any region. This mode of training served several functions: it weakened intra-regional consolidation; among its graduates, it was meant to foster a feeling of solidarity and produce a common culture, an incipient national consciousness; for the otherwise dispersed bureaucrats, it put to the fore the centrality of the capital, because they had all to return there from time to time. Thus, a sense of nationhood was generated, above all, by two factors: what Anderson calls 'print capitalism' and the pilgrimages to the centre by the intellectually trained.

Anderson's imaginative analysis is recognized as both powerful and provocative. Like Gellner's however, his model can be criticized for failing to square with the historical record. Also, some have voiced concern that Anderson concentrates on the imagined at the expense of 'the socio-political realities of power and the organizational structures of the state'.[29] Further, his approach appears less concerned with explaining nationalism than with concentrating on the preconditions which might enable a sense of national belonging. According to the French political scientist Christophe Jaffrelot, 'It is a case of nations without nationalism, not only because the processes described by Anderson are explicitly "unconscious" – there is no actor – but also because there is no political ideology at stake.'[30] By this refusal to take the contents of nationalisms seriously, Anderson's account can be branded as culturally reductionist. Tim Edensor, a practitioner of cultural studies, takes a slightly different tack: he regards Anderson's focus on literacy and printed media as excessive and grounded on a reductive view of culture. For nations are imagined not just on the page, but in a rich complexity of manners, including 'music hall and theatre, popular music, festivities, architecture, fashion, spaces of congregation, and in a plenitude of embodied habits and performances, not to mention more parallel cultural forms such as television, film, radio and information technology'.[31]

In sum, despite their various strengths, Deutsch's quantitative approach appears an unachievable dream; Kedourie's is functionalist, as is Gellner's; while both Gellner's and Anderson's are reductionist. In this intellectual context, what might an anthropological approach to the study of nationalism offer?

[27] Anderson 1983: 44, orig. italics
[28] Ibid: 56
[29] James 1996: 7–8; Edensor 2002: 7
[30] Jaffrelot 2005: 18
[31] Edensor 2002: 7

Here much of the most illuminating work by anthropologists has been that done on ethnicity, which in so many ethnographic cases overlaps with a nationalist project. One of the earliest to stake out a particular position was Clifford Geertz. An Indonesian specialist, he wanted to understand the tensions in recently modernized societies between their distinctive features (material progress, social reform, a sense of citizenship, etc.) and the sustained power of what he termed 'primordial attachments', derived from kinship, language, locality, religion and culture. For him these 'givens' were so resilient because they were so irreducible; they 'are seen to have an ineffable, and at times overpowering coerciveness in and of themselves'.[32] And their existence can cause much strife in a modernizing society:

> Though it can be moderated, this tension between primordial sentiments and civil politics probably cannot be entirely dissolved. The power of the 'givens' of place, blood, looks, and way-of-life to shape an individual's notion of who, at bottom, he is and with whom, indissolubly, he belongs is rooted in the non-rational foundation of personality.[33]

Geertz's polemical primordialism is often opposed to a stark instrumentalism. The Africanist Abner Cohen is a good example here, for he argues that ethnic identities develop to fit functional organizational requirements. To him, ethnic groups are informal political organizations who deploy their cultural resources in order to delimit and so secure their group's resources. He thus stresses ethnicity as a means by which members of otherwise informally organized bodies can come together politically to pursue their collective self-interest.

> Ethnicity in modern society is the result of intensive struggle between groups over new strategic positions of power within the structure of the new state ... Ethnicity is fundamentally a political phenomenon ... It is a type of informal interest grouping.[34]

Of course, primordialist and instrumentalist approaches need not necessarily exclude each other. Instrumental manipulation and primordial sentiment may go hand in hand; they may also conflict, as may different sentiments or opposing instrumental goals.[35] However, what each position does serve to illuminate is, in turn, the potentially affective power of ethnicity and the interested political ends it may further.

It was the Norwegian anthropologist Fredrik Barth who, in the late 1960s, put forward the most radically informative approach to ethnicity. Opposed to those who saw ethnicity as the property of a clearly bounded, culturally defined, usually static group, he argued that we need to focus on the interface between groups. In other words, ethnicity was the dynamic product of interaction, where members of one group chose from their cultural repertoire certain aspects which would highlight their difference to

[32] Geertz 1973: 259
[33] Ibid: 276–7
[34] Abner Cohen 1974a; 1974b: 96–7. For a more modern statement of ethnicity in instrumentalist terms, see Appadurai 1996: 14–15. The classical satire of nakedly self-interested 'professional minorities' is Wolfe's essay 'Mau-mauing the flak catchers' (in Wolfe 1970).
[35] Jenkins 1997: 23, 46. See also Eriksen 1993a: 54–6; Jaffrelot 2005: 38–40

others. A crucial consequence of this 'transactional' perspective, as Barth's approach is termed, is that the key definition of an ethnic group is not decided by academic commentators, such as anthropologists, but is self-ascribed by its own members. This entails that any analysis of ethnicity must start by studying the viewpoint of those members, and the ways they strive to maintain boundaries between 'us' and 'them'. Others, however, members of 'them', frequently seek to impose their categorization of the group onto its members. In these circumstances, the fieldworker's job is to trace the varied consequences of the political struggle between proponents of both sides for, as Richard Jenkins has pointed out, the twin processes of collective self-identification and social categorization might be distinct but are still routinely implicated in one another. Moreover, as he emphasizes, just because ethnicity may appear variable and manipulable in these processes does not mean it is infinitely variable nor that it is perpetually in flux.[36] Exactly what pertains in each case has to be elucidated by anthropological investigation.

Several commentators in the social sciences have noted the remarkable congruence between theories of nationalism and anthropological approaches to the study of ethnicity. Though this congruence is unsurprising, it has been surprisingly neglected until recently, most likely because of well-grounded insularity: academics tend to stay within the boundaries of their own discipline. Despite this habit of not venturing beyond one's turf, it has became clear to some that national identities share many features with ethnic identities: both are historically contingent constructions, reliant on notions of culture; both are contested, negotiated and relational; both need to be sited into their various contexts, local, regional, national and international.[37] To say that ethnicity and nationalism are congruent is not of course to conflate the two. An ethnic movement does not necessarily have an explicit political agenda. A nationalist ideology usually relies on a notion of national culture, but that may well be understood in pluriethnic terms. That said, we have still to recognize that many nationalist movements today do have ethnic dimensions as key to, if not even constitutive of their ideologies.

Barth, in a famous passage, stated that anthropologists of ethnicity should study 'the ethnic *boundary* that defines the group, not the cultural stuff that it encloses'.[38] What he intended by 'cultural stuff' was language, religion, traditions and laws, material culture and so on. However, as several have since argued, Barth's statement appears counter-intuitive. They find it hard to believe that the constitution of the cultural stuff on which ethnic differentiation is grounded is largely irrelevant. Jenkins proclaims

> This surely cannot be true. For example, a situation in which the As and the Bs are distinguished, *inter alia,* by languages which are mutually intelligible for most everyday purposes – as with Danish and Norwegian – would seem to differ greatly from one in which the languages involved are, as with English and Welsh, utterly different.[39]

[36] Barth 1969; Jenkins 1997: 51
[37] E.g. Bauman 1992: 678–9; Eriksen 1993a: 97–120; Jenkins 1997: 143; Jaffrelot 2005: 45
[38] Barth 1969: 15
[39] Jenkins 1997: 107

Cornell has similarly argued that attention should be paid not just to the boundaries of ethnic groups but to their content as well. Categorizing these internal factors in terms of interests, institutions and culture, he focuses on the variable content of ethnic identities and on the role content plays in patterns of ethnic persistence and change. Anything less, he argues, leads to an incomplete understanding of ethnic processes.[40] A corresponding criticism has also come from within Basque academia itself. The prize-winning Jon Juaristi, a former member of ETA (*Euskadi ta askatasuna*, 'The Basque Country and Freedom') and now virulent anti-nationalist, has raised parallel doubts to those of Jenkins and Cornell about the transactionalist approach to ethnicity. Classing Barth as a structuralist, he has stated, 'The structuralist reduction of identity to a frontier, to an opposition, does not completely convince me. Identity is also – and above all – I think, a discourse on identity.'[41]

I am not the first anthropologist of Europe to study cultural dimensions of nationalisms. For example, in the 1980s a series of students of Edwin Ardener at Oxford focused on peripheral ethnicities and nationalisms within Western Europe. Their ethnographies include Maryon McDonald on the Bretons, Malcolm Chapman on the Celts, Sharon Macdonald on Gaelic Scots.[42] At much the same time, or later, others have carried out fieldwork on matching examples elsewhere in Europe, e.g. Joseba Zulaika in the Basque Country, Loring Danforth and Anastasia Karakisidou on Greek Macedonia.[43] But, save the odd worthy exception, the majority of these anthropologists have tended to investigate the same, well-established general topics: party politics, language, religion and the land. In contrast I, in a vainglorious effort to be distinctive, to give other topics their due prominence, and to plough my own furrow, have chosen a set of phenomena normally passed over: football, cuisine, graffiti, bones, teeth, blood groups, etc. It is also true some anthropologists have written enlightening papers on everyday, unofficial nationalisms[44] but none, as far as I am aware, have given it the monograph-length attention I argue it deserves. Hence this book.

Basques

The books published on Basque nationalism could fill shelf after shelf of an academic library. I have no wish to repeat what they state. Instead I give here a bare-bones account of the history, mainly political, of Basque nationalism. My aim is to put the following chapters into their appropriate contexts, nothing more. Moreover, since I did all my fieldwork among

[40] Cornell 1996; Cornell and Hartmann 1998: 86–9
[41] Juaristi 2006: 357
[42] McDonald 1989; Chapman 1992, 1993; Macdonald 1997. See also contributions to Tonkin, McDonald and Chapman 1989
[43] Zulaika 1988; Danforth 1997; Karakisidou 1997
[44] Eriksen 1993b; Linde-Laursen 1993; Wilk 1993; Foster 2002

Basques living in Spain, I have nothing to say about Basques in France.[45]

It was above all Sabino Arana, the son of a local lawyer, who in the last decade of the nineteenth century stimulated the rise of Basque nationalism as a political force. Though other Basques in previous decades had fomented a literary and romantic sense of Basque distinctiveness, frequently based on dubious historiography and philology, it was Arana who was primarily responsible for the creation of both a reasonably coherent political ideology and a fledgling, but increasingly well-established political movement.

A key reason for this success was the fact that in the last two decades of the nineteenth century the Basque Country experienced the fastest and most extensive industrialization of any area in the world. Ascendant industrialists increasingly exploited the high-quality coal deposits of the area, whose product they used to feed the rapidly growing iron- and steel-making industries. This in turn greatly boosted the production of the long-established local ship-building yards. Thousands of villagers left their homes to come to live in the grim shanty settlements which grew up on the edge of industrial towns. There they were joined by very large numbers of job-hungry migrants from regions of Spain beyond the Basque Country. Arana and his supporters, mostly members of the local petite bourgeoisie, correctly perceived the astonishingly rapid industrialization of their country as a real threat both to their own position within local society and to the traditional way of rural life. In the emerging new society, customary values linked to a predominantly agrarian way of life did not hold as much sway as before. On top of that many well-to-do Basques felt keenly the loss in 1876, after the final surrender of Basque Carlist forces to the army of central government, of the local *fueros* (provincial charters of autonomy).[46] The sum result was that Arana and his fellows conceived of these tumultuous social, political and economic changes as ones affecting the very nature of the Basque Country. In reaction to this unwanted degree of accelerating flux, they propounded a nationalism which aimed to arrest the potentially destructive effects of laissez-faire capitalism within their own land.

Their words had resonance in the local setting. Within a few years, and despite centralist opposition, they had started to win seats in the municipal, provincial and national assemblies. In the early twentieth century they expanded their base of support, till then primarily urban-centred, by focusing on rural initiatives and by slowly extending a homeland-wide network which covered both the cities and the countryside. By the time, in 1936, that Francisco Franco made his armed bid for power, the Basque Nationalist Party (el Partido Nacionalista Vasco, PNV) was sufficiently strong to be able to bargain successfully for the establishment of an autonomous regional Basque Government. They were only to see it suppressed two years later when the insurgent's troops conquered their land.

---

[45] For anthropological work on the area of France in which Basques live, see Ott 1981, Terrio 2000; on Basque nationalism in southwest France, see Jacob 1994, 1999
[46] On the Carlists, see MacClancy 2000

The dictator's regime effectively squashed almost all manifestation of nationalist life for more than two decades. By the late 1950s the latest generation of local youths, impatient with the perceived passivity of their parents, embarked on a new programme of nationalist activism. Their organization, ETA, began as a broad cultural and humanist movement. In the late 1960s one section of its membership took up arms to pursue their struggle and slowly began to turn it into a terrorist organization with separatist, irredentist and revolutionary socialist ends. Armed action led to a heavy-handed reaction, which affected almost all those in the Basque Country, not just militant activists. In the last fifteen years of his regime Franco imposed five states of exception in Vizcaya, Guipuzcoa, or both. At one point it was said that a quarter of all the Civil Guard were stationed in the Basque Country, so of course giving substance to long-held nationalist claims that their homeland was an occupied country. In the process, ETA soon became greatly popular, though always polemical, throughout Spain and was generally seen to be in the vanguard of radical change.

In the Basque Country, local *cuadrillas* (very stable groups of friends, especially youths, who spend almost all their social time together) act as the backbone and organizers of activities in public space. The Basque sociologist Ander Gurruchaga has argued that the regime's heavy-handedness both pushed members of these groups towards the nationalist camp and forced them to adopt a 'code of silence'. To Gurruchaga, this practice of keeping mum was not a passive ploy but 'an active and transgressive behaviour'; since one could not express dissent publicly (except in illegal demonstrations), a code of silence was a way to create throughout broad sections of Basque society a sense of profound difference from the forces and institutions of the state. Within a *cuadrilla*, news of the latest ETA bombing might be met by a nudge and a remarkable lack of further comment.[47] Ironically, Franco himself might have appreciated this strategy, as he instructed Prince Juan Carlos, his king-to-be, in the ways of government: 'One is master of what one does not say, and the slave of what one does'.[48]

People could express themselves more openly at home. Within the domestic circle, nationalist parents were able to inculcate their offspring in anti-regime values and the central importance of being Basque. Just like the local Carlists who, from the nineteenth century on, had generated a sense of identity so strong it was transmitted within families through the generations, many nationalists quietly but proudly bore their badge of belonging, almost as though it were a family inheritance. It is partly for this reason that, in the early 1970s, with the increasing age of the dictator heralding the end of his sclerotic regime, the PNV could quickly refashion itself as a functioning major party. Come the first elections after Franco's death in 1976, it was immediately established as the prime centre-right party in the Basque Country, while a variety of radical groups, all products of schisms within ETA, populated the mid- and far left of the nationalist spectrum.

[47] Gurruchaga 1985: 130
[48] Quoted in Tremlett 2006: 49

Since then the PNV, despite its own schisms, has gained, and maintained, a hegemonic position within the mainstream political life of the Basque Country. Ever since the creation of a Basque Autonomous Region in 1978, the PNV has run the Basque Government, often in coalition, sometimes not. In the meantime, several of the smaller radical nationalist groups shut up shop, while the majority of the rest formed a coalition. Initially called Herri Batasuna ('Popular Unity', HB), at the turn of the millennium the conservative central government had it declared illegal, only to do the same to its successor a few years later. The mid-left party, Euskadiko Eskerra, formed when the 'politico-military' wing of ETA disbanded in 1978, disappeared a little under two decades later when it merged with the Basque branch of the nationwide Partido Socialista Obrero Español (PSOE).

PSOE is a centre-left party widely seen as representing the interests of non-Basque immigrants, whose numbers were massively boosted by a second great labour immigration into the Basque Country from the late 1950s to early 1970s. What is so remarkable here is that even though the migrants are now in the majority on the electoral rolls, that numerical difference is not turned to political advantage. According to the anthropologist Marianne Heiberg who did fieldwork in a 'mixed' town in the mid-1980s, many migrants are fragmented into networks of fellow migrants from the same area of origin and 'feel dependent on a closed, self-sufficient Basque community in which most social benefits are held . . . Open, direct criticism of this community is not thought a practical proposition. Group action against it is not conceived as possible.'[49] Voting follows very stable patterns, within the two blocs: nationalist and non-nationalist. Thus locals might shift their vote from one end of the nationalist spectrum to the other, and back again, but very rarely would they vote outside the nationalist camp. Similarly, the great majority of migrants will vote for either PSOE or Partido Popular, the nationwide centre-right party. The only significant exception here is the adolescent or adult children of migrants who may embrace the nationalist cause and go over to that side. I know of no examples whatsoever of Basques making the opposite move.

In sum, Basque nationalism continues to set most of the political agenda of the Basque Country, with PNV ideologues as its disputed hegemons. Radical nationalists still command a loyal minority, albeit a very gradually decreasing one, of the electorate. ETA, which once had the tacit approval of much of the Basque Country, continues to lose support, also very gradually. The longest-running terrorist organization in Western Europe, it is now regarded by many as a 'problem', whose dissolution is called for by an increasingly broad section of the Basque public. At the time of writing (June 2006), it has recently called a permanent ceasefire, as a prelude to a negotiated end to the conflict. The initial reaction of the main Spanish parties has been both cautious, with those on the left optimistic, and those on the right sceptical. At the very least, we can say the possibility of a lasting

---

[49] Heiberg 1989: 97

resolution to the armed dimension of the Basque conflict now appears better than it has for decades.

Of essence, the exotic and anthropology

There is one central, polemical point I have to raise, in order not to disquiet certain readers, particularly in the Basque Country. At first, social scientists studying contemporary nationalisms thought it was all very well for them to dedicate themselves to highlighting the essentialist nature of many groups' vaunted identities. However, a perhaps unexpected political dimension to their work was quickly made evident. For example, the postmodernist James Clifford has described what happened within American academe:

> A whole range of formerly marginal and excluded peoples and perspectives were fighting for recognition: women, racial and ethnic minorities, new immigrants. These groups, for the first time entering this public sphere, often felt the sophisticated cultural critics to be, in effect, telling them 'Oh yes, we understand your gender, race, culture and identity are important to you, but you know, you're just essentializing.' Well, the insurgents were not amused. . .[50]

The differences of opinion between teachers and activist students led to 'bitter polemics around . . . the potentially reactionary effects of rigid anti-essentialisms'. Clifford recognizes this tension, and so values the support he and his colleagues receive from insurgent scholars and activists who, while criticizing essentialism, do so in 'a non-absolute, historically contingent, dialogically and politically engaged way'. His own personal solution to resolving this tension is to acknowledge that he flirts closely with essentialisms in order to remain engaged with the concrete situation he is in. By taking this tack he hopes to avoid pretensions to a 'philosophical or political purity which would evade the historical conjuncture and its cultural politics'.[51]

I take his point. It is often all too easy for Western academics to adopt a thoroughgoing anti-essentialist approach and think that they are bent on a purificatory project unveiling the essentialist obfuscations of those they study. However, unlike Clifford, I do not believe that this implies we should act as meretricious handmaidens of essentialists whose movements we might admire. Indeed it could be argued that Clifford's position here tends towards the condescending and the neo-colonial, because it is to grant others a special status: as though their essentialism was somehow more acceptable than that of activists promoting movements which American liberals did not admire; as though their being on the side of the political angels was sufficient reason for us to stay our intellectual hand. On the contrary, instead of regarding anti-essentialism as a politically destructive strategy, it is not difficult to underline the potentially highly positive contribution a discriminating, self-consciously partial version of this style can make, for several reasons. First, by scrutinizing in a detailed, sensitive,

[50] Clifford 2003: 64
[51] Ibid: 65

historically grounded manner the essentialist strategies of ideologues and activists, whatever their political stripe, scholars of identity can strive to lay bare the conceptual parameters within which people may be urged to action. This is not necessarily to rob political messages of their emotional and motivating powers, for as Lucien Lévy-Bruhl stated in the 1900s, knowledge of the source of one's ethics has no necessary effect on their normative power. To locals, the significance of their ethnic identity may be very variable: in some cases it is just part of the background; in other cases it may be all-pervasive, a core part of locals' definitions of themselves and of the broader situation in which they find themselves. Here, in Jenkins' felicitous phrase, ethnicity is imagined but very much not imaginary.[52] Cornell and Hartmann, using a more academic terminology, make much the same point when they speak of 'constructed primordiality'. By this, they mean that the emotive power of an ethnic identity comes, not from anything genuinely primordial, but from the rhetoric and symbolism of primordialism which is attached to it.[53] In these cases, ethnic identity matters greatly to many locals; it is a central structure of their daily lived reality. The Basques are one example. Furthermore, uncovering the constructed nature of an identity is not necessarily to question its authenticity. In this context we must not forget that all social identities are, after all, socially constructed, as are all notions of authenticity. To that extent, the remarks I make about the Basques could well apply, equally well, to any other social identity, be it ethnic, nationalist or ethnonationalist. As one Basque historian has put it, 'To ethnic nationalism, it is unimportant if its invention of tradition and the nation is unmasked, nor does it matter how detailed or precise this unmasking is. The only important thing is loyalty.'[54]

Secondly, by demonstrating how the serial essentialisms of an ideology evolve over time, social scientists can evidence the variety of versions of a particular identity and so, however indirectly, encourage plurality, even within the supporters of a particular ideology. Thirdly, by recognizing that concerns about essentialism may be a matter of explicit debate within this political arena itself we enable an academic, hopefully non-partisan discussion of it. After all it was Alfonso Guerra, former Vice-president of Spain, who criticized the nationalism of modern PNV leaders as 'dangerous', 'exclusionary' and 'essentialist'.[55] Finally, by engaging with essentialisms and their consequences, we academics may reflexively make ourselves more aware of the essentialisms, however limited or not, which support our own postures.

I raise these points as I wish to forestall potential criticism that this book is a politically naïve, if not reactionary exercise in deconstruction. While I am keen to shun that charge, one critic of my work did think I had already

---

[52] Lévy-Bruhl 1905: ch. 1; Jenkins 2002
[53] Cornell and Hartmann 1998: 90. To them, one benefit of this approach is that it does not lose 'touch with how ordinary human beings in many cases experience their own ethnicities' (ibid.).
[54] Díaz Nocí 1999: 3
[55] *M* 2 iv 1998: 9

fallen into a well-known trap which contemporary anthropologists are meant to avoid: exoticism. An anonymous Basque academic, the reader of a much earlier version of Chapter Five, which I had submitted to a journal as a potential article, accused me of promoting the very arguments I was striving to examine critically:

> I believe that the author, by focusing on some physical anthropology and anecdotal references, which overlook the overall racist situation in Spain and Europe, contributes to this tendency, thus reifying the argument the author is trying to analyse . . . Attempting to racialize the other (Basques) by analysing its racist tendencies without a clear and respectful understanding of the historical and political context (Spain and Europe at least) is something that must be strongly condemned.

He/she added, 'Let me just say that this article offends my Basque sensibility.' Once again, I take the point. I recognize that I have to tread very carefully, especially given that I am writing about a literate, educated population, a few of whom will be paid to read my words. I have thus endeavoured in the subsequent re-writing of that chapter to remove any taint of exoticism and have reviewed the whole manuscript with precisely that caveat in mind. After all, as an anthropologist, one aim of mine is to comprehend the apparently strange, not to compound strangeness.

One sub-theme which emerged, somewhat to my surprise, in the writing of these chapters was the integral role of anthropologists and anthropologies (both academic and popular) in the evolution of the Basque nationalist process. This 'nationalization' of social scientists is not, of course, unique. Herzfeld, for instance, has already analysed the role of Greek folklorists in the nascent rise of modern Greek nationalism.[56] Thus if the academic encounter, in the Basque Country, with nationalistic forces is not novel, it has been at least surprisingly sustained. Joseba Zulaika, a leading Basque anthropologist, has argued that anthropology was made a substitute for religion in the Basque case. According to him, anthropology played a 'canonizing role in Basque discourse: supplying debatable origin hypotheses, noting ethnographic differences, justifying claimed biological differences, as well as consolidating the profoundest convictions that *lo vasco* is an autonomous political and cultural fact'.[57] On this point another indigenous anthropologist, Juan Aranzadi, is in complete agreement: 'PNV as much as ETA have always known full well that the essential task of reaching "a consciousness of solidarity as a people" in order to construct itself as a nation has three dimensions: political, historic and cultural; and that to achieve the third, the labour of anthropologists is fundamental, whether they be explicitly nationalist or not.'[58] As critically summarized in Chapters Five and Seven, the first Basque anthropologists both made themselves and were made protagonists in the first decades of the emergent ideology, and even influenced the painting styles of some of their contemporaries. In the

[56] Herzfeld 1982
[57] Zulaika 1996: 8
[58] Aranzadi 2001: 396

postwar period their writings and those of their successors were used to feed a popular anthropology profitably deployed to political end, as discussed in Chapter Seven, while more recently Zulaika has been one of the most outspoken and forceful critics of the ground-breaking franchise of the Guggenheim Foundation in Bilbao, whose polemical establishment and operation are considered in Chapter Eight. Even today the writings of Basque anthropologists on their compatriots and their predicament are given column feet in the local press, may be referred to in local novels and, if sufficiently polemical, receive public replies from leading Basque politicians.[59] For instance Xabier Arzalluz, President of the PNV from the late Francoist period to the beginning of this millennium, was quite prepared to rebuke publicly both Zulaika and Aranzadi for their learned opinions.[60] In an area where intellectuals are still granted public weight, the comments of anthropologists are taken seriously. They continue to be able to play a public role.

This experience is a further reminder (if one is needed) that anthropologists are not just commentators on the sidelines but may well perform a circumscribed though still lively role in the very process they are studying. That is, they are not merely flies on the wall but may, in their small way, be part of the buzz.

Fieldwork, chapters

I call my approach 'anthropological' because, above all, it is grounded on long-term fieldwork, which has been extensive in time and intensive in manner. Since I started publishing on the lived reality of contemporary nationalism in 1988, scholars in other disciplines have produced their own work on this general topic, particularly Michael Billig in social psychology and Tim Edensor in cultural studies. But none, as far as I can judge from their reports, has done intensive fieldwork for an extended period.[61] Whether, in this case, this archetypal anthropological method reaps the results it should produce, I leave for you to decide.

I have to be guarded here. I do not want to promote the benefits of fieldwork in some unmindful way, as though that technique promised to unlock every door, to reveal every hidden fact. For I am only too well aware that though the people I lived with were amazingly candid much of the time, they were not nakedly open with me. For instance, though at times my landlady would hint that there were widows and widowers in the village who formed common law unions which they did not declare for tax reasons, she was always careful never to state who they were. Another

[59] For instance Miguel Sánchez-Ostiz, the much-garlanded Navarran author, casually refers in a recent novel to the controversial Basque anthropologist Mikel Azurmendi and his ideas about the Basques needing enemies in order to define themselves (Sánchez-Ostiz 2001: 171).
[60] E.g. Arzalluz's attack on Aranzadi, *Deia* 10 iv 1994, p. 13.
[61] Billig (1995) is an insightful study of British nationalism, based on the discourse analysis of focus group discussions. It is difficult to discern from Edensor's book (2002) what methods he relied on.

example: one summer in the mid-1990s when I returned for a month spell, I showed my landlords my photocopy of a section from a recent local book about sensational events in Navarre during the first half of the last century. The section discussed an event which had occurred in the village during the Second Republic and whose shameful dimensions no one had ever revealed to me. 'Oh yes, that's quite true,' they said, checked the author had got his facts right, asked me where I had got the information from, and then gently moved the conversation onto other topics.

I am also deeply aware that, despite villagers' relative openness, there may well be subtleties of local life which I never came to appreciate fully. My comprehension, I have to assume, was always limited. This point was energetically brought home to me one Sunday evening towards the end of my main period of fieldwork (almost two years in total). I was in a popular village bar; the television was on, and the volume turned up. A news reporter stated that an ETA pair had killed someone that afternoon. A female friend, incensed by this news, began to berate ETA, loudly, and in the strongest terms. She then turned to me, 'You think you understand us. But you never will. You could be here for ten years, but you'll never understand us.'

I have also to add that doing fieldwork in an area where armed activists operate meant there are further limits to what one can learn. There were certain things I had no wish to learn. In 1979 a Basque anthropologist had asked ETA members if he could do fieldwork within the organization itself.[62] I had no intention whatsoever of doing anything similar (his request was turned down). Even if one puts aside for a moment all the ethical questions raised by doing fieldwork among an armed group, I had already discovered, when researching the history of a small group which had once carried out armed operations in the area, the great difficulties of studying such a unit. Some ex-members of this band were very reluctant to talk while others seemed almost over-keen to polish their activist memories. Sifting out a credible account was not easy.[63]

Poorly armed with a little Castilian, I went to live in the Old Quarter of Pamplona, Navarre, in March 1984. I spent the next nine months trying to learn more about the local way of life, politically, historically and culturally. Some of this time I passed with friends involved in a local pirate radio station. In September the next year, fortified by the funds of a post-doctoral fellowship, I returned to my old flat in Pamplona. Over the next three months, which I mainly spent attending an intensive course in the Basque language, I slowly worked out which Navarran village might be a suitable place in which I could base myself. In December I was introduced to a poet from a village which interested me greatly.

His name is Milu and his hometown, Cirauqui, is a medium-sized village in what is known as the 'Middle Zone' of Navarre. Milu persuaded a

---

[62] Zulaika 1988: xxvii
[63] MacClancy 1989

neighbour to let me rent the unoccupied part of his second house, the basement of which he filled with cows, and in the attics of which he and his wife hung hams, sausages, herbs, and clothes to dry. I stayed there for twenty-two months and have since been back every year, for at least a brief while, sometimes for a few months. My landlords, his parents, and their daughter provided me with lunch daily and offered me friendship constantly. Milu was similarly accommodating and had me immediately made a member of his *cuadrilla* ('age-group') within the village.

During fieldwork I also began to meet Basque academics, mainly historians, sociologists and anthropologists, some of whom have become close and valued friends. Since then, I have spent a cumulative, significant period of time in Basque universities and, guided by my Basque peers, in local academic institutions and archives. I helped teach the Jakitez Master's course in Basque Studies between 1998 and 2000, gave several papers to Basque academic audiences, and in 2003 was made the Oxford Delegate for Eusko-Ikaskuntza (the Society for Basque Studies), charged with assisting the annual Visiting Basque Fellow to St Antony's College, Oxford. Much of my work has previously been read by Basque colleagues and I value their comments.

Even though my Basque work is ultimately grounded on long-term fieldwork in two sites – a village (Cirauqui) and a small city (Pamplona) – it is clear from reading almost any chapter of this book that much of the material discussed there is not primarily based on conventional fieldwork. Instead, and in step with modern anthropological approaches, my work is multi-sited. Focusing on a particular issue, item or concept, I have followed my topic wherever it led me. Thus I have interviewed Basque academics, journalists, chefs, politicians, civil servants, curators, pirate radio broadcasters, football supporters, football administrators, and any others who seemed relevant (for my purposes) and available at the time.

The first ethnographic chapter of this book is perhaps the one most based on traditional fieldwork methods in one site. For here I wish to give a strong sense, based on events I witnessed, of the lived reality of a highly politicized area (Pamplona, and more generally Navarre) where people often divided themselves along the lines of a left-wing nationalism and a reactionary regionalism. Though this chapter is grounded on events and attitudes current in the late 1980s, recent enquiry leads me to believe that much of the analysis still holds true. At the same time, it remains a valuable historical analysis of an otherwise undocumented way of life at a certain moment in time.

Chapter Three investigates the role of a football club within local life and the nationalist process. Athletic Club de Bilbao (also referred to as 'Athletic' or 'Athletic de Bilbao') is one of the most successful teams in the history of Spanish football. Its other main claim to fame is that it sees itself and is usually seen as distinctively Basque because its players have to be Basque or to come from a Basque province. For these reasons Athletic is commonly regarded as one of the greatest, most unifying symbols of Basqueness, which has played a noteworthy part in the development of Basque national pride. Given that anthropologists of nationalism should be investigating the invention of modernity as much as that of tradition, researching the evolving social roles of this team is a particularly good way to examine the development of a distinctively Basque modernity. Moreover, since the anthropology of sport is still a fledgling sub-discipline which continues to be viewed with scepticism in some quarters of our subject, this chapter may be regarded as a contribution to the effective establishment of this relatively novel zone of study.

Chapter Four is an attempt to delineate the parallel evolution of Basque nationalism and of an idea of '*la cocina vasca*' ('Basque cuisine'). Local styles of cooking are among the most appreciated in the whole of the Peninsula. Exactly how this came about, thanks to whom, for what reasons, and to what consequence are central themes in this chapter. At the same time, the renown of Basque cooking is boosted because of the interest shown in the 'gastronomic societies', historically centred around the coastal city of San Sebastian and much vaunted as working examples of Basque egalitarianism. The extent to which this is in fact the case is a subsidiary theme of the chapter. Anthropologists have long paid attention to the social and nutritional use of food (e.g. Richards 1932) but none, to my knowledge, have studied the ideological role of the idea of a particular 'cuisine'. This chapter is an attempt to redress that balance and also to assist in the creation of a still-emerging interdisciplinary 'Food Studies'.

Chapter Five summarizes and presents ways of assessing the nature and local roles of biological and genetic information in the Basque Country today. After first reviewing the information available on the prehistory, physical anthropology, haematology and genetics of the local population, I critically review the work done by Basque anthropologists over the course of the last hundred years or so into the nature of their compatriots. I then examine the evolving relations between nationalists and the production of this knowledge. For these data, though usually scientifically verifiable, are not produced in a disinterested, anationalistic vacuum. Another way of putting this would be to say that this chapter is concerned with biological anthropology, social anthropology and the social anthropology of biological anthropology. A supplementary aim is to add to the surprisingly scanty literature on racist discourse and on the connections between conceptions of 'race', 'nature' and 'culture' in Western Europe today. In this sense, the Basque case is a particularly interesting one, given its long-standing interconnections, with respect to 'race', of politics, science and popular attitudes.

In Chapter Six, I trace and comment on the intertwining over the last hundred years of Basque politics and an idea of '*el arte vasco*' ('Basque art'). In particular, I strive to follow the, at times intense, debates which have repeatedly surfaced between ideologues of Basque nationalisms, journalists and artists about the nature and value of *el arte vasco*. Anthropologists of art continue to worry about the appropriate level at which to pitch their central concept. 'Art' is not a term derived from anthropological analysis or one whose usage outside of academica is highly restricted. The very opposite: the concept is deeply embedded in the historically particular evolution of European cultures. It is therefore significant that, as far as I am aware, no anthropologist of art has recognized that the term 'art' or synonyms for it in other cultures may themselves become a cause for internal contest between interested parties. Given this apparent lacuna, in the Basque case the question 'But is it art?' is not seen as a hoary chestnut to be ignored but as a politically motivated interrogatory to be studied.

The next chapter is more of a visual excursus, which draws together threads from Chapters Two and Six. In the Basque provinces over the last twenty-five years, political graffiti has been ubiquitous, polemical, dense and imaginative. They may be regarded as visual statements by believers of direct action, and at times as a form of painterly dialogue between members of opposed factions. Either way, for anthropologists, it is an unstudied mode of representation and politico-visual performance. Some scholars have studied gang graffiti and their ilk in American cities but none, to my knowledge, whether in the USA or Europe, has studied contemporary graffiti put up by political activists.

If most of my chapters deal, in one way or another, with different manifestations of Basque modernities, the last one attends to the only example, so far, of a distinctively Basque 'super-modernity': the Museo Guggenheim Bilbao. This extremely striking, large shiny new building has immediately become an emblem of contemporary architecture for the world. It has been made the flagship for the revitalization of the formerly grim and grimy city of Bilbao. Its success is so great, city authorities from all continents are studying to see if they can imitate its example. Within the Basque Country, it has been just as successful, as a stimulus to polemic and to social change. Just how big and diverse an effect one construction can have on the inhabitants of a city and its region, and on who they think they are, is the central theme of Chapter Six. Since the debate about the Museo looks set to continue into the future and since it continues to stimulate the question of what kind of identity today's Basques want, it is an appropriate chapter on which, however provisionally, to end.

2
At Play with Identity

Identity is a catch-all term of our times. It is an empty vessel which can be filled with almost any content. As a quick perusal of recent volumes on European communities shows, astute anthropologists can use identity as a general framing device for a surprising variety of ethnographic data. In these books discussion can span from the individual to the regional to the supranational, from styles of dress or dance to religious faith. The range of possible topics seems to be limited only by the imaginative power of the compiler. The worry, of course, is that we anthropologists may well impose a notion of identity upon unmarked aspects of others' cultures. The danger is that we may extol or assiduously analyse a part of others' lives which they themselves regard as of little importance or as not just restricted to themselves but as common to many. We start to find symbols where none at present exists. The resulting ethnography may tell us more about the classificatory ingenuity of its author than about the way the people studied regard themselves. In these conditions identity begins to seem primarily an anthropologists' category; it appears to be an unjustifiably arbitrary manner of delineating others' lives in academic terms.

In his Scots ethnography *Whalsay*, Anthony Cohen worries about the implications of anthropologists inferring symbolism in other people's behaviour. He argues that in the analysis of other's social identity the interpretations anthropologists make are the ways that they, rather than the locals, make sense of what the natives do. The reasons the locals give for their action need not coincide with the explanations anthropologists proffer. Cohen suggests that an anthropologist's only defence for an interpretation can be its plausibility.

> What [an anthropologist] calls 'symbols' are the constructs of meaning which he sees surfacing repeatedly and which are thus commended as significant to the analysis. While this apparent consistency may itself be a figment of the analysis, it is the only basis on which interpretation can proceed.[1]

Cohen's problem arises because Whalsay folk do not have a strong, collectively acknowledged sense of identity; there is usually no need for them to agree publicly on what being 'Whalsay' means.

However, Cohen's qualifiers, doubts and self-imposed restrictions have no place in the analysis of politicized ethnicities. In these ethnographic situations,

[1] Cohen 1987: 94

26

there is no need to *posit* an identity, to classify these people according to one's own criteria, and then worry about the status of the construct. Local political parties or energetic factions which claim to speak for an ethnographic group organize their own symbolism; in their speeches, writings, and graffiti they provide their own exegeses of their own actions. In this sort of contested social arena an anthropologist has the privileged opportunity to see the game of identity at play. And the rules are openly discussed as each side attacks the strategies and manoeuvres of the other. Here anthropologists do not need to hunt down or discover symbolism where little or none at present exists. Rather they may compile and re-present in a linear, written mode the different, contested aspects of local identities as they are today expressed by their exponents. It might be said that Cohen falls at the first hurdle, with his almost paralysing query about the nature and status of ethnographers' classificatory strategies. But this obstacle can easily be jumped by simply paying attention to what people themselves say. And in an area as politicized as the Basque Country, they have a lot to say about themselves.

Some ethnographers may try to catch 'The Identity of the X' in their writings, but this effort is all the more difficult in societies, such as in the Basque area, where the very notion of identity is part of the local debate. The problem is compounded where 'Tradition' is itself a political term, the ideological property of a solidly right-wing group – in my ethnographic case, the Carlist Traditionalist Communion. The original focus of my field-work was to elaborate an account of the confrontation between Basque nationalism and the regionalism of Navarre, a northern Spanish province. This ideological battle provides differing conceptions of prehistory, history, race, religion, territory, language and political destiny. Identity and ethnicity cannot here be taken as ethnographic givens as Navarrans argue over who they are: Basques or Spaniards? Clearly in these sorts of context ethnicity is mutable *strategy* grounded in historical circumstances, not unchanging datum coasting in some timeless ethnographic present.

Where divisive politics permeates so much, people are made much more sensitive to their acts – no matter how seemingly 'trivial' – and of the possible political meanings that they can be given. Their lives become more dense and their behaviour takes on tones of significance absent in more peaceful provinces of Spain. Thanks to the elision of politics and ethnicity in northern Spain, people are being reminded and are reminding one another of their ethnicity far more frequently than, say, Oxford postgraduates who don't read the newspapers. Adults living within the geographical area where Basque nationalism is a political force may have organized their way of life so that they can avoid being charged or charging others of being Basque nationalist or Navarran regionalist but the point, of course, is that they have had to *organize* their lives that way by deliberately avoiding certain places, turns of phrase, and habits. A Basque patriot friend mentioned that my yellow lighter with its red top had the same colours as the Spanish flag; others said that my red braces reminded them of Manuel

Fraga, the highly patriotic right-wing leader who sometimes sports Maryle-
bone Cricket Club suspenders, bought while he was ambassador to Britain
in the days of Franco. A mother sharply tells her son to turn off the radio,
because the gentle love song broadcast is being sung in Basque. During the
annual fiesta of the village that I lived in one ardent Basque patriot criticized the playing of the hired Zaragozan band. 'They're just bloody *españolistas!*' he cried. Politicos can make their nationalist or regionalist strategies
apply to any aspect of culture. Anything can become marked politically and
so be regarded as positive or negative by different factions. Nothing escapes
the political eye.

Of radical nationalists and *el rock*

In Navarre most Basque nationalism is revolutionary socialist. At the time
of my main fieldwork, its main organization was Herri Batasuna ('Popular
Unity'), a radical coalition of small political parties, most of them originally splinter groups from ETA. To members of the coalition, Basque nationalists are *abertzales* (Basque/Euskera: 'lovers of the fatherland'). In Guipuzcoa,
Biscay and Alava, the term may apply to a nationalist of either the left or
the right. But in Navarre, where supporters of the PNV are few and not
very active, the label *abertzale* is usually applied to radical nationalists only:
those on the left to the far left, who tend to put their beliefs into action.
Since this chapter is primarily about Navarre, it is the usage I will follow.

To be an *abertzale* is not decided by birth but by performance. An *abertzale*
is one who actively participates in the political struggle for an independent
Basque nation with its own distinctive culture. You are not born *abertzale*.
You make yourself one. I have met people whose parents emigrated from
southern Spain and who, though not born in Basqueland, identify with the
Basque movement, learn Basque, and join demonstrations against the latest
threat to the integrity of the Basque people. One told me, 'Not being born
doesn't matter. I *feel* Basque.' His gathered friends nodded agreement. To be
abertzale is defined both prescriptively and proscriptively. *Abertzales* must
totally shun *chivatos* – 'informers, people thought to have any connection
with the police'. My first month in Pamplona, friends of my Basque flatmate
told him I was a *chivato* because they had seen me chatting (innocently) to
an armed policeman during a small riot. He corrected them, saying I was
just an ignorant foreigner newly arrived in town. Later, angrily, he put me
right about local rules of life. Locals recognize the danger of being branded
chivato by their own peers and that it is necessary to demonstrate the
unfounded nature of the charge as quickly and as effectively as possible.
People branded *chivato* can be so ostracized that the only community left in
which they can find friends is the police. The *chivato* is pushed into
becoming a real informer, sometimes with fatal consequences, for ETA
gunmen shoot informers dead.

Radical ideologues speak of *la gran familia abertzale*, a social unit where political attitudes are often inherited and one broad enough to accomodate both militant nationalism and revolutionary socialism. Members of Herri Batasuna had so successfully appropriated left-wing metaphors that in Basqueland it was difficult to be left-wing but not *abertzale*. (In the dying days of the dictatorship, being a member of ETA was a way to assert opposition to Franquism and members of the opposition looked well on ETA because it helped their aims. Anti-Franquism and armed Basque nationalism were seen to go hand in hand, and were confounded by many.) Almost all left-wing issues were discussed within a Basque frame. To *abertzales, el Pueblo Trabajador Vasco* ('the Basque Working People') is a *pueblo* oppressed by the occupying forces of the Spanish state and exploited by centralist capitalists. (The concept was first created by members of ETA in 1967.) Following their line of metaphors, the Basque people is already a 'nation' with its own 'popular army' (ETA) and whoe gunmen are its 'best sons'. Basque politicians who do not advance the Basque cause are 'traitors', the attempt to build a nuclear power station on the Basque coast becomes 'genocide', and the entry of Spain into NATO is damned as subversion of 'Basque sovereignty'. In this way radical Basque nationalists have created an explanatory world-view with great interpretive extension.

This rhetoric can turn deadly, for when in 1987 gunmen put two bullets through the head of an ex-leader who had renounced terrorism and returned to a quieter life, a Batasuna leader argued that 'an army cannot allow deviations, and even less so from one of its generals who appears strolling through territory occupied by the opposing army'. The quite literal appropriative power of radical nationalism was exhibited at the funeral in 1988 of the first ever gunwoman to be shot in a police action. Though the funeral was the usual mass event such occasions are, her father (a well-known nationalist moderate) removed the Basque flag draped over the coffin, and tried to prevent radical militants from entering the graveyard, raising their fists over the descending casket and singing 'Eusko Gudari', the popular song to ETA combatants. He was strongly criticized in *Egin*, the Batasuna organ, which stated that the corpse belonged to the 'people' and not to its father, and that the 'people' could not be stopped claiming political kinship with their fallen sister. In dying for the cause, she had forfeited the rights of her family for those of *la gran familia abertzale*.

Abertzales wish to increase the number of Basque speakers, to increase the sorts of occasions on which it is spoken and thus, if necessary, to create social events in which Basque is the language of communication. In an attempt to 'Basquize' Castilian *abertzales* impose Euskera orthography on Spanish: *tx* is used in place of *ch* (e.g. *txorizo*, 'sausage, thief'), *b* instead of *v* (Nabarra). Where possible Euskera, rather than Castilian, terms are used (e.g. *arrantzale* 'fisherman'). Political slogans are preferably shouted in Euskera, words for new Basque institutions came from the Euskera, not the Castilian, lexicon (e.g. *ikastola*, a school where Euskera is the medium of instruction), and parents give their children Euskera names – a practice banned during Franquism. In Euskera-speaking areas place signs are often bilingual, and with the Castilian toponym usually painted out by some midnight *abertzale*.

In this general context learning Euskera becomes an exercise in left-wing politics for politicized youth, and speaking the language in non-Euskera speaking areas (police stations, for instance) becomes a political statement. In the intensive course of Euskera I attended in the provincial School of Languages in Pamplona, posters used in the class often centred on political themes: pollution, demonstrations, dropping flower-pots on policemen, etc. Every soldier or policemen in these pictures looked distinctly ugly and clearly had not shaved in the last few days. In reaction to political events outside the school, teachers staged (bilingual) democratic assemblies in which people decided what action was to be taken: our committment to the cause was unquestioned. Bars run by radicalized youth are given Euskera names and barpersons will reply in Euskera if spoken to in the same tongue, though neither they nor their clients may be able to utter more than a few phrases. In one new bar I saw the sign, 'Castilian is also spoken.'

In fabricating their own social events, their own fiestas, and, to some extent, their own language, *abertzales* create a novel, functioning sub-culture of their own, one broad enough to include urban activists, punks, young villagers and skinheads. (Some *abertzales* are particularly proud of the fact that Basque skinheads, unlike their bald counterparts elsewhere in Europe, are not automatically associated with the violent end of the right wing.) Students of Euskera collectively camp out for days, and sponsored thousands run in marathons pacing out the extent of Basqueland, all for the sake of raising money to promote the teaching of the language. They also participate in fiestas celebrating marked aspects of 'Basque' culture, such as wood-choppers, stone-lifters, dancers, troubadours, Basque musicians, and the *olentzero* (the Basque equivalent of Father Christmas). In fact there are so many of these modern fiestas that committed nationalists can spend many of their spring and summer weekends going from one event to another. Public gatherings held in homage to murdered Batasuna leaders, to dead gunmen (or their mothers), or to *abertzales* killed by police in demonstrations become the frequent occasion for further, congregated celebration of the radical version of how to be 'Basque'. The range of this constructed culture is shown by the articles in the radicals' newspaper, which may laud the pre-capitalist way of life of Basque villagers in the last century, or describe the latest developments in 'the Basque novel', 'Basque painting', 'the Basque cinema', 'the Basque video', 'Basque sports', 'Basque cuisine', or (very popular) 'radical Basque rock'.[2]

Herri Batasuna coined the phrase '*el rock radical vasco*' in 1983 as a cate-gorical strategy to give shape to, to stimulate further, and to politicize a pre-viously uncoordinated collection of Basque rock bands, whose names often

---

[2] This construction of a nationalist subcommunity within Basque society is not novel. During the Second Republic, the activities of the PNV went far beyond those of a classical political party, constituting instead a 'microsociety within the heart of Basque society' (De Pablo, Mees, and Ranz 1999: 231–6).

advertise their countercultural attitude: La Polla ('prick') Records, Delirium Tremens, Vómito, Cicatriz ('wound'), Virus de Rebelión, Barricada, Porkeria T. ('dirt, disgusting mess'). Promoting *el rock* was a way for the *abertzale* organization to reinforce its connection with energetic youth and to radicalize rock-concertgoers. The coalition gave consistent publicity to these rock groups in a weekly *Egin* section devoted to their music and repeatedly hired them to play in Batasuna fiestas. *El rock radical* is seen as a direct result of the contemporary socio-political situation in the Basque country. And this makes it different, if not also superior, to rock movements in other regions of Spain, which are regarded as but mere imitations of fashionable transatlantic music, not reflecting the life in their own towns. *El rock radical* is loud (usually very loud), it is not very subtle, and the sense of protest is meant to be clear. When the promoters of one concert learnt that the front guitarist of the Galician band they had hired was a member of the National Police, the event was hurriedly cancelled. A strong sense of rebellion controls the stage; some bands set the tone by shouting '¡Gora ETA!' ('Long live ETA!') as they stride on; at the more charged concerts, members of the audience may pelt the musicians with bottles or beer-cans; the more excited ones may invade the stage, where some of them will start to sing while others strive to embrace the singer or strum the guitar.

Several bands display their stance by singing in Euskera, some of whom learnt it solely for the sake of their songs. One very successful band, Hertzainak (the Euskera term for the Basque Autonomous Police), sing all their highly charged numbers in Euskera, though none of the group can speak the language. The songs of *el rock* concern the level of unemployment, the pervasive drug culture (especially the heroin flood), the lack of change, the chances of revolution, the hatred of State militarism, the oppression by the forces of legitimate violence, and the need to act. Sex is a more common theme than love. With their pounding rhythms, high decibels and frenetic lead singers these locally produced bands are seen to be one way of carrying on 'the struggle'. And they do not take well to those who promote a more narrow-minded commercial view and dare to point out, as did one journalist from a Madrid-based newspaper, that 'Their autochthonous character will impede their expansion beyond the Basque Country.' In reaction to the question 'Given you could sell much more in Castilian, why do you sing in Euskera?', one musician replied, 'Well, if that question is in your questionnaire, either you are from Madrid or your soul is lost.'[3]

A comic strip in a special issue of the *abertzale* newsmagazine *Punto y Hora* issued in August 1986 summarily depicts most of *el rock radical*'s rebellious aspects. The lead singer of the fictious band, 'Txakurrak' ('dogs' in Basque), is first shown in bed with a woman, making love and smoking joints. Praising marijuana he complains about the hallucinations produced by heroin, the irritating tickle in the nose on sniffing cocaine, and the stomach indigestion caused by amphetamines. He is next seen on stage singing, 'We're just going to keep beating up the national police.' His sim-

---

[3] Both quotes in López Aguirre 1996: 60,101

ulation of anal intercourse with a guitarist of his band while singing, 'Don't worry. All this about AIDS is a lie', provokes the arrival of the police whom he single-handedly beats into submission. The strip ends with the protagonist joining his friends (a punk, a rockabilly, a skinhead and a rocker) in what promises to be a violent demonstration.

This music is seen as specifically Basque both because it is made by Basques and because it sometimes blends Punk, New Wave, Heavy Metal, and Ska with strands of traditional Basque music. Leading *abertzales* regard these groups as a part of the emerging self-created Basque society, one generated 'from below', not imposed 'from above'. *El rock radical* is played in the bars run by Basque youths, it is produced by independent Basque record companies (with names such as Discos Suicidas), it is discussed in the numerous fanzines published in the area, and it is broadcast by the plethora of pirate radio stations found in almost every Basque (or Navarran) town of any size. The effectiveness of these stations is clear: when, in November 1985, on the tenth anniversary of Franco's death, I suggested to friends in Pamplona that we make an irreverent interview with the dictator, especially resurrected for the programme, the radio station subsequently received several very threatening phone calls from outraged franquists.[4] Meanwhile music-halls are losing their audience to locally organized festivals, frequently improvised, free events, often held in out-of-the-way places: hamlets, homesteads, *frontones* (Basque *pelota* courts). This is a world which Basque youth can regard as having been effectively constructed by themselves. In the words of one irreverent musician, speaking against the perceived oppression of the Basque land,

> What we say is that we would like to change it all. And if we could write and make a free and tropical Euskadi, we'd like that because it would be more amusing. The problem is that we can't. What we can do is to try to tell the people to raise their consciousness, to break the seat in which they are sitting, and to move themselves. If the people move themselves and search, they will find something good. If they go out into the street, we'll see one another there. The unity of our movement is based on action in the street.[5]

The members of these groups are not mere puppets of experienced politicos, being cynically manipulated for political ends. In the best anarchic tradition of rock and roll rebels, some are deeply uneasy being associated with a political label and some reject any association with *el rock radical vasco*. As the leader of Hertzainak put it, defending a song of theirs,

> Although it's sure all the members of the group have voted, or vote, I don't know, for HB some time in their life, that is not to say that we are like them nor that we think exactly like them. The problem is that HB, because it is a marginal and, in some way, persecuted group, is more difficult to attack, but Drogak Aek'n (Drugs in AEK, the abertzale Euskera language academies) is a song against people with closed minds . . . and is a way of saying that, deep down, those in HB are old fogeys just like those in the PNV.[6]

[4] On the power of pirate radio stations in the Basque Country, see Urla 1995
[5] 'Hau dena aldatu nahi nuke', *Punto y Hora*, monograph, August 1986
[6] In Espinosa and López 1993: 89

The more independent of these rock and roll rebels do not want any ties to a particular political party programme and are very well aware HB is keen to support activities beloved by *abertzales* or members of the broad counter-culture. When Herri Batasuna staged a round table on 'Music at the service of the pueblo', the lead singer of Cicatriz spoke his mind:

> I said the bloody truth; that it was all a montage to catch the votes of punk youth . . . I told them it seemed to me a trick, and that for me rock and roll didn't vote or have politics. I also told them that, before, they called us frustrated Basques because we smoked joints, and now they call us happy and combative. No, my friends, no, we have changed from revolution to joints, and full stop.[7]

At about the same time as the creation of '*el rock radical vasco*', Herri Batasuna began to use the slogan '*Martxa eta borroka*' (perhaps best trans-lated as 'liveliness and struggle'). This rallying-cry connoted both the need for young *abertzales* to enjoy themselves while still working for the cause, *and* their need to remember the cause whilst enjoying themselves in town and village fiestas. '*Martxa eta borroka*' is a way both to enliven the struggle for Basque independence and to politicize traditional fiestas in a radical mode. For, as so many examples show, these collective parties of sanctioned licentiousness with excited and inebriated crowds filling the streets can easily turn into major demonstrations. The bloody conflict between the festive par-ticipants and massed groups of the police in the Pamplonan fiestas of 1978 was so sustained that the municipal council was forced to stop the festivities after only two days of the week-long event. In the same fiestas eight years later I witnessed two hapless *nacionales* who had to change the wheel of their police-car in the main Plaza. They were quickly surrounded for the duration of the operation by some sixty whistling youths. Since they were not being violent, the police did not reply. They did not want to provoke a major riot. Outside of fiestas, the same scene would have been unthinkable; the police vans would have arrived in minutes to clear the area of the disrespectful whistlers.

Though *abertzale* culture is a mix of modern events and a selective taking-up of former ways, it gains prestige by association with the glorious past of Basque culture and history. But by claiming to be the rightful heirs to Basque tradition, nationalists can be criticized by others for acting incon-sistently. When I watched a display of Basque dancing in an anti-war fiesta, one Pamplonan friend said to me that it was good dancing, but what was it doing here in Pamplona? The dances performed came from a fishing village miles north of the city. Traditionally it would not have been staged in Pamplona, and certainly not by Pamplonans. Though the annual festival of Basque dance brings together performers from many different areas, it also decontextualizes and reduces the distinctiveness of regionally based dance routines by making them all assimilable parts of a generalized 'Basque culture'. The confusion here is between culture as a static bounded entity, its content legitimated by traditional use, and culture as a dynamic, interpretative product, its content continually redefined by its present

---

[7] Espinosa and López 1993: 100–1. For later work on Basque punk, see Kasmir 1999

practitioners. *Abertzales* want the reflected prestige of the Basque past: they do not want to be confined by it. The culture they manufacture is a modern mix of the present and the past in the present, a continuing construction. Here, marked 'cultural' events are appropriated by a party programme which, in turn, is judged by political effectiveness.

Some Basques, like my critical friend, regard the social milieux created by *abertzales* as akin to a cultural monster, an unwanted hybrid threatening the existence of supposedly 'purer' growths. Yet, as defenders of this novel sub-culture argue, these invented contexts are absolutely necessary if Euskera is to survive, let alone thrive. Since the rural social structure which underpinned the traditional usage of Euskera is gradually disappearing, defenders of Basque need to create new arenas within which its usage may be considered customary. However, even this imaginative fabrication of novel contexts together with the expansion of the system of *ikastolas* is not enough to ensure the continued existence of Euskera as a viable language into the next millennium. In the Navarran village where I do fieldwork, some of the young men and women (the offspring of Basque nationalist but native Castilian speakers) were educated solely in *ikastolas*. Yet they do not normally speak Euskera because some of their friends do not understand it. For if a circle of acquaintances gather, even if only one of the group is not a speaker of Basque, the language used is Castilian. Similarly, professional teachers of Euskera, who have learnt the language as youths or as adults, do not usually employ it when talking casually to one another. As one put it to me, shame-faced, to them emotional terms in Euskera do not carry the same personal psychological force as their Castilian equivalents. She confessed they 'ought' to speak Euskera amongst themselves but failed to do so because it did not provide a sufficient degree of personal satisfaction. Its words were not charged with the autobiographical associations that imbue the terms of one's mother tongue. In these sorts of circumstances, the danger is that, in social encounters, initially speaking some Euskera becomes a form of tokenism, a dutiful acknowledgement of its symbolic importance, before getting down to the business of the day, the latest gossip, or the deeply felt expression of opinions about recent events. Usually, when I was first introduced to committed nationalists, we would utter a few formal phrases of greeting in Euskera and then switch to Castilian. But that was normally enough for me to be accepted. The fact I had studied their language intensively for a few months was taken as sufficient evidence that I took their language (and implicitly their political aims) seriously.

A further obstacle to the perpetuation of Euskera is the very process of politicization which galvanized its revival in the last decades of the dictatorship. For some Basques, uninterested in or disenchanted with the nationalist struggle, have reacted against the language movement as part of their rejection of politically motivated Basque patriotism. Some Navarrans, though the children of Basque-speaking, Basque surname-bearing parents, deliberately make no effort to speak the language and may even go so far as to claim they are not Basque.[8] To them, the ethnic adjective has become so tainted by terrorist acts that they do not wish to be associated with it in any way.

The politicization of Euskera has also affected, negatively, its usage among the most moderate of nationalists. For if, in the time of the dictatorship and the first years of the transition, learning the language was an integral part of the general oppositional culture of nationalists, then the granting of autonomy and the establishment of a Basque Government with steadily increasing powers has, for many, removed the justification for the continued existence of this culture. Hence a major reason for learning the language has effectively disappeared: speaking Euskera is no longer a way of manifesting opposition to Franco and his epigones but just a means of personally defending a nationalist notion of Basque culture.[9]

Running with bulls

An integral part of this nationalist culture is political demonstration and I must emphasize the frequency, size and often spontaneous nature of these gatherings. Since elected representatives of Herri Batasuna long maintained a policy of not attending any of the national or regional legislative assemblies, they manifested their political clout by the number of activists they could rapidly mobilize into the street. These demonstrations could be seen as doubly democratic because they are a way for 'the people', without the aid of any political representatives, to state their politics with their feet, and because everyone within the demonstrating crowd is equal: there is no apparent hierarchy within their number during the event. When in 1987 units of the then newly formed Basque Autonomous Police first went into action against a riotous assembly, journalists in *Egin* asked what these men were doing. Did they not realize they were part of the Basque people themselves, and why were they trying to prevent fellow members of the Basque people from expressing their grievances?[10]

The street is openly recognized by all politicians as urban territory to be contested. This attitude is best exemplified by the famous statement in 1973 by Manuel Fraga, then Minister of Government, about the efforts of the police to control public space in the face of mass and sometimes violent demonstrations: *'La calle es mía'* ('The streets are mine'). As the Batasuna newspaper said, demonstrating is almost the duty of an *abertzale*: it is part of their performance. It also acknowledged as a necessary *rite de passage* for radicalized teenagers. In the words of one, 'You have to suppress your fear.'

[8] A Basque colleague informs me that this strategy would not occur outside Navarre. 'Your Navarran bias comes up very clearly here; that happens only in Navarre; Basques from Biscay, Guipuzcoa or Alava would never claim, however much they may disagree with nationalist politics, that they are not Basque; they will claim that they are Basque *and* Spanish, or more Spanish then Basque' (S. Leone, pers.comm.)

[9] MacClancy 1996a discusses bilingualism in the contemporary Basque Country

[10] On the subsequent evolution of attitudes by *abertzales* to the Basque Autonomous Police, see Aretxaga 1999

2.1 To do is to be; to be an *abertzale* one must act as one: the central character runs carrying the *testigo* (lit. 'witness'), the specially sculpted baton used in the annual *Korrika* sponsored relay run, to raise funds for the teaching of Euskera. The three bubbles issuing from his head show a runner chased by a bull in Sanfermines, a demonstrator chased by an armed policeman, a beret-clad local chasing a pig for the annual domestic pig-killing (for the production of pork and pork products). The words read, 'In Euska Herria always running'. Pamplona 1987. (© Patricia Houston)

Participants discuss these demonstrations in the same terms and phrases used to talk about the bull-running in the Pamplonan fiesta made famous by Ernest Hemingway. People ask beforehand, 'Are you going to run?' and afterwards, 'Did you run? How often? Where? How long? How close did the bulls get?' (for the police are sometimes called 'bulls'). And people run, on both occasions, along the same narrow streets of the Old Quarter in Pamplona. This conjunction was exploited in the Navarran television advertisment put together by Batzarre, a hard left radical nationalist coalition separate from Herri Batasuna. The beginning of the advertisment interspersed clips from violent demonstrations in the Old Quarter with shots of the crowd being chased by the bulls in the fiesta. One leading member of the coalition told me these two aspects were juxtaposed 'because they show the reality of Navarran life today'. When a member of ETA died in prison (of natural causes) *Egin* followed its usual pattern of devoting several pages to the life of the dead man. Amidst the general panegyric typical of such events, the paper emphasized the athletic ability of the late terrorist. He had been nicknamed 'El Olímpico' because, in one well-known demonstration seen on television, an armed policeman swinging a truncheon had chased him for several hundred yards but had been unable to reach his target. El Olímpico had acted like a true *abertzale* and had done so in an exemplary, swift-footed manner.

The meeting between the police and the crowd is almost as ceremonialized as the encounter between bulls and people in the annual Pamplonan fiesta. Demonstrators provoke reaction by spilling the contents of bottle-banks across one entrance to the main Plaza. The police arrive, to the expectation of their opponents: I once heard the crowd *cheer* when the vans belatedly turned up, others have seen demonstrators impatiently stamping their feet while waiting for the opponents to show themselves. The police push open their van-doors and charge towards the fray. The demonstrators run to the relative safety of cars pulled out across the street, or stay behind smelly barricades of burning bags of rubbish. The police use tear gas, rubber bullets, and long rubber truncheons. Those behind the barricades shout slogans, whistle, maybe let off firework rockets and smash small drain-hole covers against marble shopfronts to make stones for throwing: windows of banks are a common target for these fervent anti-capitalists. The taunting, challenging nature of their jeers is patent. I have heard demonstrators cry, '!Vago! !Vago!' ('lazy, indolent') when the police paused in their firing. The police charge again, their opponents retreat, and so on, until the crowd is dispersed. Both police and people recognize the similarities between bull-running and demonstration, but the unpaid participants in these duels emphasize that they run because they are against the police. If they enjoy it, then that is merely a secondary benefit. The fight may have ritualistic elements: it is still a fight for political ends.[11]

The demonstrators do not just aim at any cop in uniform: their target is more specific. Members of the paramilitary forces, the National Police and the Civil Guard, are the focus of their assaults. It is in their stations that suspect terrorists are questioned, are tortured, and sometimes die. Municipal police do not usually carry arms and are not normally concerned with

---

[11] Local satirists are well aware of the parallels between demonstrations and fiestas. In his *Clowns in the Launderette*, Alex de la Iglesia portrays the picaresque adventures of a local holy fool. Towards the novel's end he comes upon a meeting of riot police and masked youths:

> The line of police in black was ever closer. A lad who ran at my side suddenly kneeled and threw one of his rockets towards the police. They just managed to avoid it. It exploded at their back, on the façade of the city-hall. Gosh, it seems that this infuriated them quite a bit. They replied with a shower of rubber bullets and gas canisters, some coloured. This is fiesta! Excited, I ask one of the lads for a rocket. I light it and it explodes, beautiful, in the sky.
> 'You an idiot, or what?'
> 'That is the last time I take a rocket from anybody. Next year I bring my own' (De La Iglesia 1998: 151–2).

Bernardo Atxaga, the most renowned Basque writer ever, has written a song *Ni hooligan* ('I hooligan'), about a hooligan who visits the Basque Country, looks at the scenery, the bombs, the burning kiosks, and calls a hooligan-friend in Liverpool to say 'Come! This is marvellous, a paradise; above all they call you a patriot for burning cars' (*El País*, Babelia supp., 12 viii 1995: 15).

maintaining the peace in the face of violent disorder. On the whole they are left alone by *abertzales*. When a mob of two hundred used a heavy log to smash their way through the locked entrance of the Pamplona city-hall, they were disappointed to find just a few municipal policemen inside as the only guards. It was not worth their while fighting these relatively untrained officials, and they turned away in disgust, in search of a more suitable, more qualified foe. But the agitated youth on the streets still recognize the official nature of the *munis'* position. One municipal policeman told me how he had come upon a riotous gang who had just started to tear up the street to build a barricade. As he walked towards them, they quietened down, only to start up again as soon as he had gone a distance past them. Both sides in this casual encounter knew the *nacionales* would have to deal with the situation but the barrier-builders still made their token gesture in order not to compromise the *muni*.

One day in late 1984, while teaching an English language class, I commented to the class about the violence of the police, who at that moment were beneath our windows, ripping *abertzale* posters off walls and firing rubber bullets at potential targets. A mature student surprised me. 'How long have you been here?' he asked. 'Don't you realize the police need the demonstrators?' No one disagreed. According to this argument, the police and the demonstrators lock themselves into a repeated engagement of violent force. The physical aggressiveness of one side justifies that of the other. Without demonstrators, the police would be much fewer in number and those few twiddling their thumbs. Without aggressive police, the demonstrators would simply be gesturing to the air, to the bemused regard of passers-by. Instead, the two sides engage in a dangerous tournament of street-battles where the stakes are made high.

Navarrismo

Historically *navarrismo*, or Navarran regionalism, is a reaction to Basque nationalism. It is a reactive ideology which is forcefully re-stated whenever Basque nationalism appears threateningly strong. *Navarristas* have no desire to *change* the configuration of the Spanish state. Their stated aim is merely to increase the autonomy of Navarre within the broad national frame. They do not have a very well developed world-view as they do not radically stress difference nor are they trying to change fundamentally the political order of society. Basque nationalists underline the Basque nature of Navarre, historically, linguistically and culturally. They argue a *singular* view of the whole Basqueland. They want 'their' ethnic region treated as a single unit. *Navarristas* stress a plural view of their province, linguistically, culturally and ethnically. To them, the unity holding this diversity is the *fueros*, antique particular rules of self-government granted to communities at the village, urban, regional and provincial levels. They claim Navarre is the only Peninsular example of a province (once an ancient kingdom, mentioned by Shakespeare and Dante, home to Chaucer for two years) which has kept its *fueros*. Such a central concept is open to several different interpretations and when the *abertzales* are attacking the *navarristas*' version of them, the Basque patriots deride the *fueros* wholesale as 'antediluvian privileges' which do not respect the popular sovereignity of the Basque people. Similarly, they crab any institutionalized extolling of Navarran identity, such as the newly created 'Day of Navarre', any tentative proposals about establishing any sort of 'Community of the Ebro' (i.e. a superordinate organization co-ordinating particular services between the three provinces, Navarre, Rioja and Aragon, which border on the river Ebro), and the activities of the Principe de Viana, the cultural wing of the Navarran Government. Just as *abertzales* see their fight in both nationalist and socialist terms, so they crab *navarristas* as being both reactionary regionalists and members of a controlling elite. For committed patriots these enemies within their geographical camp are not merely anti-nationalist but also members of an exploitative class. And they are to be hated for both reasons.

Politics also pervades human geography as Navarre is one of the geographically most varied provinces of Iberia, descending from the snow-capped peaks of the westernmost Pyrenees on the border with France down through successively shallower and wider valleys to the Ribera, the visually dull flat plain that borders the river Ebro. Support for the radical nationalists comes mainly from the hilly north and industrial centres while the regionalists rely on their support in, above all, Pamplona and the southern half of the province. *Navarristas* play up the stereotyped psychological differences between those of the mountain and those of la Ribera. *Montañeses* or *los del monte* (who fit almost all the criteria of most definitions of Basqueness) are said to be withdrawn, grave, quiet and not very sociable. They are men of the mountain. But when they finally offer you friendship, they give it completely. *Ribereños* or *riberos*, however, are said to be loud, joyful, gay, boastful and extremely friendly. *Abertzales* acknowledge these temperamental differences but call the *montañes* sincere and truthful, the *ribereño* insincere and often deceitful. They are said to lack manners, have an unlikeable sense of humour, and at times are to be considered animals. One Saturday night, in a village bar in the middle of Navarre I saw the local dwarf using a towel to bull-fight with a dog, to the hoots and laughs of his inebriated friends. On throwing in the towel he turned and farted loudly into the faces of two sitting men, both *abertzales*. 'Oi!' one of them responded, 'That's done in the Ribera!' that is, not here, not in the village. *Navarristas* do not denigrate *ribereños*. In fact, many of them are *ribereños*.

In this factious context the ambiguity of almost any image is exploited by both parties. Nationalists put forward the independence of mountain-dwelling Basques from invading Romans as the reason for the successful maintenance of much of their distinctive mythology. To them Basque Christianity is both distinctively fervent and neo-pagan in many aspects. But to the distinguished Spanish historian Sánchez Albornoz this same lack of romanization explains Basque backwardness' and their 'irrationality': it is only the descendants of cave-dwelling pagans who could be prepared to shoot or blow up so many Spanish policemen.

The limit case to the pervasiveness of nationalist politics is the highly popular Navarran football team, Osasuna, normally to be found in the lowest ranks of the First Division of the Spanish league. For financial reasons (it's a cheap way to get players) the Osasuna Football Club supports juvenile football teams throughout the province. Until 1984 all its players were born and bred in *la cantera* ('the quarry'), i.e. the province itself. In a recent effort to end the seemingly constant threat of relegation to the Second Division, the club started to buy in players from overseas, predominantly England. Some supporters reacted immediately claiming that the ideals of the club, as a representation of Navarre, was being betrayed. But as the new players have improved the team's game, the opposition quietened. The owners of the club have taken particular pains that the team not become politicized. Unlike their peers in leading football teams in the Basqueland, players for Osasuna do not appear in newspaper advertisments recommending that people respect their heritage and learn Basque. (The term *osasuna* is Euskera for 'health'.) But if the players do not actively support Basque nationalism, nor were they criticized politically in *Egin*. It seems that the *abertzale* parties recognize the broad popular following of the team and so, in an effort not to alienate potential support for the radical camp from among the ranks of fans, they succumb to the apolitical stance of the club. However nationalist friends in Pamplona, grumbling quietly, have told me that the players are *fachas* (a derogatory term with the same significance and political accuracy as the British 'fascist'). If they're not with us they can only be against us.

The benefit of being radical

In the contemporary context of Spanish politics, where many nationalist forces seek an advantageous accommodation with the central government, Herri Batasuna remains exceptional. Unlike other Basque parties which have diluted their demands or modified their position, the political wing of ETA persists in defining the radical edge of nationalist politics. On almost any issue that is under discussion, Herri Batasuna takes an extremist stance, in order partly to show up their nationalist opponents' moderation and preparedness to compromise. The disadvantage of this ideological immobility is that what adherents might value as a morally upright steadfastness can appear to others as a refusal to accept the changing realities of the day. When the British Hispanist Michael Jacobs visited an *abertzale* in Bilbao, he comes to regard his host as out of touch:

> I spent that night on a sofa below a crowded bookcase, in a time-warp. I had regressed to a world of innocence and idealism. The books were those which might have been found in a student flat of long ago: Marx, Engels, Walter Benjamin, Rosa Luxemburg, Lenin, Che Guevara, Regis Debray, Marshall

McLuhan, Mao Tse-tung, Simone de Beauvoir.[12]

The advantage of this immobility is that *abertzales*, by not shifting their position, do not have to worry about the present nature of their identity. By not changing their political place, they have the satisfaction of continuing to know where they stand, as a radical nationalist friend in Cirauqui explicitly stated to me.[13] The point is also made by the Spanish writer José María Merino in his short story *Imposibilidad de la memoria*. The central thread of his tale is contemporary Spaniards' loss of identity through the persistent compromises necessitated by the establishment and maintenance of democracy:

> We would go mad if we were capable of understanding up to what point we can manage to change. We convert ourselves into other beings. That double ghoul of some horror story,' he thought, repeating a topic habitual in his reflections.
>
> Javier had changed much, but perhaps it was true that the loss of identity was one of the signs of our times, and that there no longer remained in the world anything human which could conserve its substance. He himself had affirmed it in rotund phrases, on one of those occasions in which they had a conversation which rose above the strictly domestic.
>
> 'Identity now only exists in the day-dreams of ayatollahs, of abertzales, of people like that'.[14]

Unlike the protagonist Javier who disappears in a highly mysterious manner, *abertzales* do not lose their identity, do not have to question their own integrity. By continuing to uphold the slogan 'Those not with me are against me' they maintain a strong sense of political and linguistic conflict which serves to animate their efforts to see Euskera re-established as the common vernacular of their homeland.

The undercut

I wish to make a point here which, even though it is an anthropological commonplace, I have yet to see in any writings on Basque nationalism. My point is that though radical leaders might wish to underscore and deepen the divide between themselves and the forces of the state, there are committed members of both sides who will, on occasion, put domestic allegiance before political kinship. For it was suggested to me during fieldwork that members of an extended family, even if they were each entrenched at opposite poles of the political spectrum, might put aside those differences during family gatherings, e.g. weddings, and might even quietly assist one another.[15] When I tried to follow this matter up, some of the people I spoke to acknowledged this cross-factional fraternization did occur on occasion,

[12] Jacobs 1994: 311
[13] On the local, fundamental importance of knowing where one, and others, stand, and of not being a turncoat, see MacClancy 2000: 70–71
[14] Merino 1993: 114
[15] For further examples of kinship transcending political division, see Harris 1972; MacClancy 2002: 6

but none wished to give further details, not surprisingly given the great sensitivity of this information. In the first chapter, I mentioned possible limits to my fieldwork. This was clearly one of them.

In other words, despite the powerful rhetoric of *la gran familia abertzale* and the passionate conviction shown by nationalists and their opponents, the emotional tie of a more intimate sense of family could still predominate at times, perhaps especially at celebratory occasions. Ideologues and propagandists might wish to draw clear lines along political boundaries but locals, even avowed members of one side or the other, could decide to discreetly sidestep them, on a strictly contextual basis.

2006

While the majority of this chapter is grounded on my fieldwork of the mid- to late 1980s, I am today (September 2006) somewhat surprised that the main changes since in Navarre are more ones of degree not kind. Most importantly, the ranks of the *abertzales* have both thinned and split. After the ETA ceasefire in 1999 Patxi Zabaleta, a Pamplona lawyer and local Batasuna leader, left to form a new party, Aralar, which positions itself on the nationalist left but rejects armed violence. It has at present four representatives in the 50-strong Parliament of Navarre. The sum consequences of these changes are twofold: it is now possible to raise local left-wing issues without automatically adopting a nationalist dimension; *batasuneros* can no longer dominate debates on what it means to be an *abertzale* in the province. There are other indicative shifts: today local pop music fans no longer speak of *el rock radical* while teachers of Euskera can not assume their students are on the nationalist left. When in 1997 a Pamplona class, attended by a local colleague of mine, found the word *iraultza* ('revolution') in a text, no one knew what it meant. Their teacher commented that previously *iraultza* was the one word of Euskera all introductory students already knew.[16]

Despite these changes, the basic oppositional stance of the radical nationalists persists, as does their sub-culture. While the number and size of demonstrations might have diminished in recent years, during the prolonged ETA ceasefire from 1998 to 2001 the radicals took full advantage of police reluctance to make arrests, by creating the *kale borroka*, the highly organized management of violent youth gangs in city-streets. Their joint movements co-ordinated by mobile phones, they repeatedly intimidated anti-nationalists. The ceremonialized nature of this urban violence continues and may even be openly recognized. When, in August 2006 during the negotiated peace process, a PNV spokesman tried to downplay the recent urban attacks of some *abertzale* youths, he stated that acts of street violence and the staging of demonstrations are just part of 'the ritual of every summer' of the radical nationalist left.[17]

---

[16] S. Leone pers. comm.
[17] *Información* 23 viii 2006: 29

On 7 May 1998 a pair of *etarras* (ETA combatants) shot dead the UPN (Unión del Pueblo Navarro) spokesperson in the Pamplona town hall. He was the first victim of terrorist violence in Navarre in several years. The next day a newspaper published a cartoon of a hooded *etarra* stating, 'Now we kill Navarran politicians so that it is seen that we consider them as if part of the family'. Unsurprising then that the *navarrista* arguments against the radicals' irredentism do not go away but resurface whenever the latter revive the Basque claim to Navarre.[18] Indeed *navarrista* attempts to downplay the Basque dimension of the province have strengthened since UPN gained control of the Deputation in 1996, and which it has held ever since. Their president Miguel Sanz, as leader of the Deputation, has vigorously pursued policies, sometimes in the face of mass criticism, which reduce support for the teaching of Euskera in the province, and which strengthen the constitutional independence of Navarre from some possible union with the Basque Country.[19]

To these important extents, the analysis of this chapter still holds good today. The debate on identity remains fresh.

[18] On this, see MacClancy 1999
[19] For information on the policies of UPN, see their website www.upn.org. For an example of the criticism levelled at UPN's policies towards Euskera, see *Deia* 12 iv 2002: 24.

3
Football

Johan Huizinga was right: play is central to life. In his seminal and much-praised *Homo Ludens*, first published in 1938, Huizinga argued that play had an essential role in the development of civilization. To understand humanity in any rounded sense, it had to be taken into account. And of course, one key latter-day manifestation of play was the rise of organized sports from the nineteenth century on.[1] It is thus surprising that until relatively recently mass sport was not thought an appropriate topic of research for serious social scientists. The attitude seemed to be that nothing so enjoyable could be worthy of sustained analysis. From the 1990s on, however, a belated and continuing series of studies into the ever-more prominent phenomenon that is modern sport has begun to dispel that prejudice.[2] Since the attitude, however, still lingers and since the roles of mass sport in the development of modern Basque society have been significant, an aim of this chapter is to unravel the socio-political contexts of a very particular and nationally famous Basque football team, one whose sense of identity is central in the hearts of minds of its supporters: Athletic Club de Bilbao.

This chapter, however, also has an even more important aim: to understand, via the study of local football, how the Basques have constructed their own version of the new. As stated earlier, nationalists may laud both certain splendid moments of Basque history and distinctively Basque variants of modern Western culture. While they wish some of the glories of the past to reflect back on to them, they do not want to be constrained by an obsessive fidelity to history. Instead they wish to create a culture broad and supple enough to include both bereted farmers and guitar strummers. The American anthropologist Jacqueline Urla makes a related point in her work on current Basque ethnonationalist culture: that many nationalists wish to be seen as both the heirs of a laudable history and also as 'up-to-date' as those of their contemporaries in other lands interested in both the renovation and the recuperation of their way of life. Peering backward does not mean that nationalists cannot also be as 'advanced' as some of their neighbours. They want their way of life to be seen not merely as different, but as simultaneously different and the same, as culturally distinct in certain time-honoured ways and as culturally common in others – modern

[1] Huizinga 1949
[2] E.g., MacClancy 1996b

44

others. Thus, if we are use Hobsbawn and Ranger's terminology, they are as much involved in the 'invention of modernity' as in the invention of tradition.[3]

In this chapter I wish to underline this Janus-like character of Western ethnonationalism, its continual concern to create an ever-dynamic, distinctive cultural mix of the antique and the contemporary, by discussing the remarkably close and evolving relations between one nationalistic community, those of the Basque province of Biscay, and its most famous football team, Athletic Club de Bilbao.

It was the British who first brought the game to the Basqueland. In the early 1890s, in the environs of Bilbao, sailors whose ships imported coal to the United Kingdom and engineers working for local coal-mineowners and shipbuilders would occasionally play football wherever they could find a flat piece of free ground. To most residents of Bilbao these games were their first sight of football, though many had already read about it in the newspapers or heard of it from those sons of the local bourgeoisie who had been educated in British Catholic public schools. Interest grew rapidly, and the first 'friendly' match between British and Basque teams was played on 3 May 1894. The expatriates won 6-0.[4]

As the popularity of the game continued to increase, locals and expatriates started to form their own joint clubs. Athletic Club de Bilbao, formed in 1901, gained renown two years later by winning the first-ever Championship of Spain, held in Madrid. This was merely the very first of an illustrious record which the club has been able to maintain up to recent times: besides gaining a host of other trophies, it has won the national championship twenty-three times, has been top of the league eight times, has participated in all the main European championships, and has never been relegated to the second division – a distinction it shares with only two other clubs in the country, Barcelona and Real Madrid. Over sixty of its footballers have played for Spain, one of them (the goalkeeper José Angel Iribar) holding the record for number of games (forty-nine) played in the national team. When Athletic Club de Bilbao won the league in both 1983 and 1984 it is estimated that, on each occasion, crowds of over one million came to greet the ceremonial arrival of the victors into the city. To put that figure into perspective, when in May 1994 Manchester United both came top of the league and won the F.A. Cup (and thus became only the fourth British club last century to do so), the crowd that greeted their ritual tour through their home-area failed to number more than several thousand.

Local support of the team, however, is based not just on its sporting achievements, deeply impressive though they may be, but on what it represents, because Athletic Club de Bilbao is seen as *the* team of the Biscayans. Moreover, in national contests 'Athletic' aspires, often successfully, to be seen as *the* team of the Basques, though many supporters of Real Sociedad,

---

[3] Urla 1993; Hobsbawm and Ranger 1983
[4] Much of this historical section relies on Mugica 1982 and Athletic Club Bilbao 1986

based in San Sebastian and the only other consistently top-grade Basque team, might question that.[5] In this chapter, I examine the sources, extents and futures of this identification. For football is here not a peripheral passion, played out in ninety minutes every Saturday, but a central strut of modern notions of who the Basques are.

Identification

When trying to account for the degree of identification between the team and its supporters, the key characteristic which locals most often emphasize is Athletic's much-vaunted rule that only Basques (broadly understood) can play in it. This rule distinguishes Athletic from all other clubs in the Spanish League. Some other clubs used to uphold a similar rule for their own territory but all, bar Athletic, have now given it up. In the first years of Athletic a significant minority of its players were resident Englishmen: Alfred Mills, an engineer, was one of its thirty-three founders, and noteworthy players of its first decade include Langford, Dyer, Evans and Cockram. But by 1919 the team had become exclusively Basque and in that year the Junta Directiva of the club decided that it would remain so as a matter of principle. At first Basqueness was defined in almost Aranian terms: a person born and brought up in the Basqueland, whose all four grandparents had Basque surnames. The criterion of surnames was gradually relaxed and, in the 1950s, the rules were further eased to allow those born in the Basqueland, whatever their parentage, to be considered for the club. Thus local-born sons of immigrants, like their Basque friends, could start to dream of making it to Athletic's first eleven. But even this relaxation of the rule could still lead to unfortunate occurrences. Manolo Sarabia, who went on to become a great player for the team in the 1970s, recalled what had happened in the mid-1960s to his brother, a promising forward who was twelve years his elder:

> They called him to come sign up, but on his filling in the form, they realized that he had not been born here, but in Torres, in the province of Jaen, where my family comes from . . .

> My brother returned home very upset, almost crying, because, of course, his dream, like that of all the lads round here, was to play in Athletic. I was just a kid then, but seeing him so unhappy, I went up to him and said, 'Don't worry, Lazarus: I'll play in Athletic, because I was born here, and they won't be able to say no to me.' For that reason, getting to play for Athletic was for me like a sacred commitment, something that I had to achieve, whatever it took.[6]

In the 1970s the club re-interpreted its rules again, allowing those who had

---

[5] The formerly nationalist and now fiercely anti-nationalist Basque journalist Patxo Unzueta, who has greatly influenced the work on Basque football by British social historian John Walton (e.g. 2001), states that 'Athletic has continued to be considered an exclusively Biscayan institution' (1999: 149). My own experience, based on years of fieldwork in urban and rural Navarre, and of repeated periods spent in San Sebastian, rural Guipuzcoa, and Bilbao, is that Athletic is seen as a predominantly but certainly not 'exclusively' Biscayan institution.
[6] Quoted in Unzueta 1986: 120

not been born in the Basque provinces but had been brought up there from an early age to be considered for Athletic. This broadening of the club's pool of potential players coincided with the extended definition of Basqueness that radical nationalists had started to propound at that time; to these activists 'a Basque' was not someone who fulfilled the conventional ethnic criteria, but someone who lived and sold their labour in the Basque Country. As one member of Athletic's management put it to me in 1994, *'Lo importante no es donde se nace sino donde se pace'* ('What is important is not where one is born but where one grazes.') He admitted that the club's definition of 'the Basque Country' would include the three historic Basque provinces of southwestern France; it was merely that 'we have not yet gone there to look for players'. In 1997, Athletic, influenced by its new French trainer, did hire its first French Basque player, Bixente Lizarazu, a member of the French national squad. But he did not play particularly well within the team and within a year decided to transfer to a German club. Athletic's Junta Directiva admitted that this experience was not a happy one but that it would not discourage them from seeking possible players from over the border in the future. Since the 1990s the rules have been re-interpreted yet again: Athletic will now consider players who were born and brought up outside the Basqueland, yet have at least one Basque parent. The club is also now prepared to consider people not born and brought up inside the Basqueland and who have no Basque parents, yet learnt to become footballers within the area.[7] Despite the progressive re-interpretation of this symbolically fundamental rule of eligibility, the great majority of players for Athletic are still men born and raised in the area, and the rule is still popularly spoken of as 'Basques only'.

An important financial consequence of this rule is that Athletic, unlike all other important clubs, does not usually spend a sizeable part of its income on purchasing stars from other teams. Instead, since 1971, it has spent much of its money investing in the youth of its region: in the Bilbao suburb of Lezama the club has set up what has become a virtual academy of football, with five grass pitches, another of artificial grass, a covered pavilion also with artificial grass, a gymnasium, a *frontón* (for playing the Basque ballgame of *pelota*), and a medical centre. There teams of adolescents (some of them boarders) receive years of intensive training in the finer points of the game from famed ex-players. Students at Lezama form eight junior teams, graded by age, which play in their respective regional and national juvenile leagues, often with great success. 'Graduates' of Lezama help form the second team of the club, known as Bilbao Athletic, which plays in the Second Division of the Second League. They also participate in the affiliated club, 'Basconia', which plays in the Third Division and is so successful it has its own junior side. Furthermore, Athletic maintains seven schools, 'mini-Lezamas', spread throughout Biscay and just into the neighbouring Basque provinces. In each, local boys are trained twice a week and the more promising among them are offered places at Lezama. On top of all

[7] *Deia* 15 iii 1998: 43

this, Athletic has formal agreements with 100 clubs in Biscay and ten others in Alava, Guipuzcoa and Navarre. In return for economic and professional support and occasional provision of graduates from Lezama, these clubs, which belong to lesser divisions or leagues, agree to transfers of their best players for a reduced sum for Athletic, if so requested. Moreover, since 1998, Athletic has set up an annual series of meetings with those in charge of sports in over 300 Biscay schools, in order to ensure that methods of training in the province are up to the latest standards. This policy of generally cultivating local talent rather than purchasing already proven players for extortionate prices is known as *la cantera* ('the quarry'), and is one major reason why people of the area have been able to identify so easily with the club. For it means not only that many supporters at a home match know they are witnessing the efforts of their fellows, but that if local boys display ability they may dream of being seriously considered by the selectors.

From time to time, Athletic may well spend large amounts when buying established players from other Basque teams but there is a clear limit to the number of such transfers it can make. For if *la cantera* is 'one of the basic pillars of (the club's) existence and its *raison d'être*' then, in order to maintain a high level of general enthusiasm, Athletic has effectively enforced itself to take advantage of its more promising Lezama products. In this sense, sustaining any real sense of *la cantera* creates its own obligations. In a 1998 interview, the Assistant to the President of the club strove to downplay the significance and possible number of expensive transfers. Instead he chose to underline the centrality of the club sustaining itself with 'people from home': 'One must not create anxiety in the lower teams, because all the lads who defend the Athletic strip should see reaching the first team as something possible.'[8] If, as occurred in the 1996–7 and 1997–8 seasons, too many promising players are bought for the immediate requirements of the first team, they may be 'rented' out to other clubs in the First or Second Divisions, or integrated into Bilbao Athletic. There they can continue to participate in top-level football and to mature as players. If they are seen to fulfill their promise (which very few in fact do), they are taken back by the club to join its premier squad. In this way, Athletic can strive to balance the competing demands of buying in young hopefuls and sustaining the spirit of *la cantera*.

There are, of course, other disadvantages to this policy. For instance, a lesser or local amateur club may threaten to pull out of its agreement with Athletic or seek the sponsorship of a different Basque First Division team, unless Athletic raises its financial contribution significantly.[9] Also, some fans complain that other clubs exploit Athletic's restricted choice of purchasable players by raising the transfer price of any Basque member of their teams. For there is such a small pool of footballers which Athletic might be interested in that at times it may well feel forced to pay over the odds.

[8] *Deia* 15 iii 1998: 43; '*raison d'être*' quote from *M* 22 iv 1999: 54
[9] See, for example, *M* 9 v 2000: 66

Players, when speaking publicly, stress the advantages of the 'Basque-land-only' rule. According to Joseba Etxebarria, one of the team's leading players in the late 1990s:

> The best squad does not always win. Besides having good players, it is necessary to make a team and make it work. In this sense we are already winning because in our changing-room we all speak the same language, we are all from here.[10]

Players wishing to emphasize the inner harmony of the team and its lack of divisions speak of it as 'like a family, we understand one another, and there are no problems of being together.' When the team did very well at the end of the 1998–9 season, players stressed comradeship as the main reason for their success, for their ability to overcome bad moments. One member tried to explain it so: 'Here we are all clear about what we love. In other places they have many foreigners and perhaps they do not all have the same objective.'[11] One indicator of the camaraderie among the team was the spontaneous agreement in late November 1998 of all the players and their trainers to donate collectively over two million pesetas towards the Central American victims of hurricane Mitch; during training that week all players wore T-shirts proclaiming 'El Athletic con Centroamerica'.[12]

This strong sense of fraternity and belonging has its price though. In the words of one player, Athletic is a club which 'involves you 24 hours a day' and which 'like it or not, leaves its mark'.[13] The first team's trainer suffers similar consequences. As a local journalist stated, when discussing Luis Fernandez, Athletic's trainer in the late 1990s:

> Not any trainer will do for any team. Athletic needs one who fully takes on its philosophy ... Athletic, all things considered, needs someone who believes in what it does and gives himself up body and soul to the entity.
>
> This is the secret of Luis Fernandez. He arrived in Bilbao and understood that he was not just in another team. He understood the significance of *to be of Athletic*. And he made himself of Athletic.[14]

This sense of Athletic as a highly distinctive club is reinforced by its strongly maintained traditions. We have already mentioned some. Another is the custom for the players of a team, newly ascended into the First Division and competing in San Mamés for the first time, of leaving a bouquet of flowers at the sculpture to Pichichi, in memory of the great Athletic goal-scorer of the 1910s. Also, Athletic may recognize and honour the contribution made by locals who have performed outstandingly well in a particular sport by ceremonially presenting them with a badge of the club

[10] *M* 21 iv 1999: 55

[11] *M* 17 v 1998: 50. One player stressed that the squad was so united and could incorporate new members so easily because 'We are all from here, with very similar ways of seeing things and of living' (*M* 28 vii 1999: 42). See also *M* 24 viii 1999: 34.

[12] *M* 29 xi 1998: 55. This was not the first example of such a gesture by the team. After the devastating flooding of Bilbao in August 1983, the players spontaneously agreed to give their bonuses for the first six games of the following season towards its victims: in total, over seven million pesetas (Alonso 1998: 172).

[13] *M* 3 viii 1998: K5

[14] *M* 15 ix 1998: 49, orig. italics.

made in gold and diamonds.[15] In 1998, as part of its centenary celebrations, Athletic remembered the English component of its origins and commemorated the 1894 game against a British team by staging a match between eleven former players for Athletic and a team of English expatriates resident in Biscay.[16]

As we have seen, fraternity has its price. In the same way, the history of the club may be glorious but it brings with it its own burdens. Boasting of Athletic's past may puff up a supporter's chest but the gesture tends towards the ridiculous, or just the sad, if the team's present performance cannot withstand the implicit comparison. As one migrant to the area said to me, 'Athletic? Bah! If they were so good why do they lose so many matches?' In newspaper interviews, players may ask not to be compared with distinguished predecessors who held the same position.[17] Also, they are highly conscious of the constraints that come with the policy of *la cantera*. One player even pleaded that they not be compared with richer teams:

> We do not want that as much is demanded of us as of a Madrid or a Barcelona. We want demands on us but not at the same level as for those teams which have a great advantage over Athletic because they hire whom they want, from where they want and almost when they want.[18]

Similarly, Athletic's traditionally well-developed sense of self-esteem may clash badly with modern requirements. In April 1999 when the referee at an away game forced the team to change their shorts for those of a different colour, a columnist complained vehemently against those the home team generously supplied: 'horrific shorts with the colour of potato stew in green sauce with heads of hake. The resultant frightening combination was an aesthetic crime *en toda regla*, a tremendous lack of respect for a centenary institution.'[19] Further, though Athletic's philosophy limits its potential income, it was not until the centenary celebrations of 1998, when it invited Luciano Pavarotti and the Rolling Stones (for separate concerts), that the proud club finally opened the doors of its stadium, popularly known as *La Catedral* ('The Cathedral'), to anything other than a football match.[20] The *sancta sanctorum* had been breached.

The relatively inexpensive strategy of nurturing 'home' players dovetails with the club's self-constraining financial policy, which itself constitutes another key component of Athletic's general philosophy. For Athletic, unlike most Spanish teams, is not a limited company but a 'Sociedad Deportiva' ('sports society/club') jointly owned by its members (*socios*, at present

---

[15] E.g. the presentation to the cyclist Jesús Loroño in *M* 25 vi 1998: 56
[16] *M* 21 vi 1998: 58
[17] E.g the comments of one interviewed player in *M* 13 ii 1999: 52. After a string of particularly poor performances, one journalist pointed out that 'the weight of history hangs over the heads of the players' (*M* 12 vi 2001: 63).
[18] *M* 4 vi 1999: 57
[19] *M* 26 iv 1999: K4. See also *M* 28 ix 1999: 59
[20] *M* 30 iii 1998: 9. Some may take the idea of San Mamés as hallowed ground beyond the metaphorical. In 1999, for example, one ageing fan asked that his ashes be strewn on the pitch (*M* 8 x 1999: 57).

numbering some 32,000). Further income is usually raised, not by allowing a wealthy person with spare cash to invest to take it over, but by increasing the annual subscription. Directors of the club, supported by a majority of *socios* on this point, strive to ensure that the total value of *socios*' subscriptions constitute at least 30 per cent of the club's annual income. Of course this policy severely limits the amount of money Athletic can raise in any one year. Members, however, would rather have it that way, and so feel in some sense that the club 'belongs' to a broad section of the community, than allow it to fall into the hands of a single person, who might have designs on his new possession. As a recent President of the club put it, 'I am aware that at times it costs to be a Sociedad Deportiva but it is a constraint which is worthwhile because Athletic has to be of everybody and not of a few.' In 1999, in an effort to deepen yet further this sense of belonging and to reinforce the sovereignity of *socios* as responsible for the government of the club, the Junta Directiva agreed to conduct elections on-line, to establish an annual open meeting of the directors with *socios* and, generally, to make its workings and decisions more transparent and thus more accountable to the club's members.[21]

In the first decades of the club all its players were amateurs, albeit dedicated ones, who only received payment for the expenses they incurred in away matches. In the words of José María Erice, who played for the team from 1917 to 1926, 'We were like true brothers. The same with the directors. Our way of doing things was based purely on love, on playing and sacrificing oneself for the colours of the city and the team.'[22] In the mid- to late 1920s, however, Athletic imitated the recent example of other teams by progressively placing its players on a professional footing. Supporters of Athletic took pride in the fact that members of its first team received relatively little. Even that minimal income, however, could be very important in times of general hardship. Panizo, a great player of that period, later remembered:

> I don't know if today this will be well understood but in the 1940s, after the war, with the misery that there was and everything else, for us, to play in Athletic, to play in international games, to be able to bring up a family, that you were paid for doing something that you liked doing over and above everything else, was like a blessing from heaven.[23]

Generally, members of the team were not meant to be playing primarily for the money, but for the pride that came in representing the premier Basque side, and representing it well. This supposed and proclaimed relative lack of pecuniary interest in playing for Athletic was a further reason for supporters' ability to identify with the players. For as relatively lowly paid 'workers' they could be seen by many of their followers as, in some sense, their equals if there was not much money to be earned by kicking a ball around for the first half of their lives. They could be regarded not as avaricious individuals

---

[21] *M* 19 v 1999: 62; 1 vii 1999: 59
[22] Quoted in Athletic Club 1986, vol.1: 27
[23] Quoted in Unzueta 1982

whose only end was to exploit their talent in order to accumulate capital, but as ordinary Basques making the most of their particular physical gifts for the pleasure it gave them and the renown it might win them and their community.

Of course, as the fame of Athletic grew, the indirect financial advantages of playing for the club became more and more apparent. Becoming a highly respected figure in the local community brought benefits, as Venancio, a member of the first eleven in the late 1940s and early '50s, admitted:

> For me, Athletic solved my life. In my business dealings, it opened lots and lots of important doors. I was Venancio, he of Athletic, and people received me in a different way. What I could dream of once I had joined Athletic! It was like a miracle.[24]

Within a few years of the club establishing its commanding presence in Spanish football, players for the team began to displace famous bullfighters as popular idols. Unlike these trained killers, however, who were often associated in the popular imagination with sexual excess, the players of Athletic were represented as 'eleven villagers', as men who, off the pitch, were as sober as their fellow Basques, and as religious as them. At the beginning of each season, the team and the club's directors attend a special mass celebrated by the Bishop of Bilbao at the church of San Antón, where they make a floral offering to the Virgin of Begoña, patron saint of the city. Whenever Athletic comes top of the league or wins a trophy, they return there to offer up their victory to the Virgin.[25] Until the 1970s the team would also spend a week at the end of the season cloistered in the Jesuit university of Bilbao, performing spiritual exercises. Senior priests in the local hierarchy are keen to laud the players as symbols of fraternity and honesty, and as role-models for the male youth of the region; even Pope Pius XII, who granted the players a special audience in 1956, called them 'a model team from the moral and religious point of view'.[26] As stars of Basque society, even their social life may receive great attention. When the team was invited to tour the new Euskalduna convention centre and concert hall, the visit was given prominent space in the regional press.[27] Individual players may also allow themselves to be exploited for the sake of good causes, great publicity being given to their commitment, for instance, to pro-Euskera or anti-drug campaigns.[28] Perhaps the most striking statement of their public profile was made by the local author José Mari Isasi in his novel about a recent captain of the team, Julen Guerrero, famed for his commitment to Athletic, despite receiving financially very tempting offers from other clubs. In the opening scene, the evening rumour that Guerrero has agreed to transfer to Real Madrid leads spontaneously to a massive demonstration outside the Athletic stadium, then to rioting and the

---

[24] Quoted in Athletic Club 1986, vol. 2: 187
[25] Terrachet 1969: 6; *M* 18 viii 1998: 38
[26] Terrachet 1970: 145; Uriarte 1986
[27] *M* 29 I 1999
[28] E.g. *M* 7 v 1999: 76; 13 v 2000: 7; 15 v 2000: 16

intervention of armed police. Fleeing the rubber bullets distraught fans, inconsolable at the news, wander the streets through the small hours.[29]

During the years of Franco's regime the club's twin policies of the *cantera* and of not allowing its players to become rich, together with its string of successes, won Athletic great popularity throughout the country. In provinces as distant from Bilbao as Granada and Murcia, non-Basque fans of Athletic spontaneously set up their own supporters' clubs (*peñas*), where they assiduously followed the fortunes of the team and debated the finer points of their game. Panizo remembers them well:

> There were peñas everywhere, in even the most unexpected villages. They would come to see us in our hotel, would chat with us, identify themselves with us, because they saw that we were ordinary people, that we did not think ourselves different, that we had not gone there to act like great persons. How were we going to go there and act like great persons if everyone already knew that, if it weren't for football, we'd be wearing overalls in a factory or digging up potatoes in the fields![30]

Out of the 390 *peñas* which at present exist, 129 of them form the Agrupación de Peñas del Athletic, whose membership elects its own directive team, headed by a President. One of the key functions of the directive of the Agrupación is to act as a representative of *peñistas* to the official organization of the club. In the 1999 electoral campaign for the Presidency, both aspirants to the position promised to promote fraternization between *peñas*, to augment their relation with the club itself, and to boost the use of Euskera within the Agrupación. One went further, promising to lobby the club to exploit the Internet more widely, as both an aid to *socios* and a form of control of the club itself. These *peñistas*, at least, want yet more and closer links between supporters, and also between them and the organization they so dearly uphold.[31]

Peñas are so central to Athletic's self-conception that a grand, several-day long 'Congress' for all *peñas* is held annually in Bilbao. At these highly festive, alcohol-fuelled events, attended by 40,000 supporters from across the country, Biscayan *peñas* act as hosts for those who have come from further afield. What many participants like to stress is the sense of 'brotherhood' generated among the diverse congregants gathered there for the occasion. These greatly enjoyed jamborees are also privileged opportunities for serious exchange, as a time and space is set aside for any supporter who so wishes to present his or her complaints and suggestions directly to the Junta Directiva.[32]

Basque followers of Athletic, as several pointed out to me, also take pride in the fact that support for the team, unlike that for most British clubs, cuts

---

[29] Isasi 1998. Guerrero is not the only very good player to have stated publicly they have no intention of transferring outside the area. For them the multilayered identification of the team with local society is worth more than the extra money to be gained by a lucrative transfer (see, e.g. the statement of Joseba Etxebarria *M* 3 ii 2000: 55).
[30] Quoted in Unzueta 1982
[31] *M* 29 vi 1999: 52
[32] *M* 14 iii 1999: 40; 3 v 1999: 48

across conventional class divides. It is true that in its first years Athletic was primarily a team of *señoritos* ('young gentlemen', or in its more pejorative sense 'young upper-class parasites'). Many early players did come from the ranks of the bourgeoisie: indeed, the centre-forward who led the team to victory in the inaugural national championship was a marquis, while José Antonio de Aguirre, a lawyer from a well-to-do background who in 1936 became the first President of the Basque Government, played centre-half for Athletic throughout the 1920s.[33] But as the game became generally more popular and as footballing became a full-time profession, the proportion of young men from affluent families in the team decreased while the following of the successful club extended further and further down the social hierarchy. One sign of the continuing cross-class nature of Athletic membership is that its president is usually a member of the established local bourgeoisie rather than a self-made businessman. In Britain football might be regarded as historically the reserve of the urban proletariat, but in the Basqueland it is lauded as a traditionally common interest for members of all social classes. Another indicator of the breadth of the team's following is the fact that an informal talk given in April 1994 at the Bilbao campus of the Universidad del País Vasco by Javier Clemente, a famous but controversial trainer of its first eleven in the early 1980s, attracted a far larger audience of students than would a discussion held there led by a world-famous academic. Also some senior ecclesiastics, such as Monsignor Enrique Tarancon and Juan Arrupe, respectively Primate of Spain and General of the Company of Jesus in the 1960s, were and are quite open about their support for the club. One journalist characterized the variegated social nature of the club's support by saying 'Intellectuals, film directors, rockers: all can be supporters, there's no incompatibility'.[34] Another tried to put across the same point in an even more striking manner:

> Perhaps it would be better to say that here (in the stadium) concur a crucible of diverse and differentiated attitudes, feelings, and thoughts. Here coincide a comedian, a theologist of liberation, a cobbler, a musician, a shopkeeper, a quick-change artist and a woman of loose morals who vibrates more with the goals of Athletic than with her next client.[35]

One consequence of the close identification between the team and its supporters is the statement by numerous fans that they, the loyal football-going public, contribute in an important manner to the success of Athletic. As one historian of the club put it, if the first eleven are the shocktroops, its followers are 'the faithful infantry', 'the back-up brigade'.[36] One fan has confessed the ideas he and his kind have about their role:

> In our innermost being lies the belief that Athletic wins its matches because we

[33] It is most probably the example of his career which led to the adage that in order to get to be anyone in Basque politics one had to have studied at the local jesuit university or to have been a footballer (Unzueta 1983a).
[34] Terrachet 1970: 146–7; Cerrato 1986: 216
[35] Rodrigalvarez 1986
[36] Athletic Club 1986, vol. 3: 3. See also the statements of the club's trainer, *M* 31 x 1999: 51

urge them on ... We have stimulated and urged the team on, and they have won; therefore we ourselves have won, and for that reason we are a part of Athletic.[37]

One fan, Gabriel Ortiz, became locally famous in the 1950s and 1960s for his ability to time his very loud cries of 'Atleeeeetic!' so well that he could stimulate thousands into shouting the customary response, 'Eup!' Local journalists, Athletic's directive and players all acknowledge the central role of supporters. Games without songs, shouts and cries are 'flat, lack density, do not excite'.[38] A recent Assistant to the President of the club admitted that the reaction of the crowd at a home match is the best indicator of how well they are doing their job. Felix Marcaida, a great player of the 1950s, recognized the powerful influence of the team's following: 'When San Mamés urged us on, we flew. But when the public screamed at me, everything would go wrong for me. The public is of great importance for a player.'[39]

Perhaps local sports journalists should be regarded as part of Athletic's public as well, for several commentators have referred to the traditionally close alliance between the team and the Basque press, to the affectionate and relaxed relations between players and regional reporters.[40] All the main Bilbao newspapers maintain one journalist who specializes in Athletic. Every day each of them devotes one or two pages to the activities of the club, and on the days following matches three pages, or even more if the match was important. As one of these journalists complained to me, it is permissible for him and his colleagues to criticize particular players or the way the whole team is playing, but it would be 'very difficult' for them to make fundamental criticisms about the nature of the club and its support, for that would be seen as tantamount to criticizing Basque society itself.

One effect of all the different factors which facilitate a sense of identity between the players and their fans is that Athletic has frequently been called *una gran familia rojiblanca* ('a great red and white family', after the team's colours). This metaphorical manner of portraying an ethnically bounded football-loving collection of people in terms of generic kinship has potential meaning because the links between the directors, the players, and their public are meant to be as close, as affectionate and lacking in instrumentality as those between members of a family. Moreover, these links are ones which transcend generations and are meant to be all the stronger for that reason. Even more frequent than the kinship metaphor, however, is the description of Athletic as 'something more than a club', though just what that 'something more' might be is often left unstated. One local journalist called it 'a feeling', another referred to 'those who carry Athletic inside themselves', while one historian of the club has described it as 'something very intimate, very much its own'.[41] Perhaps the most articulate on this

[37] Merino 1986
[38] Quoted in Alonso 1998: 12
[39] Unzueta 1983b; Athletic Club 1986, vol. 3: 126; *Deia* 15 iii 1998: 42. For a further statement by a player about the importance of the public's reaction, see *M* 13 ii 1999: 52
[40] Alonso 1986; Bacigalupe 1986; Frade 1986: 35–7
[41] Terrachet 1969: 147; Estévez 1986; Roca 1986

topic has been the local-born novelist Luis de Castresana, who was a child-exile during the war,

> Athletic is for me something more a football team; it is part of the emotional landscape of my Bilbao, my Biscaya . . .
>
> I suppose that, at root, we Biscayans love Athletic because we intuit that it has something which belongs to us, because we intuit that within it is a piece of ourselves.
>
> I remember how much we, Basque children evacuated overseas during the war, were animated, shored up, and unified by having a red and white T-shirt and by calling our team 'Athletic de Bilbao'. I believe that what we did then in Brussels was to discover for ourselves, from the nostalgia of a long absence, one of the characteristics which best and most deeply defines the Bilbao team: that is, its identity as an umbilical cord linking men to the land, its geographico-emotional capacity
>
> Athletic is like the river, the *ochotes* (local eight-person choirs), the blast furnaces, the *sirimiri* (a local wind) or the Arenal (a small park in the centre of Bilbao): something which, in a way, is already consubstantial with our urban psychology.[42]

Just how strong and warm the links between the club and the community it represents can be was demonstrated by the reception given to the league champions when they returned ceremonially to Bilbao in May 1984. In the words, once again, of Castresana,

> Bilbao yesterday was something more than a mass frenzy and something more than a fiesta. It was an experience. It was the communion of a people with its team and, at root, the communion of a people with itself . . . Athletic is ourselves.[43]

Durkheim could not have put it better.

Players and supporters of Athletic might all be members of a great family but they may also participate in a broader unit. And given that football is by definition competitive, playing against other Basque teams (Real Sociedad above all, but also Alavés of Vitoria, and Osasuna of Pamplona, when they are in the First Division) can promote division as much as regional cohesion. In particular the relations between supporters of Athletic and those of Real Sociedad have swung over the decades many times between friendly rivalry and outright hostility.[44] In the 1940s and '50s, for instance, the Franquist place-men running the two clubs deliberately presented them in provincial, not regional terms; it was only from the late 1960s, with the renaissance of Basque nationalism and the consequent rise of a pan-Basque identity, that this mutual antagonism began to subside.[45] Also, support for Athletic may be questioned within Biscay itself: for example, the tension I have already mentioned which may emerge between the club and those

[42] Castresana 1968. In his novel *El otro árbol de Guernica*, which in 1967 was awarded the Premio Nacional de Literatura, Castresana describes the moment when a football team of Basque children exiled in Brussels share the one Athletic T-shirt they own and so come to feel identified with 'the best team which symbolized and incarnated the whole province' (1966, ch. 12).

[43] *El Correo Español* 7 v 1984

[44] Walton 2001: 124–31 provides a historical discussion of these swings.

[45] Shaw 1987: 191

contractually obliged to pass on their best players to Athletic.

At the same time, a communal sense of 'Basqueness' can at times cut across any sense of intra- or interprovincial rivalry. This partisan switch from team to an overarching social concept is usually manifest most starkly at local derbys, especially those where one of the two teams is fighting potential relegation. On these occasions local journalists openly discuss whether or not the dominant team will maintain the unofficial policy of throwing the game to protect their Basque neighbours. Because this strategy is directly counter to the official rules of football, many of these articles are hedged with qualifiers: quotes from representatives of the clubs stressing that they will uphold common professional standards are juxtaposed with ones from fans reminding the players of a commitment which goes beyond any one team.[46]

A different kind of event, but which still demonstrated the solidary potential of the usually nebulous concept of '*el futbol vasco*', was the murder in December 1998 in Madrid of a Real Sociedad fan by members of an ultra-right gang of Atlético de Madrid supporters. At Athletic's next match after the murder, the announcement that team-members would be wearing black armbands evoked two minutes of applause from the crowd; players later dedicated their victory in the game to the memory of the deceased. The funeral was attended by thousands, including directors, trainers and players from all four Basque clubs. Three months later, when Athletic played against Real Sociedad in Bilbao, *peñas* from both sides announced their wish to recuperate the festive ambience this derby traditionally enjoyed. On the afternoon of the match, a mass act of homage was held to the dead in a central Bilbao square, from which supporters of both sides processed together to the stadium. A joint communiqué from the *peñas* stated:

> Our rivalry, always sporting, lasts exclusively ninety minutes, outside of which, as much before as afterwards, we continue to have in common our support for all the Basque teams which make up our great common project, which is the Euskal Herria selection.[47]

Style

On 1 September 1920 Spain played in the semi-final of the Olympic Games. By the end of the first half Sweden was leading 1–0. Halfway through the second half the Spaniards were awarded a free kick. As the Athletic player Sabino Bilbao ran to take the kick, his fellow Athletic player Belauste rushed up the pitch shouting, 'Sabino, kick the ball to me, I'll overwhelm them!' He caught the ball and, running towards the opposition goal chased by three Swedes, kicked it into the net. Shortly afterwards the outside-left scored another goal, the last of the match. In the legendary history of

---

[46] For examples of these see Leguineche et al.: 1998: 107–9; Walton 2001: 132

[47] *M* 10 xii 1998: 3–4, 51; 11 xii 1998: 13–16; 31 iii 1999: 46; 5 iv 1999: K5–7

Spanish football this incident is crucial, for it marks the birth of '*la furia española*'.[48] And, as every knowledgeable Athletic supporter knows, since the majority of the national team played for the club, *la furia española* was in reality *la furia vasca*, the characteristic style of Athletic.

The most lauded components of this simple, effective but distinctive style were fieriness and long passes. It was unpretentious, direct, and aggressive, with a profusion of centres at the same level as the centre-forward. It was a very quick, strong, hard, physical style, one of vigorous players who, it was proclaimed, would not give up but would relentlessly pursue the ball until the final whistle.[49] Their momentum was such that they were expected to overwhelm or crush their opponents, and they often did so. Players were seen as so courageous and furious, ready to give their all for the 90 minutes of a game, that they were called 'lions', and were meant to be as admired and as feared as the big cats. 'It is said that Athletic fattened itself on rivals who kneeled before them', and that unfortunate opponent teams were 'thrashed, pounded down, and squashed by the weight of the goals won against them'. This fury, however, was expected to be a measured, calculated one: footballers who played like 'blind hurricanes' might have impressed some spectators but would have ended up losing their team matches.[50]

This style of strength, speed and total commitment was regarded as very Basque, since it exemplified the customarily prized attributes of male force and determination. As one nationalist wrote in a 1910 article on the game, 'The Basque race is, through the conviction of its positive physical superiority, one of the most saturated with that healthy spirit of battle, of competition, summed up by Saxons in the word "struggle"'. Similarily, the professional football of other regions was said to represent their respective local ways of life: that of Catalonia was thought to be 'colder' and 'more technical', that of Andalusia 'more reckless and pyrotechnical'.[51] The Basque sculptor Jorge Oteiza even managed to include Athletic's play within his quasi-mystical characterization of Basqueness. To him, their style was a perfect incarnation of the Basque soul: 'The long, diagonal pass and the oblique run; that is the essence of the Basque game.'[52]

At the same time as being regarded as Basque, however, Athletic's playing style was also seen – as the early nationalist comment suggests – as very English.[53] According to supporters, it was partly thanks to the British and Anglophiles who had introduced the game, and to the series of British trainers hired by Athletic that the club had come to adopt and perfect this particular form of play. The best remembered of these imported instructors was Freddie Pentland, a former inside-left for Blackburn Rovers and English international, who was employed by the club for several

[48] Unzueta 1983
[49] Delgado 1986; Shaw 1987: 21
[50] Belarmo 1986; Escartin 1986
[51] Anon 1910; Mandiola 1969
[52] Quoted in Alonso 1998: 11
[53] Mingolarra 1990

seasons during the 1920s and early 1930s. It is said that he used constantly to repeat his maxim 'The most difficult game is that of the Sunday
coming'. In memory of Pentland and his compatriots, the trainer of Athletic
is popularly known as '*el mister*'. This association of the club with the
homeland of the game was seen not as detracting from its 'Basqueness' but
as a source of additional prestige, since the most successful British teams
were still then regarded as among the very best in the world.

Perhaps a vestigial sign of this Anglophilia was the claims of Javier
Clemente in the 1980s that he was a slavish adherent of what he called
'*la manera inglesa*', a highly successful but unexciting *bloque* formation where
two defensive midfielders act as a shield to twin centre-backs and a sweeper.
According to Phil Ball, a popular historian of Spanish football, Clement
'never failed to swear allegiance to the "mother" system'.[54]

Politics

Several commentators have noted that Athletic and Basque nationalism
both arose and developed in the same place and over much the same time.
It is highly probable that both fed off the other. But, in this deeply polemical
area of study, any claims to that effect need to be very well-grounded to be
convincing.[55] For instance Ball, though very suggestive, is still just highly
speculative when he argues that the 'Basques-only' rule, at least in its
earlier more restrictive forms, was a means to celebrate the original condition of the Basque community, before the mass arrival of migrants.
According to him, implementation of this rule was a way to 'turn the
emerging football club into a theatre of nationalist dreams'.[56]

The best-read of these commentators is the Basque social historian Javier
Díaz Noci. He demonstrates that early nationalist writers were divided by
the initial enthusiasm for football. The more conservative and religious
among them, who wrote in Euskera and lived in the countryside, tended to
praise *pelota* and regarded the new sport with suspicion, as a threat to the
values they upheld; the more liberal, who wrote in Castilian and lived in
the city, tended to be Anglophile and to support the rising fashion for
football. This liberal opinion became the dominant one within the nationalist camp, as by the 1930s football and other modern sports had totally
displaced *pelota* and other traditional games as popular spectacles in all but
the most rural of areas. Interest in football was stimulated by the rapidly

[54] Ball 2001: 80–81
[55] E.g. Unzueta 1999; Díaz Noci 2000; Ball 2001: 77. Unzueta, again influencing Walton
(2001), claims in his article on football and Basque nationalism that the 'Basques-only' policy
of Athletic was 'conserved precisely because of its ability to generate social unanimity'
(Unzueta 1999; 149). He provides no evidence for this statement. It is possible that archival
research in the minutes of Bilbao municipal meetings would uncover partial support for this
claim. But it would be equally important to know which kind of nationalist made this sort of
statement, at what time, and for what discernible reason.
[56] Ball 2001: 88

developed and extensive local sports journalism, whose production was often financed by prominent liberal nationalists, several of whom themselves actually managed Athletic.[57]

Fomenting a passion for the game in a nationalist mode was seen by some as a way to democratize the masses and for the Basque Nationalist Party to extend its base of support through cultural and associative means. As one nationalist writer stated in the 1930s, 'There are those who say that sport should not be mixed with politics . . . But, aren't we going to make it a nationalist, nationalizing, eminently patriotic matter, if sport provides us with a fast vehicle for our aspirations?'[58] In general terms nationalist supporters of the game viewed football as stimulating the lauded Basque values of strength, masculinity, even-handedness, and honesty.[59] Some local eulogizers also saw it as having racial and physiological benefit: it was a 'convenient and healthy sport which greatly fortified the body and kept it in a good warlike condition'.[60]

During the Republic, Athletic clearly supported the popular campaign for Basque autonomy.[61] At the beginning of the Civil War in 1936 most of its players tried to enlist in Basque militias, but many were soon required to join a freshly created Basque 'national' team which toured internationally, with great success, for propaganda and fund-raising purposes. After the tour, which included games in France, Czechoslovakia, Poland, the USSR and Mexico, all but two players decided to remain abroad rather than return to their defeated homeland, where they risked imprisonment.

The ideologues of the new totalitarian order imposed on the country lauded sport as a moral activity which expressed and reinforced the 'two magnificent virtues' of patriotism and discipline; even spectatorship had its ethical worth and propaganda value, for it was thought that a sporting spectacle could win over the thousands of stimulated young spectators. But first the Junta Directiva of Atlético was filled with place-men prepared to play their new masters' game while the team had to present itself in the appropriate manner, and its games had to take place within the appropriate frame. Thus in an effort to 'Castillianize' Basque football perpetrators of the regime forced the club to change its name to 'Atlético de Bilbao', and regional championships, seen as 'no more than an egoistical desire to cultivate an autonomy through sporting separatism', were prohibited.[62] Since Franco allowed football to become by far the most popular of all sports played in the country, the achievements of Atlético during this period had that much greater resonance. The team effectively dominated Spanish football during the 1940s, coming top of the league in the 1942–3 season and winning the national championship in the three consecutive years

---

[57] De Pablo 1995: ch. 14; Díaz Noci 2000
[58] Quoted in de Pablo et al 1999: 236
[59] Walton 2001: 29
[60] *Euskadi*, no. 3, mayo-junio 1910, quoted in Unzueta 1999: 159
[61] Shaw 1987: 21
[62] Information about Falangist attitudes to sport, and the quotations from their writings, come from London 1995

1943–1945. These triumphs were exploited within the terms of the regime's neo-fascist mythology: the physically powerful team was lauded in the national sports press as the embodiment of '*la furia española*', which was here given very strong political overtones.[63]

The value of the team in restoring some sense of local society after the devastation of the war is openly acknowledged. The bestselling Basque academic Jon Juaristi, for example, chooses to quote his father's much-repeated argument that Atlético 'represented, from the immediate postwar on, a space of tolerance where it was possible to restore a good part of the sociability of Bilbao's ruling middle-class'.[64] However, it is very difficult these days to disentangle exactly whose sympathies lay where in the 1940s and early '50s, given that so many latter-day commentators had striven to interpret much of popular life during this time in resolutely anti-Franquist terms. For instance the club's own history of itself, produced in the mid-1980s, claims that any success enjoyed by the team was regarded by many locals as reflecting well not on the present regime but on the Biscayans themselves: 'That Atlético, of the years of rationing and the black market, was the "other food" of the people of Bilbao. And an "*irrintzi*" (Euskera, 'cry, shout') by the Basque people, thrown to the four winds'.[65] Duncan Shaw, a British historian of Franquist football who was writing at the same time, has argued that since almost all forms of potentially nationalistic activity were banned, football, which Franco personally liked, became one of the very few legal ways by which Basques could demonstrate who they were and what they were made of.[66] Victories against Real Madrid, which was seen as particularly Franquist, were said to be much appreciated by Atlético's fans, especially if the dictator himself had come to watch the game. Modern historians of the team like to repeat the words of the Atlético captain, Agustin Gainza, who, in 1958, on receiving the national championship trophy from the hands of Franco at the end of the match, still had the presence of mind to say, 'See you next year.'

In the last years of the regime, as a politically organized nationalism re-arose and its armed movement, ETA, came to be regarded as part of the vanguard of the Franquist opposition, a new generation of directors and *socios* arose within the club, people 'less disposed to tolerate the arrogant centralism of the State in general and of the incompetent and antidemocratic attitudes of the sporting authorities in particular'.[67] Within this context, the publicity given by sports journalists to matches played at Atlético's home ground was considered too good an opportunity not to be exploited by politicos in the crowd and on the pitch. From the late 1960s onwards spectators on the stands would ostentatiously wave large *ikurriñas*, the

[63] Shaw 1987: 189–90
[64] Jauristi 2006: 81. For one interpretation of the ambiguous relations between Athletic and Franquists, see Juaristi 1999: 92–4
[65] Athletic Club 1986, vol. 2: 200. For examples of pro-Franquist speeches made by the President of the club during the Civil War, see Aiestaran 2001: 231, 237–9
[66] Shaw 1987: 183. Detailed research into this sensitive topic has yet to be carried out.
[67] Shaw 1987: 186

then-banned Basque flag, knowing full well that by the time policemen had managed to fight their way through the crowd the banner would long have disappeared.[68] On 8 August 1977 the recently elected president of the club solemnly raised the *ikurriña*, to the massed cheers of the crowd, before the beginning of the game; Basque dances were then performed to the sound of traditional Basque instruments, and the players ran on to the pitch down a 'tunnel of honour' formed by dancers and spinners in regional costume. The president later stated that raising the banner, though technically illegal, was 'almost a popular petition'.[69] During the transition to democracy Athletic (as it had renamed itself in 1972) openly defended the campaigns for Basque autonomy and an amnesty of political prisoners; many players also began to learn Euskera, whose public use had been prohibited by the regime.[70]

During this period the single most prominent and active nationalist in the team was its nationally renowned goalkeeper, José Ángel Iribar. When, on 27 September 1975, two members of ETA and three members of FRAP (an armed revolutionary organization) were executed, Iribar persuaded his fellow members of the team to wear black armbands during the next game. Iribar tried to protect himself and his team-mates by saying that their gesture was to commemorate the first anniversary of the death of Luis Albert, an ex-player and director of the club. During the same season Iribar, though invited, chose not to play for the Spanish team for what would have been his fiftieth time. It was widely rumoured that he had declined the invitation because the political wing of the Basque gunmen had told him not to do so. Consequently, when he kept goal for his team in away matches in Madrid and Andalusia, he was greeted not with the cheers he usually received, but with loud boos. In December the following year just before a match with Real Sociedad, played at the latter's home-ground of Anoeta, he persuaded the rival captain to agree that both sides would run on together carrying the still-banned *ikurriña*; one Madrid paper headlined its article on the incident 'Separatist orgy at Anoeta'.[71] In May 1977, at the final of the European Cup, against Juventus of Turin, Iribar, who headed the home team, came onto the pitch carrying an *ikurriña* while thousands in the crowd also waved the flag, shouting rhythmically 'Presoak kalera!' (Euskera, 'Prisoners to the street', i.e. 'Let them go').[72] When in 1980 Athletic held a game in homage to their retiring goalie, he gave the share of the gate such an outgoing player usually receives towards a technical dictionary in Euskera, although his own private business (a potato storage company) was not going well at the time.[73]

Although most Athletic supporters see the team in nationalist terms, and although all its players are thought to be nationalist unless they show

[68] Cerrato 1986
[69] Athletic Club 1986, vol. 5: 47
[70] Shaw 1987: 192, 226, 231
[71] Athletic Club 1986, vol. 5: 28
[72] Shaw 1987: 193, 232–3
[73] Unzueta 1986; Del Valle 1988: 117, n. 2

otherwise, many fans do not wish the club to be exclusively associated with one particular political party. Since the death of Franco, the PNV has tried to control its presidency, which is regarded as an important position in Bilbao society. Indeed, the first post-Franquist incumbent, Beti Duñabeitia, went on to become the successful PNV candidate for the mayorship of the city. But in the 1990 elections to replace his successor, who had also been a member of PNV, most members of the club voted in a candidate supported by an alternative nationalist party because, it was said at the time, they did not want a single political group in charge of Athletic.

Radical nationalist leaders recognize the importance of Athletic and its fraternal rivals in Alava and Guipuzcoa; one of them is even reported to have stated that he who does not like football is not Basque.[74] Herri Batasuna at times tried to control the direction of Athletic, but had insufficient supporters at the managerial and directorial levels of the club. Instead, it sought to exploit the team's popularity for political ends by getting players sympathetic to the cause, such as Iribar, to speak for it on the hustings. These political divisions within the membership of the club were expressed territorially in its stadium: supporters of PNV tended to stand at either end while *batasuneros* congregated along the two main sides down by the wire fence, where they shouted slogans and hoisted banners for whatever happened to be the radical nationalist issue of the moment. One advantage of this position by the fence was that TV cameras following the action near the ground by default gave automatic publicity to the radical slogans of the day.

While these different parties have tussled for dominance within the club, none has permanently won a commanding position; and this, it appears, is the way most members want it to be. For Athletic, like the Virgin of Begoña, is meant to be above factional politics. It is supposed to represent all Biscayans, and at times all Basques, not just a fraction of them. As one member of the club's management put it to me, the club is meant to fulfill the same unifying function in Biscay as the monarchy is meant to do in England.[75]

Present policies

In the two consecutive seasons from 1982 to 1984, Athletic twice came top of the league and once won the national championship. But these outstanding results came within a few years to be seen, not as the latest crop of successes of an exceptional team, but as possibly the last high points in the club's history. After 1984, Athletic entered a prolonged period of crisis. It started to come towards the bottom rather than the top of the First Division,

---

[74] Rincon 1985: 92
[75] In 2000, on the eve of regional elections, one Basque journalist noted that each of the leaders of all the main local parties were privately attending that Saturday's match in San Mamés (*M* 15 iii 2000: 6)

and its directors changed the top trainer more than eleven times in twelve years. It was only with the appointment of Luis Fernandez as trainer in 1996 that the club returned to anything like its former glory.

The fundamental reason for the extended reversal in Athletic's fortunes was money. Some other clubs in the Spanish league, especially 'super-clubs' such as Barcelona, now have so much money invested in them that they are able both to buy outstanding players from other teams in Spain and abroad for large amounts and also to pay their own teams very large salaries. This effect of the rising standard of rival teams was compounded by the transfer of Athletic players to non-Basque clubs. Such a move would have been almost unthinkable in earlier years, since members of Athletic were supposedly completely committed to their club. But the offers made to players became, in their minds, too good to refuse. In the early 1980s members of the team were among the worst-paid footballers in all the First Division, earning only about a quarter as much as their opposite numbers in other clubs. By 2000 there were over fifty Basque players in non-Basque teams, six of them in the Barcelona squad alone.

To stem this loss of talent, the directors of Athletic decided to end the long-established tradition of *buena vecindad* ('good neighbourliness') with the fellow Basque teams of Real Sociedad and Osasuna, and began to poach footballers from them. However, when players from Athletic saw how much was being paid for these imports, they began to ask for higher salaries. The club's directors, by agreeing to these demands, ended Athletic's even longer-established tradition of an 'economy of austerity'. The effect of this demise has passed the whole way down the club, to such an extent that Athletic is no longer keen for its younger players to participate in national juvenile selections. As one of their trainers recognized:

> In the long term, it creates problems with the players. Football has changed a lot in the last years. The motivation of the lads, which used to be to play and to enjoy themselves, is now different and if they go to the selection very young, on their return we already find intermediaries in the doorway.[76]

The combined effect of these financially oriented changes is that the statement 'Athletic is something more than a club' is somewhat less true than it was until relatively recently, and its supporters know it. In a telephone survey of 1,000 *socios* carried out in February 1992, during the worst period of the club's extended crisis, for the newspaper *El Mundo*, the most commonly cited cause of the club's poor results (29 per cent of the sample) was that its present players did not give their all: 65 per cent of them said they were too mild, their game was no longer one of force or strength, they lacked the desire to struggle, they had become a bunch of *señoritos*. As one put it to me, because the members of the first team now played for money as much as for love, they were not prepared to 'die on the field' and so were letting down their club's glorious traditions.

Yet the majority of Athletic's *socios* are not prepared to see the club's cherished traditions change any more, even if that means that it become

[76] *M* 11 viii 1998: 33

very difficult indeed for their beloved team to repeat its former string of victories. In a subsequent survey of 394 *socios* carried out in September 1992, 53 per cent said that they were against the transformation of Athletic into a limited company (22 per cent of the sample said they did not know), while an overwhelming majority (83 per cent) said they were opposed, or very opposed, to the club's buying players from abroad: they did not want a 'foreign legion' in their front line.[77] *Socios* are well aware of the possible consequences of these attitudes. In the *El Mundo* survey 76% of them said that they would rather see Athletic relegated to the Second Division than allow the club to give up the tradition of *la cantera*. They asserted this attitude even though buying already proved players from poorer countries, such as Serbia and Croatia, would be a much cheaper option. Of the sample, 33 per cent accepted the present swings of the team between highs and lows as practically inevitable, given the policy of *la cantera*, which means that only once in every so many years does the club produce a squad capable of winning titles. José Clemente, who in 1985 was re-appointed as the club's top trainer, was clear on this point when asked about it in an interview:

> There is no doubt that, above all in the league, we start out in a position of infe-
> riority, but that way things have more valour. The championship is perhaps
> more feasible. Nowadays, moreover, Basque football has also to cope with the
> consequences of the Common Market norm of the free circulation of European
> players. But I believe that Athletic will continue with its football of *la cantera*
> unless the socios say otherwise. For me, particularly, I would not like to see
> foreigners entering.[78]

In 1991 the directors of Real Sociedad, wishing to improve its performance by hiring foreigners, only managed to abolish its own exclusive policy
of *la cantera* by claiming that it had commissioned a mass survey showing
that most *socios* would not mind.

The only concession to changing circumstances that a majority of the
Athletic *socios* (78 per cent of the *Egin* sample) were prepared to contem-
plate was the introduction of publicity on players' shirts. Yet even here,
they did not want the change to be as great as it has been for other teams,
as most *socios* insisted that if the colours of their team's shirt had to be
'stained' by commercialism, the company to be granted this privilege had
to be a Basque one.

The idea of any success now being all the more meritorious precisely
because of Athletic's self-imposed limitations was very strongly stressed by
journalists in May 1998 when the team ended up second in the First
Division and thus gained entry into the Europe-wide Champions League.
This success, which led to tens of thousands celebrating in, and commanding, the streets of Bilbao was trumpeted in the press as a great vindication
of the club's stubbornly maintained policy.[79] Columnists took especial satis-

[77] *Egin* 21 September 1992
[78] Ortuzar and Rodrigalvarez 1987
[79] M 16 v 1998: 42–53; 17 v 1998: 44–50

faction in emphasizing that money wasn't everything: 'that the theory "he wins who has more" is not scientific, that in football are still influential non-quantifiable factors like strength, identity, spirit of the team and passion'.[80]

The benefits of maintaining a *cantera* have gained greater relief in recent years because of rising concerns throughout the country about the steadily increasing number of foreign footballers in Spanish teams. This importation of others is recognized as a real obstacle to the potential careers of young native-born players. In early 1999 Jordi Pujol, President of the Catalan regional government, even dared to criticize the percentage of foreigners in the extremely popular Barcelona football team, easily the most successful and richest of all Spanish clubs in modern times.[81] The extent such importation can reach, in Spanish sport generally, was dramatically displayed in early 1999 when Alavan Basques celebrated their local basketball team winning the national league Cup. A columnist relates:

> [During an interval in the final game] the players huddled together for secret chats with their respective trainers. The television camera and microphone moved towards the group of the Vitorian team. What I heard left me stupified. They were talking in English! I couldn't believe it. 'And this is the team of Vitoria?' I exclaimed.[82]

In a half-hearted attempt to stem the inflow, the national football federation considered limiting the number of non-EU players in Spanish teams, but came to no agreement.[83] In the midst of all this polemic about what is to be done, there is just one club whose members can pride themselves on the nationality of their team. In the words of an Athletic slogan popular during the 1998–9 season, 'God created only one perfect team. The others he filled with foreigners.'

Athletic is now trying to raise its income by a number of methods. It has recently commissioned paintings, inspired by the example of Athletic, by eighty Basque artists, some of them famous, some of them young hopefuls. This collection is to be the core of a future Athletic museum, modelled on the highly successful art gallery opened by Barcelona Football Club in 1997.[84] In 1999 Athletic also hired the English marketing expert who had massively boosted the income of Manchester United by creative merchandising.[85] At the same time, Athletic continues to hope for a resolution to its long-standing difficulties about an agreement on a site for a new, much larger stadium.[86] Only by offering more seats does the club think it can gain substantially more *socios*. For all the grandiloquent words about *la cantera*, this money-raising is essential because, as the club is well aware, success breeds success: by participating, however ingloriously, in the 1998–9 Champions League, Athletic's coffers were increased by over a million pounds.

[80] *M* 17 v 1998: 2
[81] *M* 20 I 1999: 56; 22 iv 1999: 57
[82] *M* 3 ii 1999: 2
[83] *M* 11 v 1999: 67; 12 v 1999: 57
[84] *M* 13 v 1998: 11
[85] *M* 14 iv 1999: 60
[86] *M* 18 vi 1999: 60

This money is now all the more necessary, to attract local boys to football and to attract the best to Athletic, as the birthrate in the Basque Country has in the last decade declined to being the lowest of any European region. This alarming demographic datum is perhaps the most grievous long-term threat to *la cantera*.

When the British first brought football to Bilbao, the game was seen as something very strange and very new. Playing on a muddy pitch in the rain in daring short trousers which exposed the knees almost scandalized those Catholic *bilbainos* brought up on *pelota*. To them the novel British practice was 'a kind of madness', 'a form of audacity', a sporting challenge to which they slowly rose.[87]

By adopting this fashionable import from a prestigious country and developing their own style of playing it, the *bilbainos* were being both very Basque and very modern. Some might single out the Basques as one of the 'most ancient peoples' of Europe, but on this interpretation they were also among the most open to the up-to-date.

Although Athletic's play was originally seen as something very modern, it has gone on to become one of the most popularly rooted traditions of the Basque Country. In fact, one might say it has become a 'traditional' part of Basque modernity, a customary component of its twenty-first-century nationalism.

---

[87] Mugica 1982: 11–12

4
Feeding Nationalism

Difficult to think of something more central to our lives than food. For we digest symbols and myths as much as fats, proteins and carbohydrates. At one and the same time food is both nutrition and a mode of thought. It enables us biologically, and structures our life socially. As both fuel for our bodies and ideas for our minds, food is common to every single one of us.

Given this, it is all the more surprising that a recognizable 'food studies' did not arise within academia until the closing decade of the last century. Economists and geographers might have paid attention to its production and distribution but the great majority of political scientists, historians, sociologists and literary critics stubbornly avoided serious work into the topic. Even anthropologists outside of Third World village settings tended to quietly pass over it. For reasons which are still unclear, these attitudes have dramatically reversed, and today a host of academics from a range of disciplines produce monographs, textbooks and readers in this new field, edit book series, hold conferences in it, and head organizations dedicated to its furtherance, such as the Association for the Study of Food and Society, in the USA, or the seminal Oxford Food Symposium, in the UK. They have come to realize the insights a study of food and foodways can give.[1]

In some societies the foods valued and the ways they are prepared are codified into a cuisine, which may even become a central symbol of the society itself. In this way a discourse of food and food practices, open to multiple interpretations, can assist in both the construction and sustaining of national community. Locals may laud this everyday mode of nationalism; some politicians may come on board as well. For they know that turning foodstuffs and dishes into bearers of national identity is a down-to-earth way to make an otherwise abstract ideology more familiar, domestic, even palatable. France is the famed exemplar here.[2]

The topic of this chapter is another well-known, well-regarded cuisine – the Basque one – internationally lauded yet strikingly little-studied in a critical manner. In the following, I investigate how an idea of Basque cuisine arose, what it entails, how it has evolved, who uses the term, and for what reasons. I regard this chapter as a still all-too rare contribution to the study of the political dimension of national cuisines.[3]

[1] Possible reasons for the rise in interest in food are discussed in MacClancy 1992: 209–13. I am also a founding trustee of the Oxford Food Symposium Trust.
[2] E.g. Zeldin 1980; Trubek 2000; Ferguson 2004. On politicians and cuisine see Coulon 2000,

Origins

Though Basque cuisine is usually presented as thoroughly traditional, its creation is above all a consequence of modernity, a result of the revolutionary changes experienced in the Basque Country during the late nineteenth and early twentieth centuries. Four key factors led to the formation of the idea of a *cocina vasca*: industrialization, tourism, folklorism, the rise of professional chefs.

Firstly, thanks to the industrialization experienced in Biscay from the 1880s onwards, a bourgeoisie based on the wealth generated by the new industries arose in Bilbao. The social aspirations of this new social stratum created the conditions for the refinement of local cooking. When Gregorio Marañon, a leading Spanish intellectual of the interwar period, looked back over this period, he spoke of 'those groups of enterprising men' who 'with their great optimism, their liberality, their lively vigour and their excellent stomachs impelled Basque cuisine towards perfection'.[4] Since the more prestigious forms of French culture were then regarded as epitomes of 'the elegant, the natural and the really fine', these industrialists tried to consolidate their status by employing French chefs in their newly built palaces. They also stimulated the opening of elitist clubs (modelled on the aristocratic clubs of St James, London), restaurants, and hotels with restaurants, all commonly staffed by French, or French-trained, cooks. These sorts of establishments, hitherto unknown in the area, offered members of the emerging dominant class novel forms of sociability, ones usually centred around commensality and which fitted their new-found position within Bilbao society. Members of the well-to-do emulated this novel culture of eating out in commercial establishments by holding mass feasts in restaurants. The new habit became so popular in the city that by the 1910s 'one could not conceive of any celebration without the accompanying banquet.'[5]

Although the menus at the majority of the restaurants were almost wholly French, some did offer a mixture of French and local dishes. These local dishes are best regarded as 'neo-local': in other words, they were traditional but refined or Frenchified dishes. The most famous example of this process was the Bilbao restaurant 'El Amparo' ('The Shelter'), which ran from 1886 to 1918, managed by the three Azcaray sisters. This trio, who had all studied cooking in France, combined French and international *haute cuisine* with a refined version of popular Basque dishes. Their menu might offer such earthy local dishes as beans with bacon fat and sausage, as well

---

[3] Examples of this genre are Wilk 1993; Gabaccia 1998; Pilcher 1998; Zubaida and Tapper 2000

[4] Marañon 1933: 10

[5] Sánchez Masas 1993 (1939): 42–6; Aguirreazkuenaga 1998: 354. The first quote is from Sota 1918a. The second quote is from Macías Muñoz 2005. On the leading restaurants of Bilbao in the late 1910s and the food they offered, see Sota 1918a, b, c, d, e. On the evolution of the Bilbao restaurant 'Luciano', see Echevarria 1999.

as sole *à la normandaise* or *à la mornaise*. Among other creations, they were famed for raising 'to the level of myth' their 'Biscayan' sauce, which went well with tripe, chops, snails, pigs' trotters, dried salt-cod (*bacalao*), and other central ingredients of local cuisine.[6]

The second key factor was tourism, which first developed in the middle of the eighteenth century. Food played a significant part in the tourist offer and at least one Basque historian has argued that local 'gastronomy was, from the beginning of the tourist influx, one of the principal attractions of our land'.[7] The main centre of tourism in the Basque Country was San Sebastian, which acted as a summer retreat for the Madrid aristocracy. Influenced by their competitors across the border in Biarritz, the hotels of San Sebastian offered French-based dishes and so stimulated the refinement of local cuisine.[8] Competition between the chefs of the city was so intense that when in 1895 a local paper referred to a particular chef as 'indisputably the best' of them all, eight of his colleagues immediately proposed to challenge his prowess in a public contest. The paper's editor however refused to take up the gauntlet and sponsor the event.[9] From the 1850s on, the port of Santurtzi, close to Bilbao, also attracted many Spanish tourists from a variety of provinces beyond the Basque Country. The town's popular restaurants, which arose to serve the visitors, prided themselves on the quality of the local sardines and their other fish dishes, especially those based on cod.[10] Gradually, over the turn of the century and into the decades following, almost the whole coast between Santurtzi and San Sebastian was developed for tourism, each coastal town boasting its own fish and seafood restaurants. During the second half of the nineteenth century, relaxing in spas was a further, important form of tourism in the Basque Country. Spas were particularly plentiful in Biscay, and their restaurants, similar to those of Bilbao, offered a mixture of local and some French dishes.[11]

Folklorism was the next factor of importance. With the rise of *vasquismo* (the broad movement for the promotion of Basque culture) in the last century and, above all, in this century, some writers and journalists produced articles and in some cases books on a broad variety of topics concerning the cuisine of the Basques. Folklorists already saw Basque cuisine as a definable, separable aspect of Basque culture, and they regarded their work as the production of culinary documents, as salvage ethnography. In a socioeconomic context of radical and rapid change, they believed in the necessity of 'saving' recipes and associated customs under threat of extinction. The most

[6] Anon 1918; García Santos 1989; Iturrieta 1997: 12. For an example of the mix of (predominantly) French and some neo-local dishes, see the menu offered in 1893 at the inaugural banquet by the Hotel Torrontegui (reprinted in Aguirre 1995: 254)

[7] Haranburu 2000: 239 and 275.

[8] See, for instance, the very French-influenced menu (even written in French) offered in 1884 at the inauguration of the Hotel Continental, San Sebastian, and a similar menu, also very French-influenced and written in French, offered by the city's Club Cantabrico to celebrate the election as town-councillors of seven of its members (Valle-Lersundi 1963b; 1970).

[9] Valle-Lersundi 1967

[10] Aguirre 1995: 244–5

[11] Sarrionandia 1989; Iturrieta 1997

revealing example of this 'ethnoculinary' approach is *La Cocina Navarra* by Francisco Javier Arraiza, a compendium of Navarran culinary customs, anecdotes and recipes.[12] During the height of Franquism, in the 1950s, articles in the regional magazine *Vida Vasca* eulogized diverse aspects of Basque culinary culture, both past and present. At the time, this was one of the few legal ways of promoting ethnic difference. If locals could not then openly promote nationalism, at least they could boost a culinary *vasquismo*. The topics of articles in *Vida Vasca* range from paeans to the geographic diversity of Basque cuisine to the catching and cooking of elvers.[13]

The refinement of local cuisine was also boosted greatly thanks to the efforts of a series of local, well-paid chefs, who valued learning, produced books, gave public lectures and taught their skills to future generations of cooks. For instance, at the turn of the century the most famous chef in San Sebastian was Félix Ibarguren, popularly known as 'Shishito'. He tried to raise local cooking standards by the banquets he staged and the very numerous articles he wrote in the local and national press. In 1901 the Real Sociedad Vascongada de los Amigos del País established in San Sebastian an Academy of Cuisine, the first of its kind in the whole country. Shishito, appointed its Director, and an assistant gave two classes, on French-based cuisine, daily: one in the mornings for domestic servants (five of them sponsored by the town-hall), and one in the afternoons for ladies, young and old, of local 'Society'.[14] Shishito also held weekly classes in Pamplona. On top of that, he and the Secretary of the Real Sociedad tried to promote culinary knowledge by publishing a collection of books on cooking. Although only one book of the planned series was in the end produced, it was well and broadly received.[15] Of the recipe books written by local cooks during this period, perhaps the most successful was that by Arias de Apraiz, which first appeared in 1912 and was reprinted annually up into the 1960s.[16] Similarly, the book of the Azcaray sisters' recipes for El Amparo, published posthumously in 1930, was so successful that in 1989 a Basque chef claimed 'it had been determinant in the culinary customs of Bilbao and province: to the extent that one can assert that half Biscay cooked as El Amparo taught them.'[17]

After the depradations of the Civil War and the subsequent 'years of hunger' (*los años del hambre*) in the 1940s, one chef in particular strove to keep a sense of Basque cuisine alive in the 1950s and '60s. Besides being an excellent cook, José Castillo wrote well, published widely and success-fully, and regularly attended well-publicized events promoting local foods.

[12] Arraiza 1930
[13] Ergoyen 1953; Videgain 1960. See also *Vida Vasca* 1955: 128; 1956: 146–7. A similar strategy of boosting Basque culture during years of particularly repressive government occurred during the dictatorship of General Primo de Rivera in the late 1920s (de Pablo, Mees, and Ranz 1999: 159).
[14] Valle Lersundi 1963a; Calera 1976: 35; Walton and Smith 1994: 11
[15] Valle-Lersundi 1967; Lapitz 1989
[16] Arias de Apraiz 1912
[17] García Santos 1989

Like Shishito several decades before, he came 'to occupy his place in the cultural scene of the Basque Country'.[18]

His efforts dovetailed with those of a group of concerned chefs and gourmets, all from the San Sebastian area, who in the late 1950s started to hold regular meetings. They were worried that popular knowledge and practice of traditional Basque cuisine was declining and that its study should be boosted. In 1961 they founded formally the 'Cofradía Vasca de Gastronomía' ('Basque Brotherhood of Gastronomy'). Their specific aims are 'to maintain, by their own example, Basque culinary traditions and, concretely, the conservation, improvement and promotion of typical Basque dishes'. Based in a former slaughterhouse for poultry, lent by the town hall of San Sebastian and converted by them in 1964, the Brotherhood organizes gastronomic competitions, courses, seminars, talks and exhibitions. The San Sebastian tourist board, mindful of the city's image, funds and promotes its regular conferences. The audience at these well-attended events include visiting members of similar brotherhoods from the southwest of France. The Cofradía also publishes its own Bulletin and, together with the Academia de Gastronomía Vasca (based in Vitoria and founded in 1992), puts out a series of books on different aspects of Basque gastronomy. Members of the Cofradía have also been ready to lobby local branches of various Ministries about the need for including gastronomy when promoting hotels and for raising the standard of cooking in Basque restaurants.[19] Through these various efforts they strive, against powerful modernizing tendencies, to keep alive supposedly time-honoured ways of cooking in a distinctively local manner.

Books

One way to approach the topic of Basque cuisine is to analyse the more important of the many books produced by Basque chefs. The first major wave of these books came in the early 1930s when nationalist fervour had reached a new height, only to be silenced by defeat in the Civil War. The next major wave started in the 1960s, when nationalism began to re-emerge and the first signs of a consumer society became patent. The key questions we can raise here are: what do these authors mean by 'Basque cuisine'? What image of the Basque Country and its inhabitants do they wish to project? Which aspects of Basque social life do they single out, and why?

Definition

What exactly is the '*cocina vasca*' of which these authors speak? This is an important question because, as one of them states, 'There is no people with

---

[18] Haranburu 2000: 285
[19] For details of the Cofradía and its events, see its *Boletín de la Cofradía Vasca de Gastronomía* and its website http://personal.redestb.es/euskalgastro

a history, without a cuisine.'[20] And as neither the existence of the Basques nor of them having a history is in doubt, they should, following this logic, therefore have a cuisine as well.

The first point to be made here is that the authors do not agree on what, exactly, constitutes 'Basque cuisine'. Some speak of its simplicity, others of its sobriety, yet others of its succulence.[21] Some say it is a cuisine above all of fish dishes, others of sauces, yet others of seasonal natural produce.[22] At a congress on Basque cuisine, held in 1994, a series of local chefs proposed a variety of competing definitions, based on particular ingredients, dishes, culinary customs, or taste.[23] What is more important here is not to attempt to judge who is right and who is wrong but to recognize that these writers think this a question worth debating. In other words, they do not have to come to agreement about what Basque cuisine is, just to acknowledge there is a 'Basque cuisine', whatever that exactly might be.

It is noteworthy, however, that the books of these chefs, most of them based in Bilbao or San Sebastian, tend to give a Biscayo-Guipuzcoan image of Basque cuisine. Many of their authors provide great numbers of fish recipes, lesser numbers of meat-based ones, some for vegetables and pulses, and almost none for puddings or desserts. In marked contrast, books specifically devoted to Navarran cuisine, reflecting the geographical diversity of the area, present a much more balanced variety of meat, fish, vegetable and sweet dishes, while those dedicated to Alavan cuisine emphasize the tremendously rich tradition in that province of making pastries and sweet dishes. Moreover, none of these books give space to the related but distinct culinary traditions of the French Basque provinces.[24] To this extent, books presenting a generalized 'Basque cuisine' tend to a give a regionally very lopsided view of Basque traditional dishes.

This generalization of 'Basque cuisine' also downplays the localism of certain valued ingredients. For instance, in the Navarran village where I do my fieldwork, locals would often praise certain foods from certain villages, e.g. the kidney beans of Genevilla, a village twenty kilometres to the west, as being especially good. They would also take pleasure in pointing out to me how even the local terms for a few fruits, such as apricots, were different in their village and those immediately around it from the terms used in the adjacent valley.[25] Perhaps the most extreme example of local culinary identity in the Basque Country comes from Manuel de Lope's novel about some local Navarran consequences of the Civil War:

> It was said that the best frogs were those of the pond at Zugarrumundi, fat like toads. The best snails were those of the cemetery walls of Vera de Bidasoa. And

[20] Santona 1987
[21] Marañon 1933: 14; Zozaya 1935: 11; Lapitz 1989: 5
[22] Marañon 1933: 14; Calera 1976: 32; *Actes. Premier congres mondial de gastronomie basque* 1994: 5
[23] *Actes. Premier congres mondial de gastronomie basque* 1995: 7–12
[24] E.g., the remarkable work of Susan Terrio (2000), an American anthropologist, on the production of French Basque chocolate.
[25] MacClancy 2004: 69

the best crayfish were those of the clear streams of Lesaka. Each village had a flag, with a batrachian, or with a crayfish, or with a snail.[26]

These cookbook writers' fabrication of a concept of Basque cuisine is a creative process of cultural ossification. Once established, Basque cuisine does not change. Instead, dishes are sited in a continuous present which emerges from a dateless and generalized past. The historical development of Basque cooking, however, is not too difficult to ascertain. Throughout most of their recorded history, the great majority of Basques survived on a highly restricted diet based on millet, chestnuts, broad beans and apples. Only the rich could afford a wider variety of foods, such as other cereals, vegetables, fruits, bread and wine; only they could eat meat, fish and dairy produce in anything approaching significant quantities. Foods introduced from the Americas were incorporated relatively late into Basque diet. Maize did not replace millet as a main crop until the eighteenth century while potatoes, haricot beans and tomatoes were not cultivated on a wide scale until the late nineteenth century. A major stimulus to the further dietary development of the Basques was the construction of the railroads from the middle of the nineteenth century on. These new railways enabled the mass importation of olive oil from southern Spain and facilitated the transportation of local produce from one area of the Basque Country to another.

Thus many of the dishes lauded today as integral parts of 'Basque cuisine' are in fact a product of just the last 150 years. Only a few originated in the eighteenth century: for instance, *salsa verde* ('green sauce', chopped parsley with the gelatine released from the fish being cooked) was invented and popularized in the early 1700s. Again, only a few dishes date from before that time: for example, references to *bacalao ajoarriero* (dried cod in a garlic sauce) can be found in the accounts of the medieval kingdom of Navarre. So when Basque chefs today eulogize Basque cuisine as essentially 'the cooking of our grandmothers', they are, ironically, speaking more exactly than most of them realize. For the dishes they are praising are not, as they seem keen to imply, the result of very longstanding traditions, but were created at about the time that their grandparents or great-grandparents were most active.[27]

The ahistoric style of so many Basque cookery writers is part of a strategic simplification. The dynamism of home-based cooks is forgotten for the sake of producing a static product, one which contributes to the establishment of a recognizable series of Basque traditions. A recontextualized recipe, once printed on the page, comes close to being the standardized version of a dish. In the transition from traditional oral transmission to literary production, variety is sacrificed in the name of uniformity, for the

---

[26] De Lope 2001: 59

[27] *Actes. Premier congres mondial de gastronomie basque* 1995: 48, 50–1; Abad 1999: 10–18, 49–50, 119; Bengoa n.d. For a detailed statement of the diet of rich, well-to-do and poor Navarrans in the early nineteenth century, see the anonymous 1817 petition to the Cortes de Navarra, reprinted in Iribarren 1956. For details of the diet of the well-to-do in Vitoria between the sixteenth and eighteenth centuries, see Porres 1995. See also Etniker 1990; Pérez Castroviejo 2000; Piquero 2000; Rilova 2003a, b; Serrano 2000; Ugalde 2002.

end of a good result every time. Just as speakers of Euskera are divided by their traditional dialects but unified by *batua* (a modern version containing elements of all seven dialects), the construction of a general Basque cuisine can be seen as the attempted creation of an edible Esperanto, joining the peoples of the mountains, the cities and the coast in a generalized culinary language, one which belongs to them all.

These books present a positive, socially acceptable and culinarily reproducible image of Basque cuisine. They do not include within their pages highly specific dishes or varieties of them which require ingredients only obtainable in out of the way places. In none of these books can one usually find, for example, recipes for that most traditional of rural dishes: roast, boiled or stewed cat. Small wonder, for these books are clearly intended to praise Basque culture, not to denigrate it.

These cookbooks serve manifold purpose: they help to emphasize the distinctiveness of Basqueness, they give more substance to the idea of Basque difference, and they thicken the cultural context of nationalism. For the production of these culinary manuals is not just an entertaining supplement to the development of Basque nationalism. Rather, they are an integral part of the evolution of nationalism. These books help to make Basques more sensitive towards the 'Basqueness' of their lives, with the food in front of them on the table coming to be a further ethnically marked aspect of local culture.

At the same time Basque cuisine serves as a useful (because seemingly innocuous politically) representation to foreigners of Basque culture. Thus the authors of these books like to remind their readers that Basque cuisine is not just singular. It is not merely able to stand comparison with other cuisines of the Peninsula. It is better than them: 'Basque cuisine represents the most successful form and the fullest and most characteristic expression of the Spanish culinary art'.[28] In fact, Basque cuisine is 'one of the most distinguished cuisines of the universe'[29].

Within this frame, Basque cuisine comes to be an example of how aspects of Basque culture contributed, or can contribute, to the world. Some have claimed its chefs raised the level of Madrid cooking and even influenced French cuisine greatly.[30] Others have argued that the origin of the apple is the Basque Country, from which it was exported to Normandy and Newfoundland, and from there to the rest of the world.[31] Basque chefs, whether famous or simply good at their skill, are meant to carry the flag of their culture wherever they place their pots.

Given this level of fame for Basque cuisine, allowing standards to slip becomes all the more serious. In a humorous article, where the local health

[28] Marañon 1933: 14. See also Sordo 1987: 88
[29] Lapitz 1980: 9. See also Mestaye 1935: 4
[30] Larrea 1977
[31] Uría 1983. According to Dr Barrie Juniper, Department of Plant Sciences, University of Oxford, who has recently carried out research into the topic, the most likely origin for the apple is the high valleys of the eastern Tien Sha, in what is now the northwestern part of the Xinjiang province of China (*Oxford University Gazette* 4 v 2000, p. 1109)

inspector of a Biscayan restaurant discovers that the much-admired gelatinous quality of the sauce for the dish of dried cod owed much to a piece of rubber in the stew, the author pronounces:

> The punishment had to be severe, and it was. Because they were not just falsifying an alimentary product, damaging it. The crime was greater, they were committing an offence against the fame of our regional dish, known throughout the entire world and throughout the entire world praised.[32]

Arcadia

Normally these books present an Arcadian image of the Basque Country, as a rural idyll where there is no class struggle nor poverty. Instead they sketch a harmonious society where people practise picturesque customs concerned with cooking, and stage banquets linked to the ritual calendar and rites of passage. This could be called a culinary *costumbrismo* (exaltation of picturesque customary ways) anchored to a utopian past. This nostalgic eulogy for an impossibly perfect rurality chimed well with nationalists' lauding of the Basque countryside and the virtues it generated.

Within this Arcadia, Basque cuisine is frequently presented as one primarily for men, as indeed 'the most masculine' of all peninsular cuisines. Basque males are themselves portrayed as trenchermen ('*comilones*') with taste, as men with large stomachs yet capable of treading the fine line between being gourmets or gourmands. They may eat a lot but they know what they are eating. Several of the authors emphasize the refined palate of Basques.[33] One mentions the impression he has that Basque cooks, however high or lowly, speak with love of what they are cooking, in the same way that some speak of flowers or a well-painted picture. The same author also claimed to know some local men who could even tell which pasture had been chewed by the cow they were eating, and which homestead the animal came from.[34]

In contrast, their wives are presented as the beating heart of this pastoral myth, with the Basque mother archetypally at home in her kitchen, the 'soul', the symbolic centre of local domestic life.[35] The sexual division of labour is made plain: the husband works outdoors or away from home, the wife runs the home. In the evening, she prepares the supper, he drinks with friends or in his local gastronomic society. 'When he calculates it's suppertime, he returns home. And if by chance, the supper isn't cooked or the potatoes are hard, salty or without oil, there's bound to be a row!'[36] And if he has such a developed palate, it is in great measure due to her, as the cook of the household is meant to accept, even stimulate, critical commentary on the dishes she prepares her spouse and children.

[32] López del Olmo 1930
[33] Larrea 1977; Calera 1976: 34. See also Echegaray 1948; Labayen 1951
[34] Castillo 1968: 7; 1983: 24
[35] E.g. Arraiza 1930: 3; Bayangel 1944
[36] Castillo 1968: 6

The central role of food comes across well in a local novel, *El Barrio Maldito* ('The Damned Quarter') by Félix Urabayen, set in Baztan, the most northerly part of Navarre, about a mature man's love for a young woman. Urabayen likes to speak of 'the only Love of Loves which the Baztanese has: the stomach'; 'The happiness of the Baztanese will always lie in the stomach.' But the stomach is both object of love and source of it; 'Perhaps the secret of this newborn passion which started to worry Pedro Mari resided in the sauces of Noemi.' One of the heights of this gastronomically laden, relatively short novel is the five-page (but still dense) description of the menu of a peasant banquet.[37]

Basque cuisine is lauded, not just for its gastronomic virtues and romantic properties, but for its curative powers as well. Thus, 'The spirit of our race will keep itself healthy, if the body feeds itself with our healthy popular dishes'; 'I still believe that, tasting their extremely delicate dishes, one understands the heroism of the race, their strength and their love for the liberation of their own piece of land'.[38] On this reading, Basque cuisine is an essential ingredient in constituting the very fibre of Basque society.

Sidrerías and gastronomic societies

The most distinctive customs mentioned in these books are those of the *sidrerías* ('cider-shops') and the locally renowned gastronomic societies. Both these shops and the societies are presented as above all popular social institutions, manifesting the popular democratic nature of Basque culture. In these establishments the preparation and consumption of the food express the equality of the commensales; they do not stimulate or reinforce social differences. As such they are taken to be splendid examples of the much-lauded, supposedly longstanding ideology of Basque egalitarianism.

Until the early twentieth century, cider, not wine, was the most popular rural drink for men. And they drank a lot: in 1828, in San Sebastian the average daily consumption per habitant of the city was up to three litres a day. Men drank in cider-shops, located both in villages and the cities throughout the Basqueland but especially in Guipuzcoa. In San Sebastian, the cider-shops were usually in basements, where men filled their glasses directly from huge barrels and charcoaled fresh fish on grills. According to their panegyrists, *sidrerías* were places for men to relax and enjoy a sense of brotherhood generated by alcohol, food, song and improvised verse. But from the late nineteenth century, wine became more and more popular as a fashionable substitute for cider, which came to be seen as almost anachronistic. The urban cider-shops closed first, followed by many of the rural ones.[39]

[37] Urabayen 1988 [1924]: 47–52; 194; 197. On references to Basque food in Pío Baroja's novels, see Martínez 1972. Baroja tended to see his compatriot trenchermen as gluttons.
[38] Arraiza 1930: 12; Zozaya 1935: 11
[39] Zapiain 1947; Aguirre 1983: 24–7; Prada 1995; Aguirre 2003. On the popularity of *chacolíes* (taverns serving *chacolí*, a slightly acidic local white wine, and meals) in rural areas around Bilbao around the end of the nineteenth century see Macías 2002.

Their social place was to a great extent taken up by the gastronomic societies. Indeed many societies were started by a group of male friends who used to meet in a cider-shop and then decided to acquire their own private, premises. The first were established in San Sebastian in the 1900s, and their numbers consistently rose in the following decades, primarily in the city but later in nearby towns as well. These societies offered recreational homes, above all, for local members of the mercantile and industrial petite bourgeoisie and for the rising number of Basque rural migrants needed to service the developing city. They were semi-private places where men could eat and drink when and how they wished, free of the increasing restrictions high-minded municipal authorities were then imposing on the opening hours of taverns and cafes. For the Basque sociologist Jesús Arpal, they were places where members could 'develop less conventional forms of social relations, ones less marked by the social divisions of work and class'. To him, these societies presented themselves 'as pure concelebration, in a pure production of forms of elemental solidarity which, if not alternative, were at least sufficiently differentiated from the model of industrial-urban society'. In other words, they were sites for the festive recreation of male cama-raderie, where men could joyously assert values not recognized by the new socio-economic order.[40] Furthermore, the Basque historian Félix Luengo has argued that these societies are nowadays so regionally famous primarily because in the early, turbulent decades of the twentieth century, they came to be seen as exemplary bulwarks of local ways. At a time of rising class division, occasional civil strife, and incipient Americanization, these homes for a resolutely male conviviality were made into the vigorous defenders of an otherwise increasingly beseiged, old-style sociality.[41]

The principles of these societies are few but clear. Each society has its own premises, which contains a kitchen and an area for eating and relaxing. Each member of a society has a key to the premises and is free to use the kitchen, where he may cook a meal for a group of fellow-members. At the end of the meal, money to cover the cost of the ingredients used is left in a box. Thus there is no control over what is spent other than the conscience of the members. Because it is so important to maintain this mutual confidence many societies, once established, rigorously control the entrance of new members.

It is often said that much of Basque cuisine has been 'saved' thanks to the societies, where male cooks had sufficient free time to prepare the lengthy, slow-cooking dishes regarded as central to local culinary traditions. Yet, at least in the early days of these societies, having fun in company

---

[40] Arpal 1985: 147. For examples of the municipal restrictions, see Bacigalupe 1995; 19–21. On possible reasons for the rise, in mid-century San Sebastian, of 'popular societies' (the pre-cursors of the gastronomic societies) see Luengo 1999. In nineteenth-century Bilbao it was a common custom for groups of male friends to acquire their own premises, known as 'cuarteles' (lit. 'barracks'), where together they would drink and eat food prepared by their wives (Sánchez Masas 1993: 45. See also Prieto (1991: 62–7) on male dining clubs in Bilbao during this period). This form of male sociability appears to have died out towards the end of the century.
[41] Luengo 2001: 142–5

seems to have been more important than gastronomy. Thus many of these societies also developed other interests, sporting, cultural and charitable. For instance, Euskal Billera, founded in 1902, organized bullfights and donated the profits to a local orphanage, while Amaikak-bat, founded in 1906, introduced or promoted varieties of certain sports in the Basque Country: fixed-bench rowing, handball, and grass hockey. In these early days, the great majority of members did not truly cook on their society's premises. Instead, some would reheat dishes already prepared at home by their wives. Alongside this they would add other foods, such as a salad, a piece of cheese, roast chestnuts. Some societies employed a female cook to prepare the meals. In others, members would patronize a nearby restaurant if they wished to eat together. It was not until after the Civil War, and above all from the 1970s on, that it became common for men to work in the kitchens of the societies. In fact it is only since the 1970s that the standard of cooking has generally risen in the societies. In league with this trend, the kitchen has come to be regarded as the 'sancta sanctorum' of a society, to which access is exclusively restricted to members only, even on the special days each year when women are admitted onto the premises.[42]

Though semi-private associations, whose activity occurs behind closed doors, all the societies in San Sebastian come out into the open every year on the night of 19 January, to participate in the *tamborrada*, a noisy celebration of the triumph in 1813 over the Napoleonic forces which had been occupying the city. In the cold, small hours members of each society, dressed as chefs, banging a drum or carrying a giant piece of cutlery, march out of their premises and then through the city streets to commemorate the glorious battle. The following night a juvenile *tamborrada*, with children in uniforms of the time, is held, an event originally organized by Euskal Billera. In 2000 over 12,500 people, grouped into 88 societies, dressed up and took part in the ritual. These two nights of drumming are the key celebration in the San Sebastian calendar, easily overshadowing the officially sponsored week-long fiesta held in the summer.

In the 1960s and '70s, new societies proliferated, not just in Guipuzcoan towns, but also in those of the neighbouring provinces of Biscay and Alava. In 1983 the historian Rafael Aguirre estimated there were about one thousand societies in the Basque Country, over half of them established since 1967. Much of this rise was due to the major wave of industrial development (and its consequent rural emigration) which the Basque Country experienced at this time. But some of it was also due to the Franquist regime which, with its highly constraining rules about the right of association, indirectly augmented the particular character of gastronomic societies as regular meeting-places, of concelebration, away from the prying eyes of the dictator's placemen. These newly established societies tend to be less restrictive, allowing members to bring in their wives and to entertain their families on the premises. The phenomenon of societies is now so

[42] V. Hayward pers. comm.

popular that in some Guipuzcoan towns, almost every adult resident has entrance into at least one society.[43] Today, for immigrants into these areas, being able to join a society and, if in San Sebastian, being able to wield a drumstick or outsize fork in the *tamborrada*, has become a definitive statement of 'belonging' in the locality, of accepted membership into its imagined community. Is this an extreme case of, 'To cook is to be'?

La Nueva Cocina Vasca

In the mid-1970s, a small group of young, innovative and dynamic Basque cooks came together to create a newly distinctive form of Basque cuisine. This creation was, in part, the result of already-voiced fears that standards were dropping among Basque restauranteurs: few were using care in the preparation of their dishes and some were even ready to add frozen ingredients.[44]

In 1976 the town hall of San Sebastian and a local savings bank agreed to sponsor a Round Table on Gastronomy, to which the rising star of French *nouvelle cuisine*, Paul Bocuse, was invited. Three months later two Basque cooks spent time in Lyon learning his techniques. On their return, they and their colleagues staged a series of monthly dinners over the next year and a half in each other's restaurants in San Sebastian. There they, and chosen guests, adapted Bocuse's ideas and tested out a host of new recipes. Sharing ideas, they were quite quickly able to put together a representative set of novel dishes based on a coherent set of culinary principles. With the great assistance of local journalists, they promoted their results, in both the Basque Country and throughout Spain, as *La Nueva Cocina Vasca*.

Their manifesto, which owed an obvious debt to *la nouvelle cuisine*, called for:

(1) a return to the 'classic' dishes of Basque cuisine, which would be made 'authentically';
(2) the seeking out of Basque dishes which, though forgotten generally, were still cooked among specific groups, such as fishermen, homesteaders, or cooks in gastronomic societies. Examples of such dishes include *zurrukutuna* (salt cod and garlic soup), *intxaursalsa* (walnut cream), *mondejuk* (white sausage of lamb fat mixed with vegetables), and *mendreska* (roasted fillet of bonito).
(3) the creation of new recipes using previously neglected foods of the area, such as seaweed and sea-urchins.

The aim of their cooking style was to produce dishes which kept the original tastes of the ingredients as much as possible. Dishes were to be

---

[43] Aguirre 1983: 23; Arpal 1985: 150–2
[44] Busca 1971

made simply, lightly cooked, and with sauces which did not rely on starch or fats but on the juices of the ingredients themselves. Those ingredients had to be of top quality and natural products of the Basque Country. To that end, chefs only bought seasonal produce, rising early to pick the best from local markets. They also spoke with farmers so that, for instance, chickens were raised in the most appropriate manner, and with fishermen so that they would catch more of previously undervalued kinds of fish.

Their most successful dishes include '*budín de krabarroka*' (timbale of rascasse/Mediterranean scorpion), '*lubina a la pimienta verde*' (sea bass in a green capsicum sauce), '*crepes de txangurro*' (crab crêpe), and elver salad. One particularly popular ingredient was the *pimiento de piquillo* (a small and slightly chilli-hot variety of red capsicums), cooked on their own or stuffed with txangurro, vegetables, mushrooms, krabarroka, baby squid or seafood.

The manifesto of these cooks, who were soon to enjoy considerable success, might have struck a radical note but, as some local commentators were soon able to observe, the reality of their practice did not quite match the prescriptions of their principles. For instance, they did not so much return to classical dishes of *la cocina vasca*, as adapt them. Very few old recipes were revived as such. However, they did introduce a new lightness and standard of refinement to local catering, and they did restore the prestige, both local and foreign, which Basque cuisine had formerly enjoyed. Even renowned French chefs were ready to recognize their talent and what their Basque counterparts had taught them. The much-lauded Lyonnias chef Pierre Troisgros called them 'superior to us in this passionate aspect of searching through the local past and the old, of bringing out the new'.[45] As one of them put it, their success also 'dignified' the status of chef, who no longer hid in the kitchen but now chatted to customers.[46]

The leading chefs of the *Nueva Cocina Vasca* are today treated as public personages, just as Ibarguren and Castillo were in their days. Accounts of their careers, the various national and international prizes they win, the popular food competitions they judge, and the public events they inaugurate or simply attend are all given feet of column inches in the local press.[47] Their achievements are also officially acknowledged. In 1998, Juan Mari Arzak received, along with the Basque sculptors Eduardo Chillida and Jorge Oteiza, the Gold Medal of Guipuzcoa, in recognition of his work and its 'world renown'.[48] And these chefs are well aware of the roles they are choosing and are being made to play. For instance, when Arzak was invited in 2004 to prepare the grand dinner for the eve of the Crown Prince Felipe's wedding,

[45] 'Revolución en Euskadi', *Cambio 16*, No. 312, 4 xii 1977: 86–91; García Santos 1986: 8–32
[46] Lapitz 1983: 21. In 1982, two of the most innovative of these cooks experimented with a variant of their *Nueva Cocina Vasca*, one centred around smells. In these dishes they made greater use of herbs and replace cream-based sauces with fish, meat or vegetable stocks. But it did not seem to have had much effect, and was quickly forgotten within a few years.
[47] E.g. *M* 8 viii 1998: 3; 10 viii 1998: 1, 6; 14 viii 1998: 6; 10 ix 1988: 5; 10 xii 1998: 16; 28 xii 1998: 6
[48] *M* 27 iii 1998: 4

he told the press, 'It is an honour, because it is on behalf of Basque cuisine.'[49]

In their desire to share some of their innovations and to raise popular standards, these chefs give open classes during the Gastronomic Week of Intxaurrondo, a San Sebastian neighbourhood. This annual celebration of good cooking was first held in 1990 and quickly grew into a highly popular event, attracting notable chefs from across the Spanish state as well as from the French Basqueland and Basque communities abroad. One chef of the group, Luis Irizar, had already set up his own school of cooking in the mid-1980s. However, in 1998 the Nueva Cocina chefs tried to revive the cooperative spirit they had originally enjoyed, to consolidate their pedagogic efforts, and to link with the newer generation of younger Basque chefs (including those in Navarre and Iparralde) by establishing a Gastronomic Forum of Euskal Herria. One of the main aims of the Forum is to lobby for, and participate in, the establishment of a higher education institute dedicated to gastronomy and catering management.[50]

'Basque cuisine' today

An idea of 'Basque cuisine' could come to the fore because a cultural version of Spanish nationalism has, in the modern period, been so weak. Since the Revolution, a particular version of 'French cuisine' has been a central part of French national identity.[51] There has been no comparable process in Spain. Instead regional cuisines have been able to gain a defined identity and the most successful of those is the Basque one. And today, there is little chance of the contemporary idea of 'Basque cuisine' declining in prominence in the Basque Country, for a number of very good reasons, primarily political and economic.

First, as the Basque Government knows well, Basque cuisine is a good image to tout. An integral part of the Government's recent tourist campaigns both within Spain and beyond, Basque cuisine is promoted as a quality product, with dishes as traditional as weather-beaten Basque homesteads and as sophisticated as the Bilbao Guggenheim. This package of food, art and futurist architecture, aimed at an upmarket tourism, is also a necessary counterweight to the bad press caused by the continuing efforts of Basque terrorists. It is a way of reminding outsiders that there is much more to the area than gunmen and radical political activity. As the Government Department for Industry, Commerce and Tourism puts it, in its promotional literature:

> Gastronomy is as much part of the Basque Country as the green of its mountains, the sea breaking on its coast, its language, or its folklore. Its cuisine has developed since the most ancient of times, parallel with the arrival of visitors to the country. Ever since the 'belle époque', Basque cuisine has been celebrated throughout the entire world.

[49] *El País* 20 v 2004: 28
[50] *M* 31 v 1998: 10; 31 x 1998: 3
[51] On the reasons for this, see Zeldin 1980; Trubek 2000

Today, with the culture of leisure established among us, Basque products, cuisine and gastronomy have become the ambassadors of a way of doing things. It would be difficult to understand present-day Basque culture without the ludo-gastronomic concept linked to everything else our country offers.[52]

It is for these reasons that Basque authorities subsidize the building of museums dedicated to local cheeses or cider, and why they are disposed to sponsor tours 'from Kenya to Mexico, from Yugoslavia to Japan' by the more renowned of the *nueva cocina* chefs, demonstrating their art to all who wish to listen. In the process these chefs come to be seen as 'ambassadors of the Basque people whose cuisine has begun to be much heard of in international dining rooms'.[53] The leader of the Basque Government expressed this sentiment so:

I have observed with pleasure these past years that there have been numerous culinary embassies which have travelled to other countries, carriers, not only of how to cook well, but also of the friendly image of our people.
. . . I see with pleasure this expansion of the Basque cuisine and I am proud of the women and men who, with their work, have managed to create an extremely important magnet for tourists.[54]

The Basque Government now funds the annual Euskadi Prizes of Gastronomy and its leading politicians are assiduous in attending a variety of promotional events for Basque foods, cider and wines. Given this interested publicity for modern Basque cuisine and its leading lights, any criticism of its renowned chefs becomes all the more damning. Thus, when in October 2004, four of them were publicly charged with paying ETA's *'impuesto revolucionario'* ('revolutionary tax'), anti-nationalist journalists made much of the fact: 'To feed ETA' and 'Nurturing the monster' were just two of the subsequent headlines.[55]

Second, nationalists of all political shades may themselves see Basque cuisine and its customs as a way to unify, possibly even to pacify local society. When a local journalist asked one leading representative of the PNV about civil confrontation in contemporary Basque society, he responded that there were 'things which bring people together, like Athletic de Bilbao, the Real Sociedad (local football teams) and the *sidrerías*', which have been enjoying a revival since the 1980s.[56] It is illuminating that Francisco Letamendía, a famous radical nationalist during the transition towards democracy, has co-argued that 'In a country torn by social and political division, culinary culture . . . will be one of the links of union, perhaps the most unquestionable, which will make brothers of all the Basques, over and

---

[52] 'La magie de la Gastronomie Basque', *Euskadi. Pays Basque. Avec plaisir*, Servicio Central de Publicaciones del Gobierno Vasco, Departamento de Industria, Comercio y Turismo, August 2003, p. 3
[53] Lapitz 1983; *Gipuzkotour magazine* Spring 2006: 12; *Gara* 13 v 2006, 'Sagardo botila' suppl., p. 4
[54] Ardanza 1987: 13
[55] *M* 17 x 2004
[56] *M* 2 x 2000: 11

above their differences.'[57] Furthermore *Egin* never once criticized the owners of Zalacaian, a Basque restaurant in Madrid and the most garlanded eatery in the country, even though the only consumers who can afford to go there are the very biggest of big capitalists. Indeed Basque cuisine is now so established a part of Basque identity that it may act as a legitimator of it. In 2004, when interviewed by a Basque journalist, a local film director, keen to emphasize his local roots and down-to-earth nature, made a particular point of stressing that one of his favorite pastimes was to cook traditional Basque dishes.

To this list of the links made between politics and cuisine must be added the use of Basque dishes as metaphors for the political process itself. Here it is as though regional modes of culinary preparation can themselves stand in for the local style of social relations. Thus in 2002 when a Bilbao writer and journalist wished to criticize the PNV and the local church for their conniving pusillanimity, he wrote:

> While ETA, with great inner peace, prepared its dynamite debut, Basque blame thickened slowly and carefully, like a green sauce of bacalao al pil-pil in the stoves of the *batzokis* [PNV club-premises], and like a red sauce of bacalao a la vizcaína in the church altars of Euskadi. The reddish and tomatoey blame of those apprehensive of the killings, for which they are not responsible. The greenish and oily blame of the nationalists looking towards an unborn nation, which neutralizes any other blame . . . Both kinds of blame fusing together in the same cooking-pot and, following the miraculous recipe of bacalao al Club Ranero, the product of a kitchen porter's mistake, but which is now repeated in the National Table [a place of negotiation for nationalists], with the premeditation, nocturnality, and planned malice of a clergyman with a bruised nose and a big gut.[58]

Third, as the seemingly uncheckable advance of global capitalism continues to erode any significant degree of structural difference between societies, then, almost by default, cultural differences start to come to the fore. In the Basque Country traditional and distinctive forms of social structure and economic organization have fallen into decay, to be replaced by more globally common forms. In the process, cultural aspects of their way of life have become one of the few remaining means by which Basques can continue to proclaim their difference from other peoples. *Pelota*, the Basque ball game, supposedly the fastest ball game in the world, was for many decades an international banner of Basque cultural distinctiveness, as local players were hired to play in the *frontones* (*pelota* courts) of Miami, the American Midwest, Mexico, the Philippines, and elsewhere. But the game has now been pushed aside as an exportable standard of Basqueness, for the sake of Basque cuisine. Why? Most likely because *pelota* is too strongly wedded to the old, overly traditional image of the Basque Country. In contrast, Basque cuisine can be presented as both traditional *and* new, both honestly simple *and* excitingly sophisticated. This Janus-like quality of Basque cuisine makes it a perfect commodity for sale in the international

---

[57] Iturbe and Letamendía 2000: 76
[58] Ezkerra 2002: 128–29

markets serving foodies, i.e. those members of the burgeoning middle classes in Western Europe, North America and Australia who have made a cultivated knowledge of food the modern hallmark of social *savoir-faire*.[59] For all these reasons, the idea of 'Basque cuisine' has today taken on a greater significance for the nationalist struggle than it formerly held.

Fourth, recent interest in Basque cuisine and its ingredients chimes with the widespread rise of the environmentalist movement in the area. For today many Basque foods are seen to be as green as what remains of the verdant Basque countryside. They are regarded as traditional, 'pure' and 'authentic', a reassuring taste of the past, at a time when change, additives and pollutants seem otherwise to be becoming the norm. For instance Basque cider is presented by local panegyrists as 'the ancestral drink of the Basques', 'authentic to its roots', 'produced in the most artisanal way possible' using 'autochthonous apples', with hope for future increased sales pinned on 'its radical naturalness'.[60] This desire for the markedly 'authentic' is one, modern way to fulfil a dream of countryside. Just as early nationalists lauded the landscape and promoted rural events presented in a traditionalist mode, so their latter-day, newly urbanized successors celebrate the Basque countryside and commemorate their version of Basqueness in this novel geo-culinary fashion. We might say these eulogizers of the neo-rural are creating a taste of what should be, a flavour of a created past, heavily oaked with an oneiric nostalgia.

Moreover, in a bid to protect Basque markets against cheaper imports and to boost the sense of local particularity, the Basque Government has created its own stamp of authentic approval, the 'Denominación de Origen Controlada'. So far it has been applied to wines, cheese, capsicums, asparagus, red peppers and a host of other foods. Their price is higher than that of their more mass-produced competitors but one is meant here to be paying extra for the sake of a guaranteed Basque product of certified origin. In this century Basque authorities have as well started to promote the meat from autochthonous breeds of livestock as 'Productos de Calidad'. Their aims are dual: to maintain local difference and genetic diversity in the face of a threatening standardization stimulated by global forces; to support local cattle farmers dedicated to the preservation of indigenous breeds, who can sell their meat as distinctive and of high quality. Many local chefs are happy to come on board, as they wish to produce dishes with ingredients which are both local and highly valued. The ultimate aim is to renovate a sector of the Basque economy, both rural (the herdsmen) and urban (the restauranteurs), by producing prestigious products with a high-profit margin

[59] Izagirre 1997: 109. On the international rise of 'foodie-ism', see Barr and Levy 1984, MacClancy 1992: 208–13. On the commercial profitability of 'Basque' restaurants in Barcelona see Medina 2002

[60] Aguirre 1996: 6, 70, 131–2. Local cheeses, produced in a time-honoured manner by shepherds in mountainous areas, have become a particular focus of interest. Every year, on the last Sunday of August in Uharte-Arakil, northwestern Navarre, the municipality holds a competition for the best artesanal cheese, followed by its auction of the winning item. The final price can reach several thousand pounds (see Hualde, Pagola and Torre 1989).

and a good Basque image, for consumption both locally and beyond.[61]

But what lies behind the rhetoric, the promotional campaigns, and the striving for authenticity? For what the politicians and the publicists of Basque cuisine fail to mention is that the daily diet of the local populace is gradually becoming less and less distinctive, as fast-food outlets open throughout the area and hypermarkets replace corner stores.[62] Over the last twenty years, I have conducted a total of over four years' fieldwork in a small Navarran village. Every day when I am there I eat with my landlord, a smallholder and his family. Even though he himself produces a significant proportion of what we eat, the rest is bought in and much of that is industrially produced food: ham, cheese, frozen rings of squid in batter, ice cream, etc. Over the years the proportion of bought-in food has increased. I have checked this fact with other locals, who admit it is a general trend within their own homes. In other words, traditional Basque cuisine is becoming more and more of a rarity, even within this agricultural, food-producing area. Furthermore, within the area's cities, producing traditional Basque dishes is coming to be seen as a luxury, as a hobby for those with sufficient income to afford the leisure time necessary to cook in the customary manner.

Some local journalists have been quick to pick up these points. Promotion of Basque cuisine is now so great that one reporter has complained of its use as 'a throwing weapon'.[63] Another found some locals annoyed at outsiders' association of Basques and good eating: 'It's as if here we did nothing else.'[64] In the words of one Bilbao columnist:

> The nationalists, almost always nostalgic for days which, in reality, have never been, are reluctant to accept the miserable truth of things, seeking difference in anything which crops up: marrows with *denominación de origen* for example . . .
>
> The reality, televisual and cruel, true as a Biblical phrase, has overcome any difference. The Basque Country, for example, being a territory presumed to be of gastronomic refinement, congregates an ever-increasing quantity of commercial macrocentres where adolescents and those who are unwilling to abandon that pitiless age, devour, day after day, cones of chips with ketchup, defrosted pizzas, onion rings, chicken à la Kentucky, plastic salads and dubious hamburgers from any MacDonalds, Burger King, Pizza Guss or Telechef.[65]

Other commentators have pointed out how some prized Basque foods are now Basque only in name. Today, the sloes (*pacharán*) for the distinctive and highly popular local drink *pacharán* (sloe anis) come mostly from Eastern Europe; the cod for *bacalao* is no longer trawled by Basque fishermen but imported, already salted, from Iceland; elvers (*angulas*) are now so expensive that they are being replaced by *gulas*: Japanese surimi fishmeat processed industrially into elver-like shapes, each tinted with a touch of squid ink.[66]

[61] Amezaga 2006
[62] Bengoa n.d.
[63] *M* 21 vi 99: 16
[64] *El País* 9 xi 1990: 11
[65] Bolland 1999
[66] *Navarra Hoy* 22 xi 1986: xxvi; Kurlansky 1997: 211–13; 1999: 259–62

Some opponents of Basque nationalism have adopted a slightly different tack, by promoting a regional cuisine whose borders cross-cut those of the general Basque area. Thus the Navarran Government and a significant number of locals are now keen to substantiate a sense of 'Navarraness' by developing its cultural distinctiveness, including its foodways. Hence, in the last decade, several subsidized books have appeared on 'Navarran cuisine', a promotional tour of Navarran gastronomy was held throughout Spain, and regional journalists devote ample column inches to articles lauding local products and their traditional methods of production. In the late 1980s, local chefs even came up with their own answer to *La Nueva Cocina Vasca* by collectively launching, with the aid of the regional press, '*la nueva cocina navarra*'.[67] It is noteworthy that the only event in the 2004 calendar of the London branch of the Instituto Cervantes (the Spanish Government body which promotes Spanish culture overseas) which included a free reception was the talk on Navarre given by the President of its Deputation: the Instituto programme stated that his 'comprehensive analysis of Navarre today' would be followed by 'a Food Sampling Session of Navarrese top quality products including asparagus, roasted red peppers, cheese, wines and liqueurs'.

These sectional tactics for fighting cultural wars lay starkly bare the political agenda behind the Basque Government's support for Basque cuisine.

In sum, 'Basque cuisine' is not an innocent term, used for narrowly gastronomic reasons. It is a constructed category, exploited by a variety of different interest groups: by nationalist politicians who wish to strengthen their own party's position, by chefs keen to promote their own careers and to fortify the standing of their own profession, and by journalists seeking copy to sell their papers. It is also an evolving category, whose content – despite claims to timelessness – develops over time, and whose ingredients may well no longer come from the Basque Country. Moreover, it is a contested category, capable of attracting criticism as well as eulogistic support. It is at the same time an idea detached from the daily dietary reality of the majority of Basques. As such, it is more of a hope than a description, an aim rather than a classification. Less 'This is the way the Basques eat' than 'This is the way we would like the Basques to eat.'

[67] Recent books on Navarran cuisine include Abad 1999, Abad and Ruiz 1986, Sarobe 1995. Newspaper articles include *El Diario de Navarra* 22 xi 1986: xxi, xxvi; 22 ii 1987; 6 iii 1987; 8 iii 1987; 14 vi 1987: 6; 22 viii 1986: 11.

5
Biology

It's very simple. We are social beings. We are also animals. Problems begin when we try to tie those two statements together. The knot becomes tighter when nationalism is involved. Indeed it tends towards the Gordian when there appears to be a well-grounded biological basis to a certain ethnic identity, and questions of 'race' and thus of course accusations of 'racism', start to raise their head. The Basques are such a case. In this chapter, rather than lunge for a sword, metaphorical or otherwise, I wish to untie this particular knot piece by piece, and to assess the evidence as I go.

Anthropologists were for long interested in 'race'. In fact in the nineteenth century, some of them were instrumental in providing it with a supposedly scientific status.[1] But in the first decades of the twentieth century, American cultural anthropologists led by Franz Boas successfully championed the academic dismantling of scientific racism. In 1930s Germany however, some anthropologists were all too ready to advance the Nazi agenda by adding academic respectability to its virulently racist programme. The complete discrediting of their work, when details of the Holocaust began to emerge, plus a decade and a half later a vigorous debate in the United States about the biology and social significance of 'race' led many anthropologists to turn away from the study of both 'race' and racism. Instead, some of those interested in social identities researched ethnicities. This did not mean that racism went away, simply that it went uninvestigated. By the early 1990s many anthropologists had come to realize how inappropriate this shift in focus was, and how popular versions of ethnic identities were often bound up with contemporary forms of racism. The sum consequence is that 'race' and racism re-emerged as important objects of anthropological study. Despite this change however, relatively little has yet been published on racist discourse and on the connections between ideas of 'race', 'nature' and 'culture' in the Western Europe of today.[2] This chapter is thus a contribution to that surprisingly scanty literature, for the Basque case is a particularly interesting, relevant example, given its long-grounded intertwining, with respect to 'race', of politics, science and popular attitudes.

[1] On racism within nineteenth-century anthropology see Ellingson 2001.
[2] Wade 2002: 97–8. See also Harrison 2002. Exceptions to the lack of work in Western Europe are Cole 1997, Gullestad 2005.

A very revealing example of that intertwining occurred on 3 November 2000 when the Basque Country edition of the Spanish newspaper *El Mundo* ran the following front-page headline and sub-headline:

'Arzalluz calls for independence invoking the Rh negative of the Basques'

The question of blood with Rh-negative confirms that this is an ancient people, with its own roots identifiable since Prehistory, as certain celebrated researchers in genetics maintain, and for that reason with the right to decide on its own destiny.

Xabier Arzalluz, then president of the PNV and hence the most prominent nationalist in his land, had been interviewed by an Italian reporter a few days before and the editor of the anti-nationalist *El Mundo* did not want his readers to be ignorant of the man's views.

It has been known for several decades that the autochthonous population of the Basque area appears to be biologically distinctive in certain ways. What is initially so startling about Arzalluz's statement is that such a prominent, modern Basque politician was so prepared to bind his group identity to blood and genes. It is as though Basques had no other conclusive ways of defining themselves. This interview, however, was not his first sally into the biological dimensions of politics. In early 1993 at a meeting in Tolosa, Guipuzcoa, Arzalluz, speaking in Euskera, had referred to the craniometric, haematological and genetic work on the Basques which, he claimed, 'showed the reality of the specificity of this people'. Four years before that, at another meeting, he had even displayed a skeletal *reliquia* (relic) of Sabino Arana, the pioneer ideologue of Basque nationalism and widely branded by anti-nationalists as an early promoter of Basque xenophobia. On each occasion Arzalluz's bio-centric bias has generated sharp criticism from a broad swathe of the political spectrum. In 1993 even a leader of Herri Batasuna had contended that his biological approach did no favours for the nationalist camp and that Euzkadi already 'possessed sufficient political, economic and cultural arguments to be able to consider itself a nation'.[3] The radical nationalist did not want any of his fellows to be held up as racist. Given this generally negative reaction to Arzalluz's words our question has to be, why would an otherwise astute politician be prepared to raise the spectre of racism?

An aim of this chapter is to place his apparently surprising comments into their various contexts: academic, political and politico-academic. By approaching the material in this way, we can come to comprehend and assess the nature and local roles of biological and genetic information in the Basque Country today. I divide the chapter into four main sections. First, I review the information we have on the prehistory, physical anthropology, haematology and genetics of the Basques. I apologize to those who might find this section scientifically leaden, but it is necessary to review and assess the relevant evidence, before moving on to the remainder of the chapter. Second, I trace the evolution of nationalists' definition of 'Basqueness'.

[3] *El País* 30 I 1993; 3 ii 1993: 18; 7 ii 1993: 23; *Independent* 23 ii 1993

Third, I critically review the work done by Basque anthropologists over the course of the last hundred years or so into the nature of their compatriots. Fourth, I examine the role of the press in this process and the resulting popular conceptions in the Basque Country of what constitutes 'Basqueness'. In other words, the following sections are concerned respectively with biological anthropology, social anthropology, and the social anthropology of biological anthropology.

Biology

Bones

Archaeologists working in the Basqueland have yet to uncover hominid bones from the Lower Paleolithic, 150,000 to 75,000BP. The material evidence they have found (mainly objects made of silex, quartz and obsidian) suggest that the first inhabitants of the area were most likely very few and widely dispersed. They lived either in coastal zones or near elevated passes in wide river valleys, where they could take advantage of the rich diversity of animals who spent time at those altitudes. It is probable that these aboriginals moved seasonally between the coast and the valleys, and that none of the sites so far discovered was a permanent residence. It is also possible that they had no permanent sites of inhabitation in the Basqueland at this time, but used the region generally as an exploitation area.[4]

The earliest hominid bones found in the area date from c.75,000BP. This mid-Paleolithic evidence, however, consists of only a humerus and a few dental pieces, discovered on two sites, the Cueva ('cave') de Lezetxiki in Guipuzcoa and the Abrigo ('shelter') in Axlor in Vizcaya. The humerus came from an adult, most likely a woman, and has Neanderthal features. Material evidence found on these and other sites in the Basqueland suggests that those inhabiting the area at this time were members of the Mousterian culture, i.e. the culture associated with the Neanderthals. Though the density of population was still very low, it seems the number of people living in the area had risen significantly since the Lower Paleolithic.

If the skeletal evidence of human occupation of the Basqueland is scanty for the mid-Paleolithic, it is even less substantial for the late Paleolithic and Mesolithic periods. The only human remains which can be securely attributed to this time are the two dental pieces found in the Cueva de Erzalla,

---

[4] The factual material in this section comes primarily from the review articles of Ferembach (1988) and De La Rúa (1990) and the book of Peñalver (1999), supplemented by Altuna 1990, Altuna ãnd Mariezkurrena 2001, Andrés 1990, Arribas 1990, Arrizabalaga 2001, Arrizabalaga and Iriarte 2001, Azkarate 1990, Beguiristain 1990, Berganza 1990, Cava 1990, Collins 1986, 1990, De La Rúa 1995, Esteban 1990, 1997, García García 1997, Gorrochategui and Yarritu 1990, Iriarte 2002, Llanos 1990, Magallón 1997, Ruíz 1990, Ruíz 1995, Straus 1990, Zapata 2001, Zubillaga 1990. BP (Before Present) is used by radiocarbon-daters, and refers to the number of years before 1950 when radiocarbon-dating was first used.

Guipuzcoa, which have been dated as Late Magdalenian; the findings in the Cueva de Isturitz, whose present whereabouts are unknown; and some pieces from Urtiaga, now regarded as deeply problematic. During this period the number of people living in the area rose further, perhaps because of a gradual influx of people forced to abandon territories in northwest Europe by the maximum glacial conditions sustained during the Solutrean.

It was during this late Paleolithic and Mesolithic period that the occupants of the Basqueland started to develop their cultural life considerably. They began to make more specialized kinds of dwelling-sites, with base camps, seasonal base camps, and seasonal base camps established for highly specific reasons, e.g. the cave of Ekain which was predominantly used by hunters of recently born deer. At the same time, locals became more specialized and better organized in their hunting techniques: for example, the use of fire by groups to channel herds towards cliff-edges. The most common prey were deer and mountain goat, though investigation of the proto-Aurignacian and early Aurignacian levels of the cave of Labeko Koba, in central Guipuzcoa, suggests its occupants hunted above all bison and aurochs, which they complemented with some deer and horse, and a small amount of shaggy rhinoceros and mammoth. People rounded out their diet by fishing and by gathering seafood, fruits, nuts, fungi, roots and vegetables. Besides using stone, they also began to make objects from bone, antler and ivory: harpoons, assegais, needles, etc. Since the silex found in Labeko Koba comes from the coast or from inland areas over 50km away, some of its occupants either travelled extensively or participated in trading networks. Much of the rupestrian art of the area (some of it of very high quality) was painted during the late Paleolithic. By the Mesolithic, it seems, the locals had stopped painting.

The Neolithic came late to the Basqueland. In contrast to what occurred in most of what is now France and Spain, the economy of the Basque area did not evolve from one based on hunting, fishing and gathering to one based on agriculture and livestock until somewhere from about 7,000BP onwards. The transition was very gradual with, for many generations, people practising both modes of livelihood simultaneously. The exploitation of domesticated animals occurred first; the shift to agriculture happened sometime afterwards, leading to the first signs of deforestation, for the clearing of space and the supply of building materials. Domesticated bovines, pigs, sheep and goats were brought into the area. It is possible that locals themselves domesticated autochthonous aurochs and boars.

Cultural change was increasingly evident from this time. People did not use caves as much as formerly, preferring to make their homes in the open air. Perhaps because of pressures from rising numbers, they also began to populate higher altitudes (up to 1,000m above sea level) and to deforest areas for the sake of extending their pastures and land under cultivation. It is during the end of the Neolithic and the beginning of the Bronze Age that people erected dolmens throughout the Basqueland, especially in areas which commanded great views. Some archaeologists think the custom of building megaliths came to the Basqueland from what is now Portugal and west-central Spain. Given the particular structure of the dolmens, other archaeologists point to the evident influence of peoples from parts of what is now France. Either way, it is clear that the cultural influences of people living in the Ebro valley, or migrating into that area from the south, had been making themselves felt from at least the transition to the Neolithic.

If we accept the limitations of the cranial typologies still used by some biological anthropologists (i.e. that we use them only as descriptive, not as classificatory categories), we may characterize the peninsular population during the Neolithic period as consisting predominantly of gracile Mediterranean (mesodolichocephalic or 'slender-headed') types, with a lesser number of humans displaying robust Mediterranean (dolichocephalic or 'long-headed') features. A minority had brachycephalic skulls (i.e. they were 'short-headed', with a relatively high forehead, together with flattened occipital and frontal regions), or of the local type known as Western Pyrenean, i.e. with a skull that is broad in the temporal region, which has been seen as a distinctive cranial type of the Basques. The particular proportion of each cranial type varied from area to area, and was not uniform within the Basque region itself. In archaeological sites of the Neo-aeneolithic period, in the region which runs from the Western Pyrenees across the Basque Country to the Cantabrian coast, skulls with Western Pyrenean characteristics are found more frequently than in sites of the same area belonging to earlier periods. In contrast, in the Upper Ebro Valley along the southern edge of the Basqueland, the majority of the contemporary population were gracile Mediterraneans; only a few were Western Pyreneans; and there were hardly any brachycephalics, who were found in greater numbers on the northern slopes of the Pyrenees.

The coming of the Bronze and Iron Ages only increased the degree of heterogeneity within the population of the Basque Country, for all the different groups of people, originally from Central Europe, who entered the Peninsula during these periods had to do so via the Pyrenees. The influence of these groups was felt most greatly in the plains and plateaux. Thus, in the Basque area, they first established themselves in the broad valley surrounding Pamplona and in the lowlands of Alava, near the Ebro valley. One new custom they introduced was the incineration of corpses. Archaeologists have ascertained that shepherds in the more low-lying areas in the southeastern end of the Basqueland began to bury their dead in cromlechs on elevated sites, while those living in the northerly, more mountainous area continued to construct dolmens.

In the period from the end of the Bronze Age through the Iron Age, northward-moving bearers of what archaeologists call the 'Iberian culture' introduced advanced techniques of metalworking, which were used for the making of arms, worktools and decorative objects. The manufacture of iron tools made agricultural tasks much more efficient and allowed locals to produce surpluses which could be exchanged or sold. In turn this production of surplus, by enabling some to play a lesser part in the cultivation of crops and the tending of animals, enabled the rise, or further development, of hierarchy within local societies. The incoming peoples, as they moved up through the Ebro river valley, also helped to create villages of houses ordered into streets on a grid system. Those villages which display the greatest degree of this so-called 'Celtiberian' influence would also be those which would later experience a greater degree of romanization.

The Roman Empire, like the Neolithic, came late to the region, with series of armies gradually subduing the whole of the population over the course of the first century BCE (Before Common Era). The Romans constructed a network of roads throughout the area and created a flourishing system of commerce with local farmers and herdsmen. Some locals joined the Roman army. As far as can be judged, no major sites of residence throughout the region were left uncontacted by the invaders.

The Visigoths came next. Originally from eastern Europe, they took advantage of the slow collapse of the Roman Empire, first commanding Gaul then moving south over the Pyrenees into Iberia. Though they frequently met resistance in certain areas of the Basqueland, the Visigoths occupied much of the region from the fifth to the seventh centuries. It was during their occupation that Christianity was definitively established among the Basques, with for instance groups of radical ascetics practising as hermits in Alava during the sixth and seventh centuries.

Work by biological anthropologists suggests that, to a great degree, the statistical profile of the skeletal morphology of the indigenes in the Basque area had been more or less established by the end of the Bronze Age. According to their studies, the biological effects of subsequent immigrations were limited but still noticeable. For instance, in the Ebro Valley town of La Hoya, which was occupied over a thousand-year period, the majority of the skeletal material uncovered displays basically Mediterranean characteristics, though some also show 'Centroeuropean' cranial features. According to the distinguished Basque biological anthropologist Concepción De La Rúa, this admixture of peoples with Mediterranean and Centroeuropean features 'makes one think of the contact with Celtic peoples who, in the middle of the first millennium BCE, reached our Country, proceeding from the Meseta' to the south.[5]

Most craniologists today regard any historical discussion in terms of skull 'type' as having dubious value. Instead of relying on typologies, they prefer to speak of graded differences in populations. Rather than compare a supposedly 'typical' Basque with a 'typical' Spaniard or whoever, they compare the differences in the shape of the distribution curve for groups of skulls from each population. Craniologists no longer regard the notion of 'type', such as the Western Pyrenean, as a natural product of the available data, but as a heuristic construct imposed by the observer on a continuum of variation. In this sense, variability in cranial dimensions is the observed reality, while a rigid cranial taxonomy is an anthropologists' invention pur-

[5] De La Rúa 1995: 306

posefully fabricated for academic (and, at times, not-so-academic) ends. Given these provisos, the most recent, methodical work on a sufficiently large sample of skulls classed as 'Basque' has demonstrated the graded, rather than the absolute natures of any difference between the indigenes of today and their neighbours. In these statistical terms autochthonous skulls can be characterized as frequently having long faces, relatively flat heads, long, inclined jaws, and angular, prominent chins. The present-day indigenous occupants of the Basque Country may be cranially different from their neighbours; but they are only relatively so.

To summarize this prehistorical sketch all we can firmly state at the present time, given the archaeological and craniological evidence examined to date in a methodical and rigorous manner, is that Neanderthals sometimes resided in the Basque Country from about 150,000BP. Since contemporary paleontology suggests strongly that there is no significant genetic overlap between Neanderthals and members of *homo sapiens sapiens* (the species to which we belong), it appears that members of the genus *homo* recognizable to us as modern humans had not begun to visit the area until c.40,000BP. However, we are unable (as yet, at least) to demonstrate any continuity between the earliest inhabitants of the Basqueland and those who established themselves in the area in much more recent times. The fossil evidence which could prove such a link is very scarce, and those few examples come from very different times and places.

Even when we move closer to our own times, interested academics are still unable to agree on who the direct ancestors of today's Basques are. Ferembach, using mainly biological anthropological material, suggests that the so-called 'proto-Basques' are descended from Neolithic Mediterraneans who came from the south and introduced agriculture and the breeding of livestock to the area, while Collins, relying on archaeological rather than craniological evidence, has argued that the present native inhabitants of the Basque Country are quite possibly descended from the indigenous Neo-aeneolithic/Bronze Age occupants of the mountainous zones. As this difference of learned opinion demonstrates, the origin of the Basques remains an open question, one which needs further evidence of all types to achieve anything approaching a satisfactory resolution.

Body

In an effort to demarcate the distinctiveness of the indigenous population of the Basqueland as finely and as comprehensively as possible, some Basque academics have also measured a variety of their compatriots' anatomical and physiological characteristics.[6] Of course, my comments above about the artificiality of 'the average' when dealing with a population of normal distribution apply just as strongly to data of this sort as they do to cranial measurements. Moreover I must emphasize how much this material side-

[6] Caraballo et al. 1985; Rebato 1985a, b, 1986a, b, 1987 a, b, c, d, e, f, 1988; Rebato and Calderón 1988, 1990

lines the influential role of ecomorphology: it is important to remember just how very plastic the skeleton can be. While taking all that into account, it is perhaps still worth summarizing this physical anthropological research.

The more significant results of this work have been taken to confirm the characterization formulated by Basque physical anthropologists in the 1920s of the 'typical Basque skull' as similar in shape to an inverted triangle. According to the works cited, autochthonous Basques are shown to have a high and broad forehead, a distinctive bulge at the temples, tall, straight and prominent noses, thin lips (especially the upper lip), and narrow chins; the ear-lobes of these 'hare-headed' characters are usually unattached; compared to Spaniards in general these Basques are tall (median 172.69cm). In terms of body-shape women classed as Basques have tall relative sitting heights, rectangular trunks, a well-developed thorax, relatively short arms, narrow hands, and legs of medium length; their heads are mesocephalic and their faces long. The only regional difference of any significance is that Guipuzcoans have taller ears and slightly narrower foreheads than Biscayans. Guipuzcoan women tend to be almost 3cm taller than Biscayan (median 158.01 cm), while Biscayan women tend to have slightly rounder faces and their Guipuzcoan counterparts slightly narrower ones.

Blood

One problem with craniology and physical anthropology as supposedly diagnostic tools for ethnicity is that a skull or a face only reveals a person's phenotype, not their genotype. Another problem is that cranial and other physical dimensions are highly sensitive to dietetic and other environmental conditions. For instance, it is most probable that the work done on autochthonous skulls in the early part of this century tended to exaggerate the degree of characteristic Basque facial features because the researchers failed to take sufficient account of the extremely bad dentition of most indigenes at that time. What they regarded as distinctive facial features of the Basques were most probably more a result of their loss of teeth and the consequent retraction of bone.[7] Given these sorts of obstacles to a more accurate characterization of the biological distinctiveness of the autochthonous population, modern anthropologists have tended to concentrate their research on genetic, rather than cranial or somatic, measurement.

Researchers have long known that a disproportionately high percentage (55 per cent) of Basques have blood of group O, while only 40 per cent of Spaniards and 43 per cent of French people have blood of the same type. It was also discovered that the Basques have the lowest frequency of blood group B in Europe: 3 per cent as opposed to 9 per cent among Spaniards and 10.5 per cent among French people. Similarly the percentage (1.5 per cent) of Basques with the relatively rare blood group AB is even lower than

[7] De La Rúa 1985: 193

the proportion of Spaniards (4.5 per cent) or French people (4.5 per cent) with the same blood type.[8] In these simple serological terms, therefore, the indigenous population of the Basque Country appears to be different from much of the rest of Europe, and certainly very different from their immediate neighbours to their north and South.

This haematological sense of difference was dramatically highlighted and given further content in the early 1940s, when an Argentinian general practitioner, Miguel Etcheverry, noted that an unusually large number of babies born within his practice to mothers of Basque descent suffered from erythroblastosis. This often fatal illness can only arise when the blood of the mother has the Rhesus negative gene (Rh–) while that of the child is the same as that of the father, i.e. Rh+. In a small but still significant proportion of such cases the mother becomes immunized to the Rh+ antigen in the fetus, and the degree of immunization tends to increase with each successive conception of an Rh+ fetus. The antibody, produced by the mother in reaction to the Rh+ antigen in the fetus passes through the placenta into the fetal circulation of the next Rh+ child, where it damages the red blood cells. In consequence, at birth or shortly afterwards, the child tends to become anaemic and may become dangerously so. Unless the condition is treated, about 50 per cent of these 'blue babies' (as they are commonly known) die before or soon after birth. After testing 128 Argentinians with four Basque grandparents, Etcheverry found that one third of his sample were Rh– : an abnormally high proportion for a group of European descent.[9] Later work in Europe confirmed these surprising results for the Basque Country itself. All the studies since carried out in the Spanish Basque provinces have shown that at least 30 per cent of the indigenous population are Rh–, while one study in the French Basque country found the corresponding level was 42 per cent. These are the highest figures recorded anywhere in the world. In the terms of this work, the natives of the Basque Country were so haematologically distinctive that they set a new serological extreme.

More modern studies on the haematological constitution of the people of Basqueland have provided us with a slightly more graded and refined understanding of local distinctiveness. These studies[10] have shown that the indigenous population cannot be regarded as a homogeneous unity. Taking as their definition of Basqueness a person whose four grandparents were all born and lived in the Basqueland, and who has eight Basque surnames, these researchers have recorded the frequency of a series of polymorphic molecules (proteins, red cell antigens, and red and white cell enzymes) in different parts of the Spanish Basque provinces. The two main results of this work are (1) that there is an increasing differentiation – in haematological terms – of the Basque population from the general Spanish one the more

---

[8] Mourant et al. 1976: 63
[9] Etcheverry 1959
[10] For example Aguirre et al. 1985; Itturioz 1987; Manzano Basabe et al. 1987; Torre et al. 1987, 1988; Pancorbo et al. 1988; Aguirre et al. 1989

one moves north from the Ebro Valley towards the inland valleys of Biscaya and Guipuzcoa; and (2) that there is a marked degree of genetic heterogeneity between different valleys in Vizcaya, and probably in Guipuzcoa. The first result fits in with the theory that the Basque country, in its more northerly regions at least, has been home to a relatively isolated population, while its southern border in the Ebro Valley has been populated at various times by peoples passing down through northern and eastern Spain from West and Central Europe. The second result suggests the relative isolation of regional subgroups from one another: a relative degree of detachment kept up by many until after the rise of industrialization, which came quite late to certain areas of the Basque country.

In order to gain some kind of idea how the Basques have maintained their haematological distinctiveness, Basque academics have also carried out a series of historical studies into the marriage customs and mating patterns of their recent ancestors.[11] Using sources such as the census, as well as ecclesiastical and civil registers, they have started to trace the evolution of these patterns over the last two to three hundred years. When evaluating these studies, however, a number of caveats have to be born in mind, for the isonomic approach adopted by these researchers relies on the assumption that one can accurately assess the degree of village or valley endogamy by following the transmission of the same surname over several generations. In the Basque Country, however, many people in the same village may well have the same surname but only very distant common ancestors. For instance, in the west Guipuzcoan village of Ataun, though the majority of the residents are called Apalategi, many residents are unable to trace any link of kinship with many of their eponymous neighbours. In the Navarran village where I have done most of my fieldwork, people sometimes remarked how many of their number were called Apesteguia, though, as far as they knew, they were not related. There is also the strong possibility that people's surnames have been changed slightly, but permanently, when they were written down by the parish scribe at a baptism or marriage. These caveats should not make us automatically discredit the following findings, just more aware of their potential limitations.

Like the work on the distribution of polymorphisms (polymorphic molecules), these geographically particular studies have tended to highlight the traditionally maintained relative isolation of regional subgroups. Studies in the south of Alava, for instance, showed that the frequency of consanguineal marriages was closely related to demographic factors (such as the size of populations) and geographical ones (such as altitude). Thus people living in small villages high up in the hills showed a very high proportion of marriages between spouses sharing many links of kinship. In the second half of the last century the percentage of marriages between cousins increased because so many people migrated out of the area.[12]

[11] For example Zudaire Huarte 1982, 1984; Mateo et al. 1985; Anasagasti 1987; Rodriguez Hernandorena 1988
[12] Guevara Aguirresarobe 1988

Similarly, in the Biscayan valley of Orozco, locals' search for a spouse has not been directed to a significant degree by considerations of kinship or place of birth. There was a low level of interparochial differentiation, while the degree of kinship between subgroups in the valley and neighbouring areas has been primarily a function of geographical distance and the scale of the populations involved. In other words, it seems geographical and demographic factors have been more influential than cultural ones in determining the degree of genetic kinship among these populations.[13]

The south Alavan studies showed that there were few marriages between first cousins in the early nineteenth century, but that, as people migrated out of the area in the second half of the century, the proportion of this sort of marriage increased. In the extreme northeastern tip of Spanish Basqueland, in the valley of Salazar, biological anthropologists (who studied the marital record for a much longer time-span than those who worked in Southern Alava) found that there was a very low degree of consanguinity in the early eighteenth century which, until the middle of the last century, rose only gradually. The proportion of consanguineal marriages then rose in a spectacular manner up until the beginning of this century, when the percentage began to decrease very sharply (mainly because emigration from the valley meant that those who stayed behind found fewer kin among the group of potential spouses). About 85 per cent of the locals came from the same village as their parents, and while almost all of the remaining 15 per cent came from neighbouring areas, about 50 per cent of those incoming spouses were themselves the children of Salazencos. In other words, the degree of genetic renovation was lower than is immediately apparent from the data.[14]

In sum, what all these studies suggest is that, if the inhabitants of the Basque Country have maintained themselves as a more or less distinct population, that, on the whole, has been more the result of geographical and demographic factors than of a particular concern for marrying a member of one's kin or natal group.

Tongue

In November 2002, Juan José Ibarretxe, the President of the Basque Government, spoke at the University of Oxford. Some of his first words were that Euskera was 'the only living feature of prehistoric Europe'. According to him the Basques were a distinctive people and a key component of that distinction was the ancient nature of 'their' language.[15] This sentiment appears a common and long-grounded one in the Basque Country and among foreign observers, but quite how to assess it?[16]

Philological evidence is usually given pride of place in any discussion on

[13] Pena 1986, 1987, 1988
[14] Toja and Luna 1987, 1988; Toja et al. 1988
[15] Ibarretxe's speech attended by author, St Antony's College, University of Oxford, 22 xi 02.
[16] On foreigners' views of Euskera see MacClancy 2005.

the origin of the Basques' ancestors, mainly because Euskera, as the only non-Indo-European language still spoken in Western Europe, is so linguistically unusual. The following grammatical examples may give an idea of just how very different it is from any language spoken by neighbouring peoples today: the definite article is not a separate word but a suffix; nouns used with numerals remain in the singular; auxiliary verbs vary according to the number of objects as well as to the number of subjects; instead of prepositions, Euskera employs a host of prefixes and suffixes which vary depending on whether the word to which they are attached refers to something animate or inanimate. Perhaps unsurprsingly, the first book on the Basque grammar was entitled *The impossible overcome.*

The origin of Euskera is so obscure and yet so fascinating a question for many linguists that a number of them have produced some almost fantastical pseudo-answers.[17] One of the more sober attempts has been the connection made between Basque and the Caucasian languages Georgian and Circassian which, like Euskera, are non-Indo-European. Some linguists have taken the 7 per cent overlap in vocabulary between Euskera and the other pair of languages as evidence suggesting the former existence of a Basque-Caucasian proto-language. However, any attempt to reconstruct this hypothetical language 'can only be made under the supposition that this proto-language possessed a common phonological system. But at present it would be quite impossible to reconstruct this system'.[18] A similar proviso applies to any attempt to link Euskera with Berber, just because they share 10 per cent of their vocabularies.

The German linguist von Humboldt considered Euskera to have been the last vestige of Iberian, the ancient language of the Peninsula. But while there are some philological and phonological parallels between both languages Iberian, so far as we can tell at present, lacked some of the most distinctive morphological aspects of Euskera, such as the nominal case system, the pronouns and the system of tenses. Any rigorous comparison is also hampered by the fact that we do not know anything definite about the form(s) of Euskera used 25,000 years ago (i.e. when Iberian was spoken in the Peninsula). All we can say is that speakers of Iberian and of Euskera appear to have been in sufficiently close contact in the western region of the Pyrenean mountains to have produced some linguistic blending between the two languages.[19] This unexceptional statement, the almost inevitable consequence of the propinquity over time of two languages, does not mean that there is no kinship between Iberian and Euskera, rather that any substantial relationship between the two has yet to be proved.

For similar reasons, we cannot yet assert that Euskera is structurally

[17] See, for instance, the list of past hypotheses compiled by the sceptical Gorrochategui (2001: 108).

[18] Schmidt 1987: 121

[19] Anderson 1988: 103–37; Untermann 1990: 151–2. The earliest known examples of common words (i.e. not proper words) in Euskera date from the fifth century, and were uncovered in 2006 by archaeologists working on inscriptions excavated from a large Roman settlement, Iruña-Veleia, near present-day Vitoria (*M* 17 vi 06).

unrelated to any other language. To date, all we can affirm is that we so far lack the linguistic methods to prove this. As the methodologically rigorous Basque linguist Joaquín Gorrochategui has put it, 'The isolated character of Euskera is, thus, a negative hypothesis, of unmarked character, upon which one cannot build any long-term historical proposal.' He is also very wary about any claims, similar to that made by Ibarretxe, that Euskera be seen as an admirable fossil, whose lexicon reflects a Neolithic or even Paleolithic culture. For, as Gorrochategui points out, an impressive proportion of its vocabulary comes from Latin while the exact age of many other Euskera terms are very difficult to date. The danger here is that we may 'concentrate on one plane an extremely broad prehistory, in which it is difficult to establish differentiated chronological strata'.[20]

Despite all these disciplinary strictures about the connection of Euskera with other languages, we can perhaps make the minimal statement that its mere survival, as the only non-Indo-European tongue left in Western Europe, does suggest the continued existence of a group (or groups) of people who, at the very least, maintained the linguistic aspect of their cultural inheritance over several thousand years. What we do not know is who exactly these groups were and where they lived, when. For instance, studies of Euskera or Euskera-like place-names in southwestern France and northern Spain suggest that Euskera (or a non-Indo-European language akin to it) used to be spoken over a much larger area than its modern confinement to the general West Pyrenean area. Some linguists have suggested that this language of the early Christian era should not be known as 'proto-Euskera' but as Aquitanian, in order to avoid implying a narrower geographical distribution.[21]

The upshot of this work, however, is to demonstrate starkly that, as soon as we start to step backwards in time, any attempt to link Euskera to notions of specifically Basque or even ur-Basque ethnicity immediately becomes problematic and very tenuous.

Genes, genomes

If the anatomical evidence from ancient human bones is too scanty, the evidence from haematology still relatively crude, and that from linguistics too indefinite, the comparative data assembled by human geneticists tends to be richer in suggestive possibilities. When Etcheverry's discovery of the abnormally high proportion of Rh– among the Basques first became known, the English serologist Mourant tried to account for this by hypothesizing that today's Basques are the direct descendants of a Paleolithic population with an extremely high Rh– frequency, who later mixed with people from the Mediterranean area.[22] He also suggested that the remarkably low frequency of blood group B among the Basques was due to a very low level

---

[20] Gorrochategui 2001: 108, 109
[21] Mallory 1989: 105; Jacobsen 1999: 28
[22] Mourant 1948

of intermarriage by contemporary Basques and their ancestors with surrounding populations. He thought it possible that a few centuries ago the gene for this blood group was completely absent from 'the inner-core of this self-contained people'.[23] It is unfortunate for these two highly suggestive interpretations that each is based on the distributive frequency of a single gene.

The difficulty here is that a gene in common does not prove a common genetic origin, for genetic similarity may arise from either common environment or common culture. Thus modern population geneticists working in the 1970s and '80s preferred to work on as many genes as possible. As the Italian geneticist Piazza and his associates stated, 'It is the *cumulative* genetic difference between populations which is expected to summarize their evolutionary history, being proportional to the time of their separation and inversely related to the migration between them.'[24]

Piazza and his colleagues carried out multivariate genetic analysis, on the basis of which they made two tentative conclusions: (1) present-day Basques are more closely related to European than to Afro-Asiatic peoples; (2) if (as their data suggested) the genetic differentiation of the Basques' ancestors from the ancestors of the modern population of Béarn, southwest France, occurred during the time of the Roman occupation, then it appeared plausible to suggest that the Basques' ancestors had already differentiated themselves from neighbouring European populations before the Celtic invasions, i.e. sometime between 1,000 and 500BCE.[25] This second conclusion, however, did not tally with the linguistic evidence that Celtic appears to have had some influence on Euskera.[26] The Basques' ancestors, evidently, were not as isolated as Piazza and his team conceived them to have been.

What this example suggests is that multivariate genetic distance analysis seems to yield only very vague results. A somewhat more exact method, pioneered by the geneticist Cavalli-Sforza, was the geographic mapping of genetic patterns of present-day European populations. When the first principal components of gene frequencies were mapped in this way they showed a major gradient from a centre in the Middle East down towards the farther shores of Western Europe.[27] This genetic gradient loosely dovetailed with the long-established theory, derived from archaeological and linguistic evidence, of a progressive but gradual Indo-European expansion which began in approximately the fifth millennium BCE from somewhere in the Middle or Near East.

In genetic terms, one important point of this mapping is that *if*, as Mourant suggested (but on the basis of only one gene), the earliest inhabitants of the Basque area were overwhelmingly Rh–, and *if* the western-bound migrants had a very *low* frequency of Rh–, then intermarriage between the Rh- aboriginals and the migrants could have produced a pop-

[23] Mourant et al.1976: 63
[24] Piazza et al. 1988: 171
[25] Ibid.: 176
[26] Anderson 1988: 111, 114
[27] Ammermann and Cavalli-Sforza 1984

ulation with a relatively high Rh- frequency, such as is found among present-day Basques. Cavalli-Sforza characterized this as interbreeding between a population of Mesolithic aboriginals and one of Neolithic farmers. According to this interpretation today's Basques are the descendants of a Mesolithic population which, for some reason, managed to survive the impact of genetic admixture with later comers better than other old European populations.[28]

In 1991 Bertranpetit and Cavalli-Sforza produced synthetic genetic maps for the Peninsula itself. The map based on the first principal components of the gene frequencies showed the major difference in the Peninsula to be that between people living in a 'Greater Basque Area' and the rest of the landmass. They pointed out that the historically documented diminution over centuries of the area where Euskera is spoken seems to correlate with the progressive dilution of the Basque genotype in modern populations (as one moves away from the centre of the Basque area). Given this correlation, they argued that 'clearly there must have been a close relationship in the progressive loss of the Basque language and increasing genetic admixture with neighbours. Most probably, Basques represent descendants of Paleolithic and/or Mesolithic populations and non-Basque later arrivals, beginning with the Neolithic'.[29]

The results and their interpretation appear suggestive. They are also deeply polemical, for Cavalli-Sforza's approach has generated both great interest and great controversy. There are several problems with his general approach and, in this case, with the specific argument of he and Bertranpetit. A general point first: synthetic genetic maps, like any methodological artefact, have both foci of clarity and blindspots; they may cloud as much as they reveal. Synthetic maps are mathematically generated by interpolation from already sampled populations within the geographic area surveyed. Since the mappers have to use the information already available (wherever it may come from geographically) rather than glean it from an even spread of sites, their interpolation may generate artificial gradients: 'the more unbalanced the set of starting data ... the stronger these artifactual tendencies.' This is a particularly acute problem here, because 'the Basque population is probably one of the most exhaustively studied at the anthropogenetic level' and because there is an almost total lack of studies in Andalucia and the Levant, i.e. coastal Spain and its inland regions from Cadiz to Valencia.[30] In other words, what these maps might best reveal is not the relative occurrence of certain genes in the Peninsula, but the relative density of studies about these genes in different parts of the Peninsula. On this reading, they are more maps of research efforts than of research results.

The specific Basque example given here illustrates further general points. First, there is no necessary relationship between the maintenance or loss of

---

[28] Cavalli-Sforza 1988

[29] Bertranpetit and Cavalli-Sforza 1991

[30] Izagirre, Alonso and De La Rúa 2001: 327. For detailed criticisms of the use of synthetic maps, see Sokal, Oden and Thomson 1999a, 1999b. See also Marks 2002.

one's language and intermarriage with the speakers of a different language. As far as we can tell, for recent times at least, language has not been a consideration in the choice of one's mate within the Greater Basque Area. Second, the documented progressive contraction of the area where Euskera is spoken occurred at least 2,000 years later than any Neolithic immigration.

Also, Cavalli-Sforza assumes that the genetic patterning he derives is the result of populations migrating, when in fact it might well be the consequence of long-term trends in very small-scale human movements.[31] Indeed his approach can not accommodate anything finer than gross population migrations, and usually in one direction only. Furthermore, it is very hazardous to assume, as Cavalli-Sforza does, a general correlation between genetic, ethnic and linguistic populations. Quite simply, we know very little about the timing of the biological processes which bring about genetic variation. As the geneticist Scott MacEahern puts it, both geneticists and linguists have yet to develop chronometric techniques with levels of precision anywhere near those of archaeology and anthropology, and this disparity 'vitiates much of the utility of the comparisons between these data types'.[32]

It was initially hoped that the new work on DNA polymorphisms, carried out since the 1990s, might overcome some of the vagueness of research done on the classical genetic markers (blood groups and plasma proteins). Instead it has manifest a new set of uncertainties. Early general work in this vein quickly confirmed that the vast majority of genetic diversity among humans was due to the differences between individuals of the same group. Only a tiny proportion was due to differences between groups.[33] I must therefore underline that any discovered difference between a Basque population and another group of humans is, genetically, a very small difference indeed. As a distinguished British population geneticist put it to me, 'If Cornwall, for instance, had been studied this intensively, the work would be bound to turn up at least some differences.'[34]

Geneticists have had to work hard to find anything different about Basque polymorphisms which can withstand critical scrutiny. One continuing problem is the small sample size of many DNA studies. Since allele frequencies have large standard errors, any inference which does not take this stochastic dimension into account may well be inaccurate or even absurd. Matters are complicated further because Basque population geneticists have themselves argued that apparent lack of heterogeneity of some Basque DNA is 'not definite proof that it does not exist, as factors intrinsic to the biology of these markers might be causing an apparent homogeneity'.[35] The same geneticists have been honest enough to caution that 'unconscious inertia' has led some researchers to magnify the suggested differences of Basque DNA

[31] Zvelebil 1998
[32] MacEahern 2000
[33] For confirmation, in polymorphic terms, of the intraprovincial hetereogeneity of the autochthonous Basque population(s), see for example Manzano et al. 1996, Iriondo et al. 1999.
[34] Mark Jobling, pers. comm. See also Barbujani 2001: 166
[35] Izagirre, Alonso and de la Rúa 2003: 329

in order that they dovetail with 'the recurrent, but not precisely defined, scenario of genetic isolation for the Basques'.[36] As the Italian geneticist Guido Barbujani warns, ad hoc, a posteriori explanations should only be regarded

> as temporary solutions until explicit hypotheses can be tested. Our knowledge of human history, especially in Eurasia, is such that almost any finding of population genetics may be associated with a historical episode potentially accounting for it but also with other historical episodes suggesting the contrary.[37]

For example, in a recent study Alonso and Armour identified a set of alleles specific to the Basque population whose estimated age precedes the Neolithic expansion. Though it seems so promising, this result in fact tells us little on its own, as a larger sample or one of additional populations could well reveal these supposedly Basque-specific alleles in other populations.[38] Work on the Y chromosome and on mitochondrial DNA of native Basques is similarly suggestive, yet in an equally qualified manner, of pre-Neolithic genetic lineages.[39] The question would still remain, however: where did these lineages come from? Arnaiz-Villena and Alonso (1998) argue that because certain distinctive polymorphisms are found within the Basque population, the Basques ultimately derive from Paleolithic north African populations. Maybe descendants of these populations, already based around the western Pyrenees, exploited some of the material culture brought by Neolithic peoples migrating from the east; maybe they admixed with them as well. At present the work which holds the greatest promise of resolving the hazy picture of Basque genetic history is the recently initiated research on ancient DNA.[40] And the first results of this work suggest that the belief in the Basques as a genetic isolate is more and more difficult to maintain.[41]

---

[36] Ibid.: 328

[37] Barbujani 2000: 145–6

[38] Alonso and Armour 1998

[39] Quintana-Murci et al. 1999; Barbujani 2001: 165–6. Jobling (2001: 174) warns that 'dating of Y-chromosomal lineages is inherently unreliable'.

[40] Arnaiz Villena and Alonso 1998, Izagirre and de la Rúa 1999. On north Africa as a possible origin of the ancestors of present-day Basques, see also Jackes et al. 1997. Rosiques argues, in a review of the evidence, that 'the biological affinity with Caucasian populations, with Atlas Berbera, or local evolution continue to be working hypotheses, never ruled out and present in the models on the origin of the Basque population. The present genetic heterogeneity could for this reason be coherent with a model of multiple origins, i.e. the three base populations: Caucasians, Berbers and local populations could have contributed in different degrees to the ancient populating of Euskal Herria. In fact the anthropology of the mountain populations has never ruled out that mountain crossroads were in the past generators of population' (Rosiques 2001).

[41] See also Izagirre, Alonso, Alzualde, & de la Rúa 2003; Alzualde et al. 2005, 2006. The Basque social anthropologist Juan Aranzadi has tried to question the integrity of *all* the above work on the grounds that it is intellectually dubious to define a biological population in terms of a cultural definition: the possession by subjects of a certain number of Euskera surnames. Further, he argues that surnames should not be a conclusive criterion of aboriginality because, as hereditary possessions transmitted patrilineally, they only started to come into existence in the seventeenth century. Until then local families or lineages identified themselves with descriptive Euskeran toponyms. On top of that many locals have 'Basquized' their surnames in recent decades (Aranzadi 2001: 450–1,458–9). It could be easily argued that Juan Aranzadi is here developing a point made by his great uncle, the renowned anthropologist Telesforo de Aranzadi, over seventy years before. He questioned the use of Basque surnames as an index of Basqueness: tracing one's ancestors back to the fifteenth century, i.e. to the great-grandfathers of the great-grandfathers of one's grandfathers, would produce a list of 4,096 ancestors.

If anything emerges as certain from all this biological and genetic investigation, it is only the consistent need to maintain a stance of critical skepticism.

Basqueness

The wealth of information about the biological anthropology of the indigenous population of the Basque Country has not come about by chance. The main reason why the indigenes occupying this particular small corner of the globe have been so well studied is the continuing stimulus of Basque nationalism. From its beginning, nationalist leaders explicitly valued Basque distinctiveness, and made it a crucial part of its *raison d'être*. According to them, the Basques were different from others and had to be recognized as such. But, as we shall see, exactly what has constituted 'difference' has varied greatly over time. 'Basqueness' was not, and is not, a stable, unquestionable concept but a problematic one, strongly subject to the political influences of its times.

A significant number of politicians in Spain, above all many early nationalists, used the same racial terminology as, and adopted many of the attitudes held by, European anthropologists of the late nineteenth century. These racist academics hierarchized the different races of the world, and gave their ordered system explicit moral overtones. According to their conception of human diversity, certain races were 'pure', and hence superior, while others were mere mongrel breeds, the unwanted products of misguided intermarriages. Pure breeds were extolled. Halfcastes were to be despised. It is also probable that the early nationalists' arguments won the audience they did because of a line of learned local predecessors who propounded Basque difference in terms of blood.[42]

To Sabino Arana, Basques and Spaniards were members of different *razas* ('races'). They were nothing to do with one another. The Basque race, moreover, was pure, while the Spanish one was not. Speaking of Biscayans

[41] (cont.) However, 'returning to that epoch, we find exotic styles of patronymics and with arbitrary choices, adoptions and changes, and who among us can be sure that their thousands of surnames are all Basque ones?' (Aranzadi 1919: 14).

It is revealing that Sabino Arana dropped the possession of sixteen Euskeran surnames as his initial criterion of membership for PNV because so few willing stalwarts could fulfill it.

[42] On the prevalence of ideas about 'race' and 'degeneration' in Spanish politics in general in the late nineteenth century, see Álvarez 1998: 455–62. My paragraphs on the racist dimension of early Basque nationalism are indebted to Larronde 1977: 119–31; Corcuera Atienza 1979: 383–90; Apalategi 1985: 86–9; and Gurruchaga 1985: 110–12. Azurmendi (2000) analyses at length the local ideological precursors of Arana, from the sixteenth to the eighteenth centuries. According to Azurmendi, these precursors established a xenophobic sense of Basque difference grounded on the purity of blood, Euskera, and the particular history of the region. See also Aranzadi 2000: 383–476.

It is noteworthy that in 1993 Arzalluz tried to defend himself against non-Basques who criticized his references to biological differences between peoples by arguing that it was the 'eternal Spain' of inglorious memory which had institutionalized 'an intense racism' by exploiting the exclusionary criterion of 'purity of blood' (*El País* 4 ii 1993: 18).

(though he later extended his ideas to all Basques), he stated.

> [The] Spanish race is a product of all the invasions that have occurred in the peninsula since forty centuries ago: the Celt, the Phoenician, the Greek, the Roman, the German, the Arab, with the Latin element as dominant. Let us turn to see what race the Biscayan is. He belongs to the race which speaks the language called Euskera. This extremely original race is neither Celt, nor Phoenician, nor Greek, nor German, nor Arab, nor is it similar to any of those which inhabit the European, African, Asiatic, or American continents or the islands of Oceania. It is an isolate in the universe to such an extent that one cannot find data for its classification among the other races of the Earth. Thus the Biscayan is not racially Spanish.[43]

This racial difference had stark and important behavioural consequences. Quite simply, the *maketos* (a derogatory term for non-Basque migrants, with the same pejorative force as the British 'wog') were stupid, when compared to the Basques:

> The Biscayan is intelligent and clever at all kinds of jobs; the Spaniard is short of intelligence and lacks the skill for even the simplest jobs. Ask any employer, and you will learn that a Biscayan does as much, in the same time, as three *maketos* together.[44]

Since the purity of a language, according to Arana, was a good indicator of the purity of a race, the patent originality of Euskera and its lack of 'contamination' by other languages convincingly demonstrated the purity of the Basque race. However Euskera, like the Basque Country, was not particularly important in itself, for Arana believed that nationhood was based not on language nor on territory, but on race. As far as he was concerned, it was better to have a society of pure Basques who spoke Spanish and lived anywhere in the world than a population of Biscaya-based half-breeds who babbled in Euskera:

> Well, the extinction of our language is of no importance whatsoever; nor the loss of our history; nor the loss of our very own and holy institutions, nor the imposition of strange and liberal ones; nor the political enslavement of our *patria*; none, absolutely none, of this matters in itself, when compared with the rubbing together of our people with the Spanish, which, within our race, immediately and necessarily leads to ignorance and a drop in intelligence, to weakness and corruption of the heart, and to total estrangement; in a word, to the end of all human society.[45]

To Arana, race signified 'the moral union of individuals born from the same trunk, who maintain among themselves relations elaborated by blood through time'.[46] One did not decide one's race, one was given it by God, and while race could not be achieved, it could be lost. Thus, those Basques who did not maintain blood relations and married outside their group were cutting their children off from the racial trunk. The easiest way to affirm a possible mate's race was by asking his/her surname: a person called Rodriguez could not be Basque under any circumstances; one called Garai-

[43] Arana Goiri 1895
[44] Ibid.
[45] Arana Goiri 1897
[46] Arana Goiri 1980: 1761, quoted in Heiberg 1989: 51

coetxea Aguirreazkuenaga Zigorraga could not be anything but. In its first years the Basque Nationalist Party would not admit anyone whose first sixteen surnames (i.e. those of his/her sixteen male great-great-great-grand-parents) were not all Basque. While Arana's definition of Basqueness was racially based, it had at the same time moral consequences. Since race came from God, one's ethics were also necessarily determined by the Almighty: full-blooded Basques had to follow the edicts of Christian law.

The traditionally deep and complex attachment of rural Basques to the land they live on seems to contradict Arana's notion of a 'rootless but racial Basquicity'. A disciple countered possible objections by contending that locals loved the valleys and woods of the countryside *because* 'they are the prehistoric habitat of the race'.[47] Anyway, the aim of Arana's political programme was not so much to provide an ethnographically credible defi-nition of his compatriots rather, to construct a sufficiently coherent concept of Basqueness which could be exploited when criticizing the Spanish immi-grants. It was meant to unify Basques in opposition to these disliked, impure newcomers, who were branded in racist terms as *beltza* ('Blacks') or as *moros* ('Moors'). Basques were fervent Catholics and upholders of God's word, the migrants were pagan anarchists: they lacked morals as well as racial purity. Committed nationalists argued that Basques had to end all form of contact with these foreigners. For the sake of the perpetuation of their race Basques had to isolate themselves from the polluting influence of these outsiders. Thus anyone ignorant or rash enough to consider commit-ting a mixed marriage had to be dissuaded.

In the first decades of the twentieth century Engracio de Aranzadi, prominent disciple of Arana and leading PNV ideologue, became the standard-bearer of this racist approach within the nationalist camp. Writing in 1910, he defined 'race' in terms of blood, 'the strongest link which exists on earth, isolating and separating its members from other ethnic groups, by differences which, because born in the very guts of nature, persist in their being and in their action while the race itself persists'. He went on:

> Do we Basques form a race? I will not bother readers by overwhelming them with torrents of cheap erudition, formed by the interminable quotes of ethnolo-gists who answer the above question in the same way as all of us.
> Treatise-writers say eleven races people the European continent: Latin, Greek, Slav, Celt, Magyar, Turk, Finn, Lithuanian, Basque and Gypsy.
> The Basque people constitutes, then, a race, so say unanimously those who dedicate themselves to this class of studies.[48]

In 1931 he was even plainer:

> Legions of the learned have tried to discover the cradle of the Basques; using history, then comparative philology and later anthropology, they have declared, with their extremely tenacious academic determination focused on the Basques, just how outlandish and strong is the personality of this people, whose territory does not exceed 20,000 square kilometres.

[47] Eleizalde 1919: 404
[48] Kizkitza (pseud of Aranzadi) 1910: 58–9

How else to explain the philological and anthropological work carried out on the Basques and their language by Michel . . . and thousands of other treatise-writers?. . .

We can believe Huxley . . . when he asserts that the language of the Basques makes philologists despair, and that the result of the formidable but contradictory labours of the learned is . . . that 'there is nothing like it in the rest of the world'.

And it is logical that it be so. Euskera, which is characteristic of this people, must be a unique, separate language; an island language, as an expression of the Basque race, which is, in the judgement of Reclus, *an 'island' race.*

Why spend more time on the proof of a fact recognized by all? Why stop to demonstrate the existence of the Basque race when all the ethnologists of Europe, admirers of the extraordinary strength of the Basque people and their disconcerting singularity, focus their attention on that in order to clarify the origins of the Basques? . . . Because the Basques live, because they have known how to resist, in a really prodigious manner, the dissolvent influence of uncountable centuries . . . For precisely this reason the Basque people are the centre on which the learned focus their piercing energies. Basque nationality is studied today because it rises up alive, with the vigour of the days of Phoenicia and Carthage.

It is right that illustrious Basques such as the Drs. Aranzadi (Telesforo de) and Eguren, professors of the universities of Barcelona and Oviedo, devote themselves to the speciality which they develop so gloriously, testifying, strictly according to the canons of modern anthropology, the Basque racial type. For us it is enough that the unanimous testimony of learned men confirms the type's existence.[49]

Two years later the National Assembly of the PNV approved a new set of statutes, which stated that only under special circumstances could non-native Basques be considered for membership of the party and that they had to have lived in the area for at least ten years. Only native Basques could occupy regional or national posts within the party. In other words, even by the mid-1930s, Arana's conception of race as consubstantial with nationality was still regnant, albeit slightly attentuated, within the Basque Nationalist Party.[50]

Many historians of Basque nationalism see its postwar period as the time when racism was finally replaced by culturalism. The key figure often cited here is the local political theorist Federico Krutwig whose 1955 book *Vasconia* is said to have inspired ideologically so many young Basques into action. Yet though Krutwig advocates a generally and strongly culturalist approach, what is never mentioned by his commentators is that it is not one devoid of racialist elements. The break with the past is not absolute. In fact, in his book he spends several pages arguing that while the Basques are not racially united and there is no such thing as a Basque race, still 'the Basque people offer a fairly characteristic racial composition', which he proceeds to detail in the terms of physical and biological anthropology, i.e. bones and blood.[51]

[49] Aranzadi 1931: 49–51, orig. italics
[50] Pablo, Mees and Rodríguez 1999: 230–1. Elorza notes the return in 1933 of an undeclared racism, with the production of 'a drawing showing a worker, an upholder of solidarity, of noble appearance, with a beret, grabbing by the neck a paid *maketo* gunman of the UGT' (a socialist trade union, well-established in Basque industrialized areas) (Elorza 2000: 52).
[51] Sarrailh 1955: 89–96

By the 1970s the great majority of Basques did not think of themselves in racial terms, but in cultural ones. Instead of worrying about the purity of their blood and the dangers of miscegenation, they were far more concerned about the survival of Euskera. A major catalyst of this change had been the rise of ETA. Members of ETA ignore people's surnames and do not worry about racial purity. Instead they stress the importance of speaking Euskera. To them, the Basque language is the central cultural prop, a besieged form of distinctiveness which was repressed by the Franquist regime and which must be maintained. As some of ETA's earlier protagonists stated:

> There is no creation more strictly and permanently national, present and live, popular and collective, than the national language. One is dealing, perhaps, with the only creation in which all the regions, all the social classes, and all the successive generations have collaborated . . .
>   In a strict sense only the Basque language maintains at an unquestionable level the objective unity of Euskadi, across the Basque-speaking zones of the Spanish and French states . . .
>   Since the times of Machiavelli it is an extremely well-known political counsel, and one which works infallibly, that to kill a people there is nothing more deadly than to kill its national language. A people which stops speaking its language is a people which has died. A people which changes its language for that of its neighbour, is a people which changes its soul for that of its neighbour.[52]

To these *etarras* (i.e. members of ETA), Euskera is 'the maximum expression of the national personality'. As the essential factor of national identity it must be not lost, nor may any effort be spared to maintain, or revive, its use.

Far from boasting about *la raza vasca*, left-wing nationalists, at least in the late 1970s and '80s, liked to speak of *el pueblo trabajador vasco* ('the Basque working people'). Marrying nationalism with socialism and taking their cue from the former Basque Communist Party, they defined a Basque as someone who sold his labour in Basqueland. The main point of this shift in definition was that, unlike Arana's deliberately exclusive characterization, this new characterization included migrants from other parts of Spain who worked in the Basque Country. Whether a worker was surnamed Mendoza or Aretxaga Etxezarreta, he or she still suffered the same 'colonial' subjection by the centralizing, capitalist government based in Madrid, as well as by others closer to home:

> For ETA it is clear that the immigrant worker is at least as exploited as the native of the [Basque] country. For that reason, in our revolutionary struggle we ask for the participation of all the workers who today live in our soil, without distinction of origin. Moreover, the interest taken in social liberation can be even greater in an immigrant than in a locally born Basque with a higher standard of living.
>   . . . We have been and always will be with the workers who, whether or not born in Euskadi, work for the establishment of a true democracy in our country. They are the base of the future Basque society. Of course, we consider them and their children rather more Basque than those capitalists with long Basque

surnames who dare to call themselves patriots while they do not stop enriching themselves at the cost of their own people.[53]

Arana defined his compatriots in terms of race; most Basques today define themselves in terms of culture (above all, their language), and radical nationalists do it in terms of politics. In other words, a human group such as 'the Basques' is not a natural given. A population of human beings who have lived and continue to live in the Spanish provinces of Alava, Guipuzcoa, and Biscay can not be considered as 'Basques' unless they define themselves, or are defined, as such. And in a complex, class-stratified society such as that found in present-day Basqueland, it is unlikely that there will be a single definition accepted by all. Instead, as we have seen, there are different competing definitions employed in different discourses and, since Arana's racist definition has proved so labile, there is no necessary reason why we should regard the definitions accepted at the present time by different sectors of the Basque population as any more stable. They are only as permanent as the discourses which constitute them.

In each case, these different examples of Basque self-definition were direct products of social conflict. Arana and his nationalist peers formulated their particular conception of Basqueness as part of their response to the threat posed to traditional Basque society by the influx of large numbers of non-Basque Spaniards from underprivileged regions. Their notion of Basqueness, expressed in the racist idiom of the day, was intended to play a double function, of uniting different sections of Basque society into an effective political group, and of emphasizing the difference between the potential members of that group and the non-Basques then migrating to the Basque Country. Since most members of the Basque *haute bourgeoisie* saw their economic interests in Peninsular rather than Basque terms, the early nationalists first tried to draw together people like themselves (i.e. members of the indigenous *petite bourgeoisie*) with members of the emerging Basque proletariat, who had recently left the countryside and gone to work in the factories of the rapidly growing towns. Villagers were only later wooed into the movement. This is in striking contrast to pre-nationalist times, i.e. before the advent of industrialization, when there does not appear to have been any general sense among Basques as a whole of their commonwealth. It appears that most people saw themselves primarily as members of a certain valley or exchange area, and did not bother much about those living in other provinces, even though they might have spoken the same language. It took the spectre of radical change to draw at least a significant number of them together, to unite them within a unitary self-definition.

The new Basque self-definition created by members of ETA was similarly a product of social conflict. In this particular case the youthful nationalists had been goaded into action by the apparent inactivity of their elders in the face of continuing cultural repression by the totalitarian state Franco had instituted. And one of the prime objects of the fascists' hate was the Basque

---

[53] ETA 1979, Vol. 3: 509

language itself. For many years it could not be taught in schools (let alone be used as the medium of instruction there), and those who used it in public ran the risk of severe punishment: a man's tongue might be cut out if he tried to buy a loaf of bread in Euskera. Of course, this very singling out of the language by the forces of repressive law and order legitimized the importance granted it by the activists of ETA in their renovatory definition of Basqueness. According to this sort of logic, the hate shown by Franco's henchmen towards Euskera only *proved* its importance: the police would not have bothered to castigate its speakers if it had been an insignificant aspect of Basque culture.

The concept of *el pueblo trabajador vasco* is, like the previous pair of group definitions, a product of social strife. However, unlike the linguistic definition of Basqueness (which is widely accepted by contemporary Basques), the notion of the 'Basque working people' remained jarringly novel to many. While the subjugatory nature of the Franquist regime was patently evident to almost anyone resident in the Basque Country at that time, not all accepted the idea that they are all equally exploited by the forces of a centralizing capitalism. This particular, revolutionary redefinition was specifically created by the radical activists in order to unite and further politicize workers resident in Basqueland. The trouble, of course, for these politicos, was that some people – whether they could be traditionally defined as Basque or not – did not wish to be politicized to that extent or in that manner. Also some resisted the idea of being placed in the same category as the disliked labour migrants. The great majority of Basques might understand the central value of their language for the survival of their culture as they know it, but not all denizens of the Basque Country understood, or wished to understand, their way of life in anti-capitalist terms or concepts which accommodated recent incomers.

Anthropologists

The work of influential Basque academics who studied their own kind is clearly central to the themes of this chapter. For their studies should not be viewed in some atemporal asocial manner, as they did not work within an intellectual vacuum, isolated from the events of their day. Instead, and to a significant degree, they need to be seen as an integral part of the very world they were investigating. They were both simultaneously analysts and actors in the scene they were describing. Their senses of 'Basqueness' and of its appropriate content are, to an important extent, both products and catalysts of their contemporary nationalist contexts. And by reviewing critically their work here we can gain a more closely-grained idea of the social nature of the definition of 'Basqueness'.

The first Basque anthropologist to achieve national renown and to give academic substance to the racial conception of 'Basqueness' was Telesforo de Aranzadi (1860–1945). While Aranzadi did not participate in conventional party politics, and is usually considered as having been a *vasquista* rather than a militant nationalist, throughout his life he vigorously championed the academic defence of the Basques, and played a major role in setting up and running the leading Basque cultural institution, Eusko Ikaskuntza (the Society for Basque Studies).[54] He also wrote a number of polemical articles in support of Euskera – then widely regarded as a language fit only for peasants – and was prepared, when attending international conferences, to call himself a representative of the Basque people.

If there is a detectable intellectual guideline to his life it was to promote Basque studies and to present his people as an individual, but not exotic, European race. Though he was ready to use the term *raza*, which he defined as 'a group of individuals whose similar features are transmitted by physical or natural inheritance',[55] he indirectly criticized Arana and his co-believers by attacking the idea of ranking races according to some preordained criteria. He thought any form of racist selection politically impossible, and that the consequences of any errors in racist classification were potentially catastrophic in scope. Though proud to be a member of the Basque race, he did not believe in a racially based theory of supremacy.

Outside of his teaching duties, Aranzadi devoted most of his working life to the study of Basque prehistory as well as to Basque physical and social anthropology. Like many at the time, he saw these three disciplines as intimately interconnected and mutually supportive. Prehistorical work gave temporal depth to studies in physical anthropology, while he regarded culture as the spiritual manifestation of race. Rather than focus on any one discipline, it was better to study all three at much the same time. He used his ethnographic work (mainly on the Basque numerical system, calendar and farming equipment) to argue against both the thesis that everything sophisticated in Basque culture had come from the Romans, and the thesis that the Basques had lived as a cultural isolate. Opposed to extreme diffusionism, he liked to highlight the possibility of independent invention: just because the Basques used a yoke similar to one found elsewhere in Europe did not necessarily mean that the Basques had borrowed it. Why could they have not invented it for themselves?

Aranzadi repeatedly stressed that, in physical anthropological terms, the Basques were a particular type among the different races of Western and Central Europe, and he contested any theory which tried to attribute an exotic origin to them. His craniological data demonstrated that the race to which he belonged did not derive from prehistoric Berber, Finnish, or Lapp migrations, nor did it descend, to any significant extent, from a Cro-Magnon population, as the British anthropologist A. C. Haddon had propounded. On the basis of his cephalometric work, he also argued both against the theory of the Swedish anthropologist Retzius that the ancestors of the Basques were

---

[54] On the work of Aranzadi and Barandiarán in the organization of Eusko Ikaskuntza, see Estornes Zubizarreta (1983). On the evolving socio-political context of biological anthropology in general during the last 150 years, see Stocking (1988).

[55] 'Antropología y Etnología', *Geografía General del País Vasco-Navarro VI:* 90, cited in Goicoetxea Marcaida (1985: 142).

brachycephalic, and against the theory of Broca that they were dolichocephalic. After measuring a much larger number of skulls than any of his
predecessors in the field, he claimed that Spanish Basques tended to be more
dolichocephalic, owing to meridional infiltrations, while French Basques
tended to be more brachycephalic, because of septentrional infiltrations.

Aranzadi accepted the idea that the shape of Basque skulls had been dif-
ferentially influenced in these ways. But he also liked to emphasize the
intrinsic character of Basque evolution. On neither side of the border had
'the Basque cranial type' lost its individuality, which he characterized in
partisan terms:

> somewhat wide but at the same time bulky in the occipitum ... a long, round,
> narrow, and not very salient chin. Head, but not the neck, inclined forwards ...
> which produces a less emphatic, less arrogant, and more benevolent posture than
> that of other races, without at the same time appearing humble, since the neck
> and back remain vertical.'[56]

If the Basques had to be confined to a particular craniological class, he considered them to be mesocephalic more than anything else. And if, he claimed,
they had made black berets their traditional headgear, that was because it
fitted well on the slightly flattened top of their skulls. Aranzadi also used to
argue, in more popular journals that local sculptors carving Public busts or
statues should follow the lines of Basque, not Classical Greek, craneology.[57]

On the whole, Aranzadi's prehistorical investigations tended to confirm
his physical anthropological characterization of the development of the
Basque race. His most controversial work was in the caves of Urtiaga,
Guipuzcoa, which he carried out together with a young colleague, José
Miguel de Barandiarán, in the summers of 1935 and 1936. Among other
human remains in the cave they found a single skull which they thought
displayed characteristics similar to those of the crania of modern-day
Basques. They took it to be a primordial form of the Western Pyrenean type.
Since the skull was discovered in a stratigraphical level thought to be Azilian
or Magdalenian, and was thus considered to be the most ancient cranium
yet found in the Basque Country, Aranzadi took it as evidence that the
Basque race had been living in the region since at least 10,000BP. At the
time it seemed fitting that Aranzadi's last work on prehistoric craniology was
also his most revelatory, 'proving' as it (apparently) did that the Basque race,
as he craniologically understood it, had been long resident on their own soil.
In this sense it is particularly unfortunate that by 1953 Barandarián was
already casting doubt on its dating, and that modern restudy of the skull
has shown it to be much less ancient than its discoverers originally wished
to think.[58] As the historian of the early Basques Roger Collins states,

> That a conclusion of such magnitude could be based upon so little evidence, too
> small even to constitute a representative sample, is quite breath-taking, and must

---

[56] Aranzadi 1889: 33–5, cited in Goicoetxea Marcaida (1985: 138). The data on Aranzadi's
life and work come from Goicoetxea Marcaida, ibid.
[57] See, for example, Aranzadi 1918
[58] De la Rúa 1988

inevitably arouse the suspicion that it is being dictated by the predetermined requirements of nationalist ideology rather than by processes of rational deduction.[59]

In the second half of the 1970s Basque anthropology was finally given a permanent academic institutional home on the founding of the Universidad del País Vasco. José Maria Basabe Prado, who had been taught by one of Aranzadi's students, was appointed as its first Professor of Anthropology. Like Aranzadi and Barandiarán (who in 1990 celebrated his first hundred years), Basabe Prado was primarily concerned with promoting Basque studies, and he created a team within his department with the intention of investigating, as far back in time as possible, the continuity of the collection of characteristics which were taken to typify the Basques.[60] It was Basabe Prado who suggested to De La Rúa, then a student of his, that she make the topic of her doctoral thesis a definitive study of modern Basque crania. His idea was that such a study would provide a baseline for comparative work into the degree and nature of evolution of 'the Basque skull'. If there is anything methodologically distinctive to the work done by his students, it is the unusually thorough series of measurements – cranial and otherwise – which they have carried out in their studies. Given these sorts of circumstances one wonders how much similarly intensive work would throw up distinctive cranial differences in other ethnically defined populations. This would appear to be a good case of nationalism indirectly generating the sorts of academic knowledge which can give further substance to the notion of Basque difference, and thus bolster the political ideology.

Basabe Prado, again like his illustrious predecessors, regarded the ancient crania he and his students studied as evidence of the antiquity of the Basques. In a popular paper intended for an educated but non-academic audience, he stated that he and his co-workers carried out their research into Basque polymorphisms by selecting autochthonous individuals 'from the natural population, from the human group which has occupied the Basque Country since time immemorial'.[61] Once again, following in the footsteps of Aranzadi and Barandiarán, Basabe Prado was not scared to use the phrase *raza vasca*, though he was keen to emphasize the distinction between raciology and racism.

Whilst all three of these academics classed themselves as *vasquistas* rather than as nationalists, the work of all three has served to legitimize and to feed Basque nationalism. Arana was himself well aware of the use his movement could make of anthropologists: 'Ethnographically there is a substantial difference between the Spanish being and the Basque being, because the Euskeran race is substantially distinct from the Spanish race, which is something we do not only ourselves say but all anthropologists as well'.[62] According to Juan Aranzadi, during Franco's reign, republication of Aran-

---

[59] Collins 1986: 7
[60] Bennasar 1987: 34
[61] Basabe Prado 1985
[62] Arana 1980, vol. 2: 1326

zadi's and Barandiarán's work in cheap, popular editions was a permissible mode of nationalist propaganda, which aided the construction of an 'ethnic consciousness'.[63] The work of all three of these academics also assisted the cause in a more indirect, general manner. For these men, brought up in a country (Spain) where learning has such a high social value, to bother to spend their time investigating Basque (as opposed to, say, Spanish) prehistory helped, and helps, committed nationalists to justify the high regard in which they hold their own people. Thus Aranzadi, Barandiarán and Basabe Prado in themselves become valuable symbols to be deployed as appropriate by the nationalist movement.[64] Whenever Barandiarán, for instance, took part in a fund-raising event in support of the teaching of Euskera, a photo of him was usually given the most prominent position in the account of the event in the nationalist press.[65] Given this political context for their studies, it becomes all the more important to isolate the *vasquista* proclivities in their thinking.

Aranzadi, Barandiarán and Basabe Prado all stated that the people whose prehistoric bones they were investigating were not so much the ancestors of the Basques, as the Basques themselves. However, it is extremely unlikely that these early inhabitants regarded themselves as Basques, for the following reasons. First, as we have noted, the Palaeolithic humans who populated the Western Pyrenees did not constitute a stable population. They did not construct permanent habitation in the area, and we do not know exactly how far, or where they roamed. Even if these people had decided to encamp themselves in the Basque Country for protracted periods of time, there is still not sufficient human fossil evidence yet discovered to enable prehistoric anthropologists to deduce any craniological similarity between these pioneers and later occupants of the geographical region. It might well just be a case of 'They came. They saw. They moved on.'

Second, even if there were craniological identity between present-day Basques and their Neo-aneolithic predecessors, that still tells us nothing about how the latter classified themselves. Quite simply, we have no way of knowing how these prehistoric inhabitants of the region now known as the Basque Country regarded themselves. Even if they spoke Euskera, which is another fact we cannot know at present, we would not know if they saw themselves *as Basques*, or any term even roughly cognate to 'Basques'. If we hypothesize for the sake of argument, that they did speak Euskera, or some primordial form of it, we still would not know whether they called themselves *euskaldunak* ('speakers of Euskera') or something similar. And even if they were to have done so, we still would not know what exactly they meant by that term: for instance, how extensive it was to be in space and time, and what cultural content it was meant to include. Since several of the present-day dialects of Euskera are almost mutually unintelligible, speakers of the language in one area may not have regarded that spoken in another region as the same language. And even if they had spoken

[63] Aranzadi 2001: 396
[64] Azcona 1984: 162
[65] See, for example, 1994: 16, 18, 143

mutually intelligible dialects, they may still have regarded one another as members of distinct generic groups.[66]

The earliest historical evidence we have on the people of the area comes from the Roman historian Strabo, who was writing two thousand years after the Neo-aeneolithic period. Unsurprisingly he does not refer to the contemporary inhabitants of the area as Basques, but as several tribes inhabiting what is now Navarre and the Basque Country. Instead of mentioning the Basques, Strabo talks of the 'Vascones', who then occupied an area roughly coterminous with what is now Navarre, and of three other tribes, each living in areas approximately coterminous with what are now the provinces of Guipuzcoa, Biscay and Alava. It is thought that the Vascones expanded westwards, colonizing or perhaps merging with the three other tribes. For this reason, those three provinces are sometimes called *el País Vascongado* (the Vasconized country) or *las Vascongadas.*

Whether this westward colonization occurred or not, it is still the case, as Roger Collins has pointed out, that historically the Basques cannot be defined, nor could they have defined themselves in relation to a common political structure or social hierarchy. Only in the last three years of the reign of Sancho the Great, a king of Navarre, were all the Basques ever under a single political authority, and Sancho's monarchy was in no sense self-consciously Basque.[67] On top of that, the little literary evidence that we have suggests that the people of the area did not even come to be referred to as *vascos*, or Basques, until the late Middle Ages at the earliest.

Since ethnicity is usually taken to mean the *self*-definition of a group of people, we have thus to understand the historically extensive definition made by Aranzadi, Barandiaran, and Basabe Prado of the Basques as statements of *their* conceptions of the Basques. It was a definition that they imposed on the dead, not one that Neo-aeneolithic persons made for themselves.[68]

Politicians, the press and the people

The politicians provide the funding; the academics do the research (while remembering where the money comes from); the politicians, popular writers and the press publicize the results, as and how they see fit. The common consequences of this process are confusion, social fragmentation and mutual ridicule.

Like Aranzadi, Barandiarán and Basabe Prado, many indigenes today consider the early inhabitants of their homeland as the first Basques. In the Guipuzcoan parish of Itziar, for example, which includes over fifty caves, some of which have been found to contain important prehistoric materials,

---

[66] Azurmendi (2000: 369, fn.1) argues the same point from a historical perspective. See also ibid.: 376, fn. 27. See also Aranzadi 2001: 429–37.

[67] Collins 1990: 41

[68] Juan Aranzadi argues that 'the Basque people' is an ethnogenetic product of early Basque anthropology and Basque nationalism. It does not pre-exist the work of these scholars and politicians, it was a conjoint creation of them (Aranzadi 2001: 396–7).

as well as ceramics, drawings and rupestrian paintings, the locals regard the original occupants of these sites as their Basque predecessors. In the words of the anthropologist of Itziar, himself a native of the village,

> Identity runs in an unbroken line from the ancestors who came from nowhere else but [the caves of] Urtiaga and Ekain, who achieved their human condition right there in those nearby underground dwellings. These caves provide for Basques the tangible context in which their imagination of the past finds its home.[69]

Such archaeological sites can give Basques a great sense of their own antiquity as a people: 'In conversations with Basques it is not unusual to hear expressions such as "that happened *only* 5,000 BC."'[70] Heiberg, who did fieldwork in southern Guipuzcoa in the mid-1970s, felt able to state, 'Regardless of academic speculation, most Basques view themselves proudly as Europe's oldest and, they claim, purest surviving race.'[71] Hence the belief among some Basques that, unlike all their near and distant neighbours, they are not descended from anyone else. In other words, according to themselves, today's Basques are not the product of some long-extinct incoming tribe or horde; they only descend from other, previous Basques. For the local archaeologist Mercedes Urteaga, this belief helps explain 'the almost mystical respect for research into prehistory' and for the relative lack of interest in the study of the Roman period and of the High Middle Ages.[72]

Locals' sense of the antiquity of their culture is also boosted in a variety of popular ways: archaeological, gastronomic, musical, athletic, artistic. Professional Basque archaeologists openly admit that local interest in digging up their past is so strong that a host of amateurs are carrying out their own excavations, though those digs be strictly illegal. Indeed this popular practice is so informally accepted that regional newspapers will even run articles on the finds of these unpaid, unsupervised irregulars.[73] A simulacrum of Ekain, a now-closed cave near the Guipuzcoan coast with fine prehistoric paintings, will open next to it in April 2008, at a final cost of more than 8,000,000 Euros.[74] Food writers extol a variety of local culinary techniques as vestiges of prehistoric procedures, especially the continued use (at least until very recently) of the *kaiku*: a wooden jug filled with milk, then rennet and hot stones, for the making of junket. Though heavy, the jug is not difficult to hold when full. Because it is forward leaning, the centre of gravity is underneath the handle, not ahead of it.

[69] Zulaika 1988: 7

[70] Ibid., orig. italics. For a Navarran example of the same strategy, of claiming the previous inhabitants of one's area as one's ancestors, see Montes Andia 1990: 26.

[71] Heiberg 1989: 13

[72] Urteaga 2003: 26. For an emphatic statement of the multiple and pervasive importance of the Romans in the Basque Country, see Urteaga 2004: 25. A local archaeologist informs me that those carrying out urban digs into the Roman period of the Basque Country are sometimes insulted by passers-by, who enquire why they are wasting their time in such efforts (Anon. pers. comm.).

[73] E.g. the article in *Deia* (23 vii 1999: 13) on the work of a Biscayan who has been excavating a particular local site for over 20 years. The fact that his excavation is illegal is not mentioned.

[74] *Gipuzkoatour magazine* Spring 2006: 29

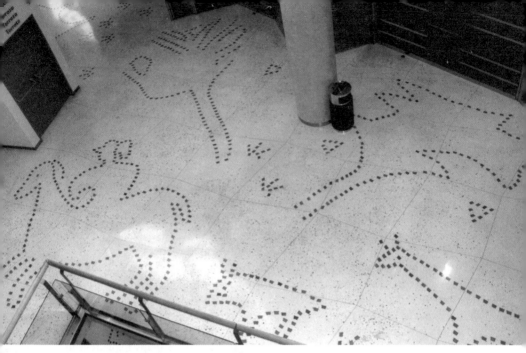

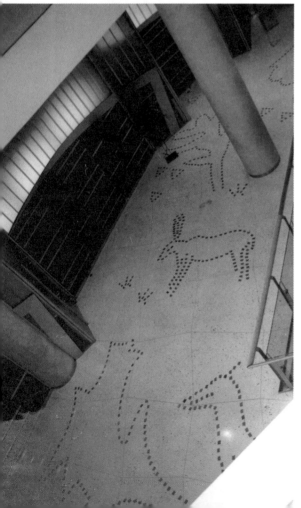

5.1 & 5.2 Stylized representations of Basque rupestrian art, as decoration for the landings of the Euskalduna convention centre, Bilbao, 2001 (© Jeremy MacClancy)

Thus this ancient utensil can be praised at both one and the same time as extremely long-established and sophisticated yet deceptively simple.[75] Some eulogizers of Basque musical traditions emphasize how old the very popular *txistu* (flute) is, as very similar instruments, hollowed out of bone, have been found on local archaeological sites, the oldest dated 27,000BP. Others point to the long-maintained rural practice of playing the *txalaparta*: similar to a xylophone, its boards are hit by a pair of performers with thick wooden sticks.[76] Aesthetic examples include Oteiza's eulogizing of Basque dolmens; Chillida's and Ibarrola's statements of how akin they feel to the artistic codes used by the prehistoric cave-painters of the caves of Santimamiñe, Vizcaya; the rupestrian floor design for the main Basque convention centre, the Euskalduna in Bilbao; Ulibarrena's grounding of Basque aesthetics in prehistory.[77] Local promoters of Basque tourism may act in a similar manner: the authors of a guide to 'Basque prehistory' openly state their aim is to foment interest in 'our most distant ancestors'.[78] These various aspects of contemporary Basque culture, plus comments such as that by Ibarretxe of Euskera as 'the only living feature of prehistoric Europe', serve to thicken locals' ideas of their ethnic group as particularly long-rooted in the area. They help indigenes to develop a sense of their own culture as, in certain aspects, a living primitivism: so long as that be understood in praiseworthy terms, as evidencing both the extraordinary depth of their ethnic legacy and the durability of some of its products.[79]

Some Basques may also make play with this prehistoric association. For

---

[75] Lapitz 1983a: 11; Leizaola 1983: 283; Busca Isusi 1987: 4–9; Hualde, Pagola and Torre 1989: 11–13; Abad 1999: 8

[76] Beltran 1998; Elorza 2000: 13; Escribano n.d. From the 1960s the *txalaparta* enjoyed a revival, thanks partly to Oteiza's writing about its cultural significance and partly to its promotion by John Cage (Zulaika 2003b: 518, fn. 171)

[77] Ulibarrena 1990; Martínez and Agirre 1995: 309; Ugarte 1996: 58. See also Kortadi-Olano 1978: 328

[78] Gómez and Darricau 1997: 8. On a more political note, they say they also wish 'to re-encounter ancient unities, forgetting ... the political divisions which have accumulated since prehistory' (ibid.).

[79] Juan Aranzadi argues that the corpus of Basque myths and legends collected by Barandarián, his colleagues and followers have been exploited in a similar manner: 'In the Basque Country one can note today a tendency to magnify the weight of these myths and legends (abusively considered as autochthonous) in the consciousness of the Basques who related them, of their ancestors, and even of present-day Basques.' He contends that, for Basques living in a traditional manner, Christianity has played an incomparably greater role than any supposed indigenous counterpart, and he criticizes Barandiarán and his circle for promoting a living autochthonous Basque paganism, systematically 'uncovered' by themselves, as a supposedly miraculous survival, directly linking local prehistory to our times, which could be used as further proof of contemporary Basques' ethnic specificity (Aranzadi 2000: 263–4, 280–319). Aranzadi concludes: 'The tendency among Basque anthropologists to exaggerate the antiquity of what is found and the "originality" of the Basque people is proverbial' (ibid: 583). In this context it is extremely interesting that the *earliest ever* representation in the world of the Calvary, with the crucified Jesus and the two thieves, was uncovered in 2006 in an Alavan archaeological site. It has been dated to the third century (*Diario Vasco* 9 vi 06: 90–1).

On Barandiarán's effort to draw continuities between the Paleolithic and the present in the Basque Country, see also Zulaika 1996: ch. 5. For an example of Barandiarán's style in this sense, see Barandiarán 1972: 11–14. Even Zulaika, such an otherwise sympathetic supporter of the man, has called him a 'humane mythmaker, a figure of shamanistic proportions' (Zulaika 1991: xv).

example, at the start of the 1985 'Korrika' (an annual sponsored relay race in support of the teaching of Euskera), a man dressed in Paleolithic style passed his bone amulet to a man dressed as a scholar, who then cried to the delighted crowd that he had found the first person to speak Euskera. According to this playlet, the Basques were an ancient people, while Euskera was both of similar vintage and its study academically legitimate. In *Napartheid,* a comic produced by radical nationalist youth in the 1990s, a Euskera-speaking caveman was often depicted in cartoons as a figure of opposition, outsmarting the forces of the state and protecting Basque culture. At much the same time, a Basque television channel transmitted 'Rompecabezones' ('breaker of big heads'), a weekly gameshow whose motif was the cave-dwelling *basajaun* ('wild man', the mythical lord of the forest), with a long beard, dressed in animal skins and bearing a club. Contestants in these jokey performances had to use 'clubs' to open doors for clues to the prizes. Perhaps the most striking representation of the Basques as unchanging since the Stone Age is 'Gu ta Gutarrak', a humorous short story by an Argentinian of Basque origin. Fascinated by the cave paintings of Orio, which make her think 'we Basques have always been the same', the protagonist and her friends construct a time machine. But with every further jump into the past, they find the landscape still unaltered and the locals yet speaking Euskera. Unable to find the original rupestrian artists, they decide to remain contentedly in the distant past, where the protagonist's children have learnt to paint in caves. In almost all these examples the caveman image is a jokey way of making a serious point: the Basques are a long-grounded people, and their language is as well.[80] In contrast to this lightly humorous vein, Txomin Badiola's play with the prehistoric motif (discussed in ch. 6) is much more ironic or destabilizing in tone. At the very least, it might be said, this local conceptualist recognizes the salience of the motif in Basque life. Making a related point but in a literary mode, *Si Sabino viviría* ('If Sabino were alive') by Basque academic and writer Iban Zaldua is a sustained satire, set in the distant future, of the local obsession with the past and indigenous genetics. Here a clone of Arana's brain, inserted into an armed robot, turns the android into a machine-gun toting killer.[81]

That so many different types of locals, whether villagers, writers, artists, or cartoonists, make the same historically extensive definition of Basqueness as did Aranzadi, Barandiarán and Basabe Prado does not affect my point that this is still an *imposed* definition on those who no longer have any voice. This similarity of definition merely serves to underline the fact that the trio of biological anthropologists were using popular, non-academic definitions in their learned discussions about the origin of the Basques. This

---

[80] Moujan 1980; Del Valle 1994: 1–4; Urla 1999: 53–5. When Moujan's story was re-published in the late 1960s in a Spanish science-fiction magazine, that issue was impounded by the forces of the Francoist state. The Basques were not to be publicly lauded, even in a witty manner. I thank Alan Bradley for showing me it, and John Linstroth for information on 'Rompecabezones'.

[81] Zaldua 2005. For a similar, though less mordant lampooning by a Basque writer of Basque ways, see Terol 2005.

sort of historically extensive definition must be regarded, not as an academically validated fact about the first Basques, but as a social fact about the rhetorical strategies employed by the Basques of the twentieth century.

Of course, journalists seeking easy copy can feed this common interest by popularizing the recent work of biological anthropologists, which at the same time gives their articles a form of academic legitimacy. *'Basques, 10,000 years before Christ'* ran the headline of one long piece published in the Sunday supplement of the Guipuzcoan paper *El Correo Español (El Pueblo Vasco)* in August 1990. Summarizing the recent studies on the craniology and the comparative genetics of the Basques, the journalist reported that the people living in the Basque Country became identifiably Basque – 'that race as strange as it is old' – thousands of years ago, maybe as early as 12,000BP. On a rather ambiguous note, the caption to the article's final photograph (of a Basque woman protecting her head from the rain with a sheet of plastic) reads, 'Anthropologists and geneticists are reluctant to divulge their conclusions, for fear of misinterpretations.'

Four years earlier, a mischievous journalist working for a Madrid-based newspaper had given De la Rúa's craniological work an unexpected twist:

THE SKULL OF THE BASQUES

Now it is known why some Basques do not accept the rules of the Constitution: their skull is different. The Basque newspaper *Deia* has run a report on the doctoral thesis of Concepción de la Rúa about this thrilling theme.

'The Basques present differential aspects in certain structures of the neuro- and esplano-cranium.' That the official daily of the Basque Nationalist Party should publish these things proves to be highly significant.[82]

Most modern-day Basques are careful about distinguishing between race and racism. When I lived in or near Pamplona from the mid- to late 1980s, my city friends were all young people in their twenties or thirties, left-wing and, if employed, held jobs as teachers, minor bureaucrats, factory workers or barmen. They were aware of some of the biological anthropology about the Basques, but they did not take it to be very important. While they might joke about the fact that Basques were meant to have large ears and noses of a particular shape, they took the political consequences of Basque culture much more seriously. To them the word *raza*, when included in the common phrase *raza vasca*, was to be understood as merely an uncommon and somewhat old-fashioned synonym for *pueblo* ('people'). They did not wish to be associated in any way whatsoever with any sort of biologically based racism.

There is, however, a small but persistent minority in the general area who maintain a racially based notion of Basqueness. Evidence for this comes, in an unsystematic fashion, from several different sources. In an interview held in 2000 Joseba Arregi, PNV official spokesperson, though wishing to distance himself from Arzalluz's Rh–centric view, did acknowledge that the party continued to grant a certain, albeit minor importance to both the evidence from surnames and studies of blood groups.[83]

[82] *Diario 16*, 6 ix 1986   [83] *M* 5 vi 2000: 13

Sociologists at the Universidad del País Vasco have been occasionally surprised, in the roundtable discussions they have organized, to find that one
or two participants defined themselves as Basque *because* of their haematological singularity. In 1991 some academics at the Universidad estimated
for me that the only Basques who were still conceiving of their group
identity in physical terms were people then in their fifties or older. However,
it is highly possible that Arzalluz's spasmodic, but repeated, pronounce-
ments about the role of academic information in the nationalist process
have helped to legitimate and have augmented popular belief about the
ethnic significance of Rh–.[84] In 1995 when local writer Miguel Sánchez-
Ortiz left his native Pamplona to live in the mountainous north of Navarre,
he was surprised to hear there some locals speaking of the Basques as a
'superior race' and to come across the odd 'layabout, who speaks of pure
blood and dirty blood, as though his business were not cheating but haematology or pork-butchery . . . It's a recurrent, occasional, surprising topic of
conversation, which arises when one least expects it'.[85]

The danger with this kind of talk is that it is all too easy to slide from
a 'racially based humanitarianism' (i.e. simultaneously acknowledging
racial difference and upholding the ideal of human equality) to racist
suprematism. When an industrial boom in the 1950s and 1960s in the
Basque Country led to the greatest influx of migrants since the end of the
previous century, one leading nationalist used a rhetorical style reminis-
cent of Arana when he branded the incomers a mass of degenerate
koreanos ('Koreans') parasitic on the local economy.[86] Many Basques
derided the immigrants, who came from poor parts of Extremadura, in this
orientalizing manner because their eyes were thought to be less rounded
and more slit-like than those of the Basques. They were also perceived to
have (perhaps because of poor diet) thinner faces and narrower jaws.
The epithet, however, has stuck, though it is very rarely used in public;
the same applies to the equally pejorative local term *manchurrianos*
(Manchurians).[87]

These sorts of racially couched insults lay bare the social, rather than the
supposed biological, basis of 'race'. Since there is far more variation within
the population of a supposed race than between races, many biological

---

[84] For further examples of Arzalluz's physical anthropological understanding of the Basques,
see Díaz Herrera and Durán 2001: ch. 6.
[85] Sánchez-Ostiz 1998: 41. See also his p. 132, and Aramburu 1996: 52. The American
anthropologist William Douglass, who did fieldwork in a Basque village in the 1960s, found
there that 'Villagers usually disparage these outsiders (non-Basque residents) in every way.
They are deemed to be racially inferior' (Douglass 1969: 13).
  For a scathing commentary on the excesses of belief in the ethnic significance of Rh, see
Savater 2001: 113–15. Wade (2002: ch.5) cautions against an over-hasty attribution of 'biological determinism' or 'genetic essentialism' in analyses of racial discourse, as determinisms
may be of varying force and racial discourse may not automatically make reference to notions
of fixity and permanence, which may themselves be variable.
[86] Sullivan 1988: 23
[87] Aranzadi (2001: 61) remembers as an adolescent in the 1950s hearing nationalist friends
singing 'Kendu, kendu, maketuá eta belarri motxá' ('Out, out, maketos and ugly ears'). On
attitudes to the migrants in the 1970s, see Heiberg 1989: 96–7

anthropologists prefer to use the scientific concept of 'cline', which refers to a geographical gradient of phenotypically expressed physical differences. Only where there is a sharp discontinuity in this gradient of differences (a discontinuity often associated with a geographical feature such as a high mountain range) do some biological anthropologists feel at all justified in employing, however tentatively, the idea of race to denote the difference between the human populations on either side of the discontinuity. In most cases, however, the particular concepts of race employed by the populace (or by *vasquista* Basque biological anthropologists) should be seen as arbitrary impositions on an otherwise continuous series of differences. In other words people's use of 'race' must be viewed, like their use of 'ethnicity', as a rhetorical device to be employed in substantiating the difference between 'them' and 'us'. And, of course, the more anthropological evidence that can be marshalled to back up one's definition of one's 'race' the less arbitrary it will seem.[88]

Though the number of such people seems to be very small, they nevertheless provide critical opponents with the excuse for branding *all* dedicated nationalists as antiquated racists, as people who judge the degree of others' Basqueness by the colour of their eyes or the shape of their head. However, it must immediately be added that, in some ways, certain Basques lay themselves open to criticism because, as implied above, *'raza'* is still part of common parlance, usually as a synonym for 'thoroughbred'. Even though this term is employed throughout Spain, its use by Basques in particular can be quickly attacked by anti-nationalists. For example, in the mid-1980s Javier Clemente, a controversial but very successful football manager from the region, was strongly criticized as 'racist' for referring, during a television interview, to Basque footballers as *'de raza'*.[89] Use of this ethnic slur against nationalists is further assisted by the publicity given to anti-racist demonstrations and similar events held by both marginalized gypsies and Third World migrants to the Basqueland.[90]

The long build-up to the 2001 electoral campaign to the Basque Parliament dramatically demonstrated, in a depressingly concentrated manner, just how easily the biological and prehistoric information about the Basques could be wildly exploited, by either side of the political divide. The year before, the moderate nationalists had tried to end the stalemate of continued killings and protracted terrorism by making a pact with their extremist brethren on the promise of legislative reform. Their anti-nationalist opponents would have none of this, which they saw as the moderates surrendering their principles to gunmen. Arzalluz inflamed attitudes by making

[88] On the social construction of the notion of race, see Boyd 1950: 200–7-, Appiah 1986; Genders and Player 1989: 17–20.

[89] For other examples, see *M* 30 vi 2000: 66. According to an editorial in the local anti-nationalist newspaper *El Correo Español, en el País Vasco*, 9 iv 1996, participants in the Aberri Eguna of the previous Sunday (31 March) had referred openly to the Basques in terms of Rh–, brachycephalia, etc.

[90] *M* 21 vi 2000:16; 25 vi 2000: 5; 8 x 2000: 5. See also Manzanos 2000. Of course, racism by locals towards Gypsies and Third World migrants is prevalent throughout Spain (see, e.g. Azurmendi 2001; Martínez Veiga 2001).

statements like the ones quoted at the beginning of the chapter, and by claiming that those who voted for PSOE were 'not from here'. He went even further by claiming that to be Basque meant not criticizing Basqueness. This assertion chimed with a proposal made by ETA at the time, that only those who felt themselves Basque, and only Basque, should be allowed to participate in the political process.

Their critics interpreted any nationalist talk of biology as racist and a cause of terrorism. They presented the PNV as on a racist par with the Klu Klux Klan, or as a group run by 'tribal chiefs'.[91] According to them, Arzalluz wished to 'neanderthalize' Basque society; the pact his party had struck with the extremists was but 'a Basque Neolithic Revolution'.[92] Yet as the anti-nationalist pacifist group, the Ermua Forum, stated in reaction to the shooting of a local journalist: in the twenty-first century, 'we don't wish to return to the darkness and confusion of the ancestral cave.' The anti-nationalists' branding of their more activist opponents as 'barbarians' skilfully exploited the term's several connotations: as the uncontrolled and the uncivilized, darker forces from darker times. Some just treated Arzalluz's outdated talk about Rh and race as, at the very least, a bad political joke: 'grotesque ... if it were not tragic'.[93]

Fernando Savater, a distinguished Basque philosopher and a leader of the Forum, jibed at nationalists' corruption of the common past. According to him, they were keen to refute history for the sake of a prehistory from which they could profit politically.[94] Other critics complained that Arzalluz suffered from a pathologic nostalgia for all the past, just so long as it was *his* version of history. One Madrid columnist was pellucid about the dangers here being run: 'The terrorism of ETA is a variant of Basque nationalism, with its same charge of racism and of contempt towards those not of the tribe, with the same wish to wring the neck of History in order to invent a totalitarian paradise of Biscayan Khmers and Edenic peasants.' In the opinion of Savater, the youths of ETA had 'imbibed a distorted history and a demential anthropology which made them believe themselves victims and converted them into executioners'.[95]

To their opponents, the PNV and their extremist associates together practised 'ethnicidal racism'. Turning the nationalists' concern with biology against themselves, one stated, 'It is as though identification with the nationalist thesis were of genetic origin.' In the words of the youth wing of the Basque PSOE, nationalists seemed to have 'ideological DNA', which disposed them to lie and deceive. In a nod towards the haematological work, antinationalists argued that terrorists were today in prison 'for supporting the

---

[91] Savater 2001: 290; *M* 18 iii 1998: 2; 5 iii 1998: 10; 4 x 1999: 9
[92] *M* 20 v 1999: 14
[93] *M* 19 ii 1998: 8; 18 iii 1998: 2; 14 ii 1999: 2; 7 iii 1999: 4; 4 iv 1999: 13; 3 xi 2000: 3; 4 xi 2000: 1, 3, 8; 5 xi 2000: 4; 6 xi 2000: 6, 10; 7 xi 2000: 16; 8 xi 2000: 6; 10 xi 2000: 12–13; 10 i 2001: 14; 18 ii 2001: 3; 28 ii 2001: 2; 3 iii 2001: 5
[94] Savater 2001: 304. For criticism of biological anthropological work in the Basque Country by another prominent member of the Forum, see Juaristi 2006: 44, 221.
[95] Savater 2001: 322

theories of those who gave importance to Rh+'; it was *because* of the belief in Rh that the Basques acted like an oppressed people; one commentator even used it as an explanation for the supposedly 'frenzied dancing of the Basques', while another crabbed Arzalluz's mythification of Rh as providing a culture of incubation for racism.[96]

In a suspiciously well-timed intervention during this electoral process, the Madrid-based Real Academia de Historia, the most august historical institution in the country, made public a report sharply criticizing the teaching in *ikastolas*. According to its learned authors, numerous textbooks used in these schools fomented xenophobia, if not also racism. In the days following its release, anti-nationalist newspapers devoted column feet to long quotes from *ikastola* schoolbooks purportedly showing the haematological, genetic and physical anthropological distinctiveness of the Basques. The timely release of this report boosted the platform of the centre-right candidate for the Basque presidency, who had proposed, among other anti-nationalist educational reforms, to not allow school programmes and textbooks 'to foment historical, geographical and anthropological falsities'. Two months later, the elections safely past, the Director of the Academia reacted to criticism from nationalist politicians and academics by admitting that it might have been 'precipitate and injust to speak of racism. But I would say, at the least, that it is picturesque.'[97]

For many critics, it was an easy step to make from accusing nationalists of politically motivated racism to branding them 'euskonazis' or 'nazionalists'; the claimed conjunction of exclusivist racism and violent totalitarianism in these purportedly parallel examples was just too tempting to ignore.[98] The Ermua Forum was explicit on this point. The Basque Government was neo-nazi because it did not defend public liberties, tolerated the street violence of extremist youth gangs, lauded cultural values over individual freedom, and imposed its views on the people.

This electoral strategy of stereotyping one's opponents in racist terms did not work. The anti-nationalist forces failed to unseat the PNV in the Basque Parliament. In the press, the general opinion of commentators was that the centrist parties, especially the centre-right Partido Popular, had striven too hard to 'demonize' nationalists, of whatever style. Overkill in the hustings had led to underperformance at the polls.

---

[96] *M* 20 viii 1999: 19. See also *M* 18 iii 1998: 2; *El País (Edición internacional)* 30 iii 1998: 10.
[97] *Diario Vasco* 8 iv 2000: 6; *M* 16 ii 2000: 16–17; 2 vii 2000, Cronica supplement, pp. 1–3; 29 vii 2000: 6, 34–5; 21 x 2000: 1, 11; 26 xii 2000: 12–13; 27 xii 2000: 8. For a further example of the politically motivated presentation of local history, see the debate about the Basque Government's refusal to support the construction of a 'Museum of Romanization' in Irun, a Basque town controlled not by nationalists, but by socialists (e.g. *M* 12 i 01: 10, 56; *Deia* 4 iv 01: 26). By the time of its opening, the Basque Government and the Deputation of Guipuzcoa had donated, in sum, 6.19% of the total donations necessary for the construction of the Museum (*Irunero* May 2006). In 2001 one senior member of local society, who wishes to remain anonymous, told me it had been relatively easy to persuade the socialist mayor to back the project as it would boost a sense of local history without feeding the nationalist cause.
[98] *M* 1 ii 1999: 11; 24 ix 2000: 11. For a particularly detailed argument of the supposed similarities between the two, see *M* 11 vii 2002: 3–4.

The ultimate question

Behind everything discussed so far lies one common question: 'Where do the Basques come from?' Or, to be more exact (since there are several competing definitions for the term 'Basques'): 'Where do the ancestors of the indigenous inhabitants of the present-day Basqueland come from?'

None of the four most relevant sources of information – the fossil record, haematology, comparative philology or population genetics – provides a conclusive answer. Even when conjoined, they only give us a series of definitive negatives and suggestive probabilities. As we have seen, the prehistoric evidence shows there is no necessary connection or continuity between the Paleolithic and the Neo-aeneolithic inhabitants of the area. The Paleolithic population may never have constituted anything more than a series of peripatetic passers-through who did not form stable communities. Moreover, until the late Paleolithic, all of those passing through would have been Neanderthals. On top of that, the number of human prehistoric bones so far examined by biological anthropologists plus the number of contemporary archaeological sites properly excavated is still far too low for us to make any firm statements about the distribution and density of the Paleolithic visitors to the area.

Thus, after all these decades of dedicated research, it appears that all we can so far say is that it is possible, maybe even highly possible, that the people today known as the Basques has shown at least some degree of group continuity since pre-Neolithic times. Whether this group of people has been based continuously and for several thousand years in the area today known as the Basque Country we do not know. This group of people may well be an admixture of Paleolithic groups who travelled north from Africa, Neolithic farmers migrating westwards or from the Ebro valley, and Neo-aeneolithic/Bronze Age mountaineers who came down from the Pyrenees. To what extent each population contributed to the resulting admixture we do not know.

What we do know, however, is that the image of the Basques as a historically isolated people who had no significant contact with any of the groups passing through or settling in the general area in post-Neolithic times is unsustainable, a myth.[99] It is also clear that, no matter which of the current definitions we chose to delimit 'Basques' by, they are not a particularly 'mysterious' people. For anthropologists, they are difficult, or as easy, to study as any other people. It is only the origin of their ancestors which is mysterious and, depending on the degree of exactitude that is being required here, the same could be said of almost any other delimited 'people' in Western Europe today. For the present, given the contemporary state of research, the strongest, most credible statement we can make is that of a qualified ignorance.

[99] For a modern attempt to maintain this image see Iriondo et al. 1996.

6
Art

Anthropologists of art have a problem: how to define the central term of their sub-discipline? Their quandary is how to compare something across cultures without the particular definition chosen predetermining the answers arrived at. If they choose too restrictive a definition they exclude a host of potential objects of study and end up producing generalizations which are neither novel nor representative of human endeavour. If they choose a very open definition they run the risk of including such a broad range of different types of objects that meaningful comparison is turned into a near impossible ideal. This difficulty of choosing the appropriate level at which to pitch a comparative concept is particularly acute in this case because, unlike terms such as 'rites de passage' or 'reciprocity, 'art' is not one primarily derived from anthropological analysis or whose usage outside of academica is highly restricted. On the contrary, the concept of 'art', like that of 'aesthetics', is very deeply embedded in the historically particular evolution of European cultures.[1] It is significant, however, that, to my knowledge, no anthropologist of art has acknowledged that the term or synonyms for it in other cultures may themselves become a cause for internal contest between interested parties. In these contexts, the question 'But is it art?' is not a hoary chestnut to be ignored but a politically motivated interrogatory to be studied.

The aim of this chapter is to study such a case, in which 'art' or its synonyms are not locally unproblematic terms but are the sites of dispute as different parties struggle to impose their own definitions. In this chapter I wish to trace the evolving roles of art within the development of that movement. In particular, I wish to follow the, at times intense, debates which have continued since the 1890s up to the present day between ideologues of Basque nationalisms, journalists, and artists about the nature and value of what has come to be called 'el arte vasco' ('Basque art').

The first decades of Basque nationalism

Nationalists

The first Basque politicos concerned about the local level of artistic activity

[1] Eagleton 1990; Layton 1991: 4-7; Morphy 1992; Weiner 1994; Staniszewski 1995

were a group known as the fuerists. These, in effect, proto-nationalists campaigned, from the mid-1870s to the 1880s, for the restoration of fiscal and administrative autonomy of the Basque Country. Acknowledging the lack of a painterly tradition within their homeland, they made sporadic attempts to promote the production of public art. To that end, they occasionally got local government to sponsor works, by local artists, of a neo-mediaevalist bent which were meant to glorify in a neo-romantic manner legendary events of the Basque past.[2]

Two decades later Sabino Arana propounded similar views about the place of painting in Basque life. But he was both much more precise and systematic than the fuerists. For him, an artist was contemptible if he was not inspired by patriotism, which was such a great and sublime emotion that, by itself, it sufficed for the creation of immortal art. Indeed patriotism was essential for the production of great works. The patriotic duty was the highest of the duties

> which man must fulfill in this world for the salvation of his soul... After the love of God, the love of the Fatherland should take up the heart of man who lives in society.
> Everything else, literature, sciences, art, etc., are secondary things, very useful, very convenient, indispensable if one wishes to add lustre to the Fatherland, in order to aggrandize it and to increase love and veneration for it; but, when all is said and done, they will never be more than beautiful adornments with which to engarland and emphasize the supreme beauty of the Fatherland.[3]

As a local proponent of the racial theory of social difference, Arana also damned those artists who did not portray Basques in what he regarded as the anatomically appropriate manner. Reviewing the illustrations to a general history of the Basque province of Biscay, he criticized many of them for depicting his compatriots as being 'microcephalous' or 'garlic-headed', and as having a 'cranelike neck, a sunken chest, a curved back, drooping shoulders'. Women, he claimed, had been portrayed as ugly and the paintings of locals in traditional dress were, in general, ethnographically inexact. 'What an erroneous and sad idea of the Biscayan type whoever wished to know them would gain from these plates!'[4]

Fellow nationalists and local sympathizers judged other painters in much the same terms. Paintings of great events of the Basque past had to be historically accurate in every detail.[5] Those of contemporary events had to display the Basques in an anthropologically authentic, if not also flattering manner.[6] Moreover paintings which portrayed Basques acting reprehensibly, for example getting drunk in a village pilgrimage, were to be criticized

---

[2] González de Durana 1983: 18–56; 1993. My early historical section is indebted to González de Durana 1983.

[3] Arana 1897

[4] Arana 1895

[5] See, for example, 'Exposición provincial', *La Unión Vasco-Navarra*, 28 August 1882; 'Un nuevo cuadro de Lecuona', *Euskal-Erria IX* No.2, 1883, p. 55

[6] See, for example, 'Cristiano', *Euskalduna* No.32, 18 April 1897, p. 253; 'Nuevas obras de Anselmo Guinea', *La Vasconia* No.223, 10 December 1899, pp. 84–5; Campión 1919

as they gave *maketos* a further opportunity to ridicule their hosts.[7] Nationalists generally praised paintings of traditional pursuits, of Basque rural architecture (especially of homesteads, symbol of the Basque family and its way of life), and of the countryside and of the coastline. Sabino Arana told one painter, 'If you want to produce the representative type of Biscay, symbolize it by a homesteader with his spades.'[8] Pictures which highlighted these marked aspects of local life and landscape served to remind viewers of what was being lost by the advancing processes of industrialization and the rise of urban life, where godlessness and immorality were thought to thrive.[9] For instance one nationalist, assessing a picture of traditional Basque fisherwomen, praised it as having the laudable 'aim of securing the life of the pueblo, with the powerful bonds which the history of its customs entail and with the eternal charm of art which sweetly links hearts with emotion itself'. To this nationalist, the recent rise of such art in the Basque Country was the 'prologue to its glorious emancipation', 'the proof of its future liberty'.[10]

For nationalists, one benefit of this sort of style was that it made the nationality of the painter patent. On simply looking at a good example of this kind of picture, the viewer was meant to be able to realize that the producer and the product were Basque. Indeed some nationalists claimed that one could recognize even the province from which the painter came.[11]

'Good' Basque painting served as permanent reminders of the virtues and beauty of their people and their land to viewers in both the Basqueland and beyond. For this reason, some nationalists thought it important that their compatriots' pictures were exhibited in Madrid and Paris. They might thus complain about the absence of Basque art in an exhibition of Spanish art shown abroad. Arana himself was ready to act in a more nationalist spirit, at times arguing against the installation, in the Basque Country, of any exhibition by non-Basque painters.[12]

The sum consequence of these nationalist attitudes was that they tended to encourage above all the production of *costumbrista* paintings which idealized an overly folkloric, impossibly ever-harmonious view of Basque rural life. (This sort of idyllic folklorism was then a common trend throughout European art.) The particular style of painting approved of by these Basque politicos was a conservative, minutely detailed realist one. For they wanted the ideological message of these canvases to be explicit and comprehensible to the greatest majority possible. It was for this reason that some opposed the recently imported novelty of impressionism, which could only be appreciated by the 'initiated'.[13] To them, art had to fulfill a propagandistic purpose for a nationalist end. Otherwise it was to be ignored, or damned.

---

[7] Anon. 1897
[8] Quoted in Lasterra 1933d
[9] See, for example, 'Barroeta', *Euskalduna* No.438, 4 April 1906, pp. 3–4
[10] Anon. 1906a
[11] Anon. 1906b
[12] Arana 1894; Anon. 1900
[13] González de Durana 1983: 82

Anthropologists

Anthropologists are not only commentators on social lives, they are participants in them as well. They do not just observe the world, they act in it
and may attempt to ensure that their work has a reflexive effect on what
they study. The Basque anthropologist Telesforo de Aranzadi is an early
example of this process. For, as one of the most eminent Basque intellectuals of the turn of the century, he tried to take advantage of the esteem in
which he was held in order to establish an anthropologically grounded
theory of Basque aesthetics. And, to an observable extent, he was successful.

Most unusually among anthropologists, Aranzadi was also a trained
artist. As a schoolboy he was tutored by Antonio Lecuona, a well-known
Basque artist of his day, while he attended night classes in drawing
throughout his undergraduate and even postgraduate years. In fact in one
academic year his grade ('Outstanding') in 'Line Drawing' was better than
that in most of the other courses he took. The benefit of these studies in art
became patent shortly after receiving his doctorate, as the first job he took,
as 'Scientific Illustrator' at the Museum of Natural Sciences, Madrid, and
which he held for six years, gave him the economic independence he
needed to prepare for professorial examination.[14]

Armed with his epitome of local physiognomy, 'the Basque type',
Aranzadi argued, in a number of articles written over the course of his life,
against those local artists who employed 'Classical' proportions in their
sculptures and paintings of their compatriots. To him, Basque use of the
Ancient Greek style amounted to an aesthetic invasion. He branded as
'Mediterraneans' those academicist artists who showed 'a marked repug-
nance to recognize the existence and to admit the aesthetic value that the
most typical features of our race have in reality'.[15] Instead of elevating
Classical statuary as the ideal by which all other art should be judged,
Aranzadi claimed that universal standards of beauty were expressed region-
ally by artists' veridical representations of the denizens of each region.
Those artists who had had the misfortune of being trained in schools where
Classicism still ruled the day had therefore to forget what they had been
taught and had to learn afresh by closely observing the people around
them. Those critics who thought anthropologically accurate portraits of
Basque women made them look ugly were, in his opinion, misguided, for it
was far better to represent the natural beauty of a people than to misrep-
resent them along the lines of a foreign ideal. Of course, as the Basque art
historian Imanol Agirre has argued, Aranzadi, though wishing to
overthrow academicism, was in fact propounding the replacement of one
sort (the Classical) by another (the Basque). For, like the 'Mediterraneans'

[14] Goicoetxea Marcaida 1985: 26–43
[15] The quote is from Aranzadi 1901. See also Aranzadi 1918, 1933; Agirre 1993: 47

whom he vituperated, he himself was upholding a normative model, based on technical perfection and the conservation of a particular tradition.[16]

Aranzadi went further, however. When 'people of other races' saw a portrait based on a Basque, all of whose features were craniometrically 'typical', he wanted them to view the result as beautiful. To that end, he recommended that artists should overstate slightly the distinctive features of the Basque type. Relying on his own training as an illustrator, he proferred specific instructions:

> In a drawing, it is sufficient to take advantage of the slightest thickness of a pencil-tip in the direction of characteristic accentuation so that an average type is converted into the typical without losing physiognomical harmony, above all in figures drawn half-size, or even smaller.[17]

By this stage, the propagandistic purpose of painting seems to have become predominant, with Aranzadi subordinating his own notion of a Basque aesthetics to the narrower end of promoting Basque distinctiveness at the risk of ethnic self-exaggeration.

The influence of his ideas is patent, however, in the paintings of many of his Basque contemporaries and their successors, especially in those by Aurelio Arteta, and the Arrue and Zubiaurre brothers. Indigenes portrayed in these pictures frequently have strong features: wide skulls, large ears, prominent noses, jutting chins, broad shoulders, big chests and large hands. Indeed, Agirre argues, the concern of so many Basque artists with the depiction of the Basque type is so marked that it has become one of the defining features of the Basque art of the first three decades of this century.[18] Aranzadi's articles had had their effect: artists had popularized his anthropologically backed notion of a Basque aesthetics by presenting it pictorially to a much wider audience than he could have ever reached directly.

Artists, journalists

The first identifiable generation of Basque artists were those sons of successful industrialists and businessmen who, in the 1870s and 1880s, were rich enough to allow their children to study art in Rome or Paris rather than enter the family firm. The most influential of this handful of artists were Adolfo Guiard and Dario de Regoyos, who introduced the Basque public to the latest European trends in painting and acted as exemplars to a steadily expanding number of youthful aspirants.

This next generation of artists, many of whom came to their different, mature styles in the first decade of the new century, faced the same problems as their predecessors: a mainly uninterested bourgeiosie, indifference

---

[16] Agirre 1993: 50 fn.3. A stern admonisher who occasionally verged on the pedantic, Aranzadi was at times also ready to criticize painters for ethnographic inexactitude (e.g. Aranzadi 1928).
[17] Aranzadi 1933: 459–60
[18] Agirre 1993: 58. See also Martínez and Agirre 1995: 159–84

from most nationalists, and a regional press staffed by journalists uneducated in the appreciation of modern art. In order to increase sales, these artists staged a series of collective exhibitions between 1900 and 1910 in Bilbao. But the Basque economy slumped from 1902 to 1906, the gallery-going public remained on the whole unmoved, and most paintings did not sell.[19]

The painters' fortunes improved, however, in the next decade thanks above all to their reformation into the well-organized Asociación de Artistas Vascos, to the economic boom experienced in the Basque Country during the First World War, and to the rise of a regional cohort of knowledgeable art critics.[20] During these years and those immediately after the war, the Association staged a number of successful collective and individual exhibitions, often managing to persuade prestigious artists whom they had befriended in Paris, such as Gauguin and the Delaunays, as well as a band of Catalan modernists, to provide works for their shows. The Association also exhibited collectively its members' canvases, with success, in Barcelona, Madrid, Seville and Paris. They further stimulated sales by allowing purchasers to pay by instalment. Several also held very profitable exhibitions in South American cities with significant numbers of well-to-do Basque migrants.[21]

As an active body primarily concerned with the promotion of the arts within its homeland, the Association staged ballets, retrospectives in homage to recently deceased painters, and banquets for distinguished Basque creative artists. It also petitioned, often with success, the provincial government for subsidies, for scholarships for budding artists, for the purchase of particular paintings by Basque artists, and for the preservation of architecturally important buildings threatened with demolition. Furthermore, its members vigorously defended their views on art in the regional press and on local podia. Some also sat on provincial and municipal committees for the selection of sculptors and architects to design public monuments and buildings.[22]

As the fame of these self-promoting artists grew and spread beyond the regional boundaries, educated locals, many of them nationalists or at least *vasquistas* (supporters of Basque culture), began to talk of the rise of a distinctive *'arte vasco'* ('Basque art'). Exactly what constituted this notion of 'Basque art' however was much debated and frequently ambiguous or unclear.[23] Juan de la Encina, the leading local critic of this period, claimed that his artistic contemporaries displayed the traditional Spanish painterly traits of spirituality and force while at the same time remaining open to modern sensibilities. To him, the Basque aesthetic was expressed in concrete realities, but that this kind of realism was always strongly conditioned by

[19] Barañano et al 1987: 214–23
[20] Mur Pastor 1990
[21] Maytia and Fernandez 2004
[22] Mur Pastor 1985
[23] See, for example, the debate between three Basque critics, Cosmos 1915a, b; Sánchez Masas 1915a, b, c; X 1915a, b, c, d

emotion. Stating anything more specific about the Basque nature of this aesthetic was troublesome.[24] A Madrid-based critic, Margarita Nelken, believed that 'What is truly significant about this Basque art is that ... these painters form an ensemble, a *bloque*, not just national but with what the French graphically and untranslatably call *l'accent du terroir.*' [25]

Encina claimed that he and his fellow Basques were

> traditionalists when the tradition that is put in front of us is a perduring tradition and not a mummy from the past. This interests us principally to the extent it can be a bearer of ferment and of future suggestions. So that for us everything ought to be oriented towards the future, towards vital change; and tradition in this sense is nothing other than a form of impelling and continuous force which comes from the most profound part of existence and which irremissibly day by day brings about reform and change.[26]

To Nelken, this 'traditional' push towards the future was both the principal force and the principal originality of Basque art, making it at one and the same time both very ancient and very modern. To her, all contemporary painting other than the Basque lacked, in an integral and profound manner, the 'very ancient'. It was this which gave Basque art its superiority over all other contemporary groups and schools, and also 'their right to be, as it pleases them, moderns of the latest modernity'.[27]

One nationalist journalist, writing under the pen name of 'Dunixi', regarded it as 'patriotic' to defend and praise the work of the Association, for its members portrayed local life and nature. According to him, what these artists needed to do in order to establish a Basque school of art firmly was to work in the area, on the area, united by a common sentiment:[28]

> If we see that (these artists) look at the race and love it and feel it, we will have the security that the community of characters is beginning to form, which later give place, by succession, by coexistence or by opposition – who knows? – of values, to the initiation of the Basque *school*, which will not confine itself to a *manner*, but would moreover involve the resulting tendency and spirit.[29]

Some nationalist correspondents argued that it did not matter if a local artist painted Basque or, say, Castilian scenes, he was still a Basque artist. Categorizing artists according to their subjects would mean that those Polish, Swiss, Hungarian, and American painters who visited the Basqueland in order to paint it would have to be counted among the exponents of 'Basque art', while by the same token those Basque artists who painted abroad would have to be considered artists of those places and not of their homeland.[30] Discussing the work of Ignacio Zuloaga, who had already achieved international renown and most of whose paintings did not portray Basque subjects in Basque settings, one nationalist critic claimed that his 'spirit' was still firmly rooted in 'the fundaments of his race'.

[24] Encina 1919. On his life and work see Alzuri 1998
[25] Nelken 1981 [1921]
[26] Quoted in Nelken 1981 [1921]: 22
[27] Nelken 1981 [1921]: 22
[28] Dunixi 1915a, b, c, d
[29] Dunixi 1915d
[30] Zubialde 1915b

If we agree that the distinctive characteristics of his genealogy . . . are force, sobriety, austerity, we have to recognize Zuloaga, not only as a Basque painter, but as the most Basque of painters . . .

And above all it is necessary to insist that Zuloaga, whether he paints Basque fiesta queens or Patagonian savages, is a Basque painter, he is alkaloid of Basque, so Basque that Unamuno could and ought to include him in the trinity of representative Basques in which he included himself in the company of St Ignatius and Sabino Arana.[31]

One nationalist journalist, using the pseudonym 'X', attacked another's praise of the Zubiaurre brothers' representations of Basques because he had not criticized their 'unbelievable' settings. 'Do they intentionally falsify the landscape, as decorative backgrounds, as though they were blurred tapestries, in order to enhance the realism of the people in the frame?' (X 1915a). To nationalists such as X, the local countryside was too important and too central a symbol of Basqueness for it to be misrepresented as a mere backdrop. In reply, X's opponent claimed that he had too narrow an understanding of art. Realism was not the only standard by which a painting could be judged. As far he was concerned, the Zubiaurre brothers, 'those aristocrats of painting, have interrogated our mountains and have extracted all the poetry of their landscapes, injected with all the yearning of their souls and drenched in feelings of transcendental passions'.[32]

The artists themselves were as vague and almost as varied as their commentators in their remarks about the nature of 'Basque art'.[33] Quintin de Torre observed that there was a common fervour among his fellow artists but that this did not justify the unifying label of 'Basque art.' Gustavo de Maeztu said that though he did not know what Basque art was, he knew it existed, in the same way that he did not know what electricity was but did know, thanks to the functioning of lightbulbs, that it existed. Julian de Tellaeche thought he and his peers shared a single, common quality: 'individualism translated into art'. The Zubiaurre brothers went further, claiming that Basque artists formed 'a harmonic unity of wills who think, love, and feel, and make others feel with them the beauty, strength and emotion of all spiritual feeling which exists and lives in the Basque Country'. Imanol argued that a common 'sacred aspiration to the summit' was sufficient for the definiton of Basque art: 'Come, Basque artists, Basques! Basques!!! They are Basque art. If they profoundly feel the Basque race, the Basque life, the Basque landscape, that is enough for the moment.'[34]

While many of these artists were prepared, on occasion, to state there was some common denominator to their work, and while many of them did portray, if not always extol, various aspects of the traditional and modern Basque ways of life, they (perhaps thinking of their extra-Basque market) were not necessarily nationalist, or even *vasquista*. Some, while *vasquista*,

---

[31] Zubialde 1915a
[32] Cosmos 1915b
[33] See, for example, Azkue 1915; Ispizua 1915; Lasterra 1933a, b, c; Michelena 1915; Tolosana 1915; Kaperotxipi 1954: 15–18
[34] Imanol 1915; Maeztu 1915; Tellaeche 1915; Torre 1915; Zubiaurre 1915

did not sympathize with the conservative politics of Arana but with the socialism then emergent in the country. Some painted portraits of Andalusian women, members of the migrant group about which Arana spoke so pejoratively.[35] In 1917 the Association publicly declared its independence by stating that 'it is neither separatist from any country nor antipatriotic of any'.[36] Maeztu was clear about his priorities. In a public speech given in 1923, he stated,

> Frankly, ladies and gentlemen, I do not consider myself a Joan of Arc of nationalities. I modestly do my civic duty, and yes I believe I have something of the Basque in me, something also of the Castilian, and if you wish, even a bit of Chinese; but what is worth something in an artist, is it the reflection of his nationality? Of course not. What is worth something in each artist is the ability to reflect his sensibility.[37]

Zuloaga was just as candid. Chatting to an Irish visitor to his house on the Basque coast, he stated:

> Though I am a Basque ... I am at my most active in my work when I live in Segovia, for there I never fail to find queer grotesque types as models ... For you should remember that though I am born a Basque from Eibar yet I refuse to sacrifice my universal heritage for any regionalism. It was Castile made Spain and every one of us whether we are Basque, Galicians or Andalusians must go forth from our narrow regions and become Castilian, for it was Castile that made the Spanish world.'[38]

Similarly, in a letter to his fellow Basque, the leading Iberian philosopher of his day, Miguel de Unamuno, he wrote:

> Very often in our countryland they have recriminated me with being a bad Basque.
> Why?
> Because I do not paint there.
> Because I do not live there.
> And I still have the desire to reply. I do not paint there ... because I do not find the land visually suitable for my temperament.
> I do not live there ... because there is no life for an artist.
> And moreover ... they live there, because they are not capable of living outside.
> I believe myself Basque to the very bone, I want a homeland as much as the best of them, but without the feeble-mindedness that reigns there.[39]

Indeed the only member of the Association who was openly, and at times actively, nationalist was Adolfo Guiard. Sabino Arana, however, detested his work and Guiard distanced himself from the movement in his later life.[40]

As well as being non-nationalist, some members, including some of the leading ones, of the Association of Basque Artists were not even Basque by any of the then current definitions: Iturrino was born and brought up in

---

[35] Llano 1977: 35; Castañer 1993: 66
[36] *Euzkadi* 8 December 1917
[37] Quoted in Manterola 1986: 15–16
[38] Starkie 1934: 97
[39] In Tellechea 1987 [1908]: 22
[40] González de Durana 1984: 68–9, 74, 117; 2004: 19

Santander, Dario de Regoyos in Asturias, while Tolosana, another 'out-sider', openly admitted that he was not Basque and that he only remained in the area because of the hospitality and kindness he received there.[41]

In fact the most prominent members of the Association may be regarded not so much as the standard-bearers of a new Basque art but as the local representatives of the Spanish nationwide 'Generation of '98', a loose collection of *fin de siècle* intellectuals, headed by Unamuno, concerned to rediscover the identity of the country and to regenerate it morally in the process. To them, this search for the 'authentic' seemed all the more imperative given both the disastrous loss of the last of the Spanish colonies in that year and the recent rise of an urban, industrial, mobile culture, epitomized by the laying of railroads across the land. In a variety of regional centres, modernist artists and writers came to proclaim in paint and in print the archetypal distinctiveness of their area.[42] Painters of Galicia, for example, emphasized the verdure of their rolling landscape, those of Valencia the luminosity and strong colours of the Mediterranean, those of Castile the 'mystic sobriety' of their plains and mountains. Generally influenced by the ethnology of their time, these regenerationists' pursuit of a *castizo* ('pure-blooded, authentic, genuinely popular or typical') art also led them to extol pictorially the peasantry of their respective areas, who were then seen as a 'living expression of the pure roots of the primitive races threatened by modernity'.[43] To this extent Basque artists' desire to underline local distinctiveness was not in itself distinctive. For by stressing, like others, regional individuality they indirectly aided inter-regional comparison. If each region was different then they were all the same in their differentiality. Thus Basque artists, by participating, from their own region, within a common, nationwide endeavour, undercut somewhat the very sense of local uniqueness that they were attempting to establish.

Indeed Unamuno and some Basque intellectuals of his generation occasionally took the process further by reiterating an old idea of Spanish nationalism: Vascoiberism. According to this theory (yet to be satisfactorily substantiated), the Basques are descended from the Iberians, the people who occupied most of Spain in the opening half of the first millennium BCE, and this geneaological connection affects them still.[44] Thus Unamuno could defend Zuloaga from those who criticized him for painting Castilian scenes by claiming that Basque painting was profoundly Spanish in tone, while Juan de la Encina asked whether the common spirituality of seventeenth-century Spanish painting and of modern Basque art did not come 'from a positive similarity between the Basque spirit and the Iberian one?'[45] But such views were anathema to the epigones of Sabino Arana.

[41] Tolosana 1915; Lafuente 1981: 14; González de Durana (2004: 34) argues that to analyse these paintings in purely Basquist terms is to impoverish them, as many of them also allude to 'universal values' embodied in famous earlier pictures by European masters.
[42] Litvak 1991; Mainer 1993
[43] Pena 1993a: 21
[44] Collins 1986: 9
[45] Encina 1919: 2

The Association languished from the mid-1920s. Come the next decade a new generation of Basque artists began to emerge, whose most promising exponents were Narkis Balenciaga, Nicolas de Lekuona, Jorge Oteiza, and José Sarriegui. Influenced by cubists, surrealists and constructivists, they were generally uninterested in their predecessors' *costumbrismo*. They regarded that as a played-out folkloristic chauvinism. Though they were still interested in developing an autochthonous art, they wanted to go beyond the strait-jacketing *etnicismo* of their forebears. To that end, they initiated a 'search for the originary state, present also in Henry Moore, in which the dissociation between man and nature has yet to occur'. They conceived of their efforts as a 'new Basque renaissance', in which indigenous art would go hand in hand with politics. Nationalists and close to the communists, Lekuona, Oteiza and Sarriegui met in 1934 with José Antonio Aguirre to discuss the contribution to policy that artists could make to a future Basque government. But the promise of this young generation went immediately unfulfilled: in 1935 Oteiza and Balenciaga left for South America to learn from its 'primitive' art (Balenciaga died there within a year); Lekuona died on the Basque front in 1937; Sarriegui, who fought in the Basque lines, was imprisoned for six years.[46]

During this period the *costumbrista* banner was borne by Flores Kaperotxipi. Kaperotxipi, whose extremely accessible style was known as 'the Basque smile', represented his countrymen as untroubled villagers in idyllic settings performing time-honoured tasks. In the opinion of Dunixi, Kaperotxipi showed the daily lot of farmers and fishermen as 'a bit of love, a bit of drink, a bit of crafty philosophy and much faith, a lot of work and continuous and happy conformity in a state of ignorance'.[47] Kaperotxipi himself described 'the Basque' of his area as

> Elegant, he has the presence and the distinction of the best aristocrats; he is good and noble, happy and brave. And, above all these things, he is a lesson, in these times, of conformity in ambition: his house, his family, his livestock, his pastures and his pipe . . .
>
> The villagers of my region live therefore happy. What could they want? A car? An oxcart serves them better. Uniformed servants? They already have their rustic dress made to measure. Sashes of honour? Titles of nobility?[48]

This sweetening approach to his totally rural subject matter contrasted very strongly with the sense of tragedy that his predecessors had lent to the locals they had portrayed. On the whole, they did not paint an alcohol-fuelled conformity with one's lot, but a sense of drama, whether rural or urban, personal or public, political or natural. However Kaperotxipi's works, unlike those of most of his contemporaries, sold well. Indeed, they were so much to the liking of nostalgic nationalists that six of his pictures were included in the 'Libro de Oro de la patria' ('The Golden Book of the fatherland') published by the PNV, while Aranzadi arranged for him to produce

---

[46] Moya 1982; Alonso 2001. The quote is from Moya 1982: 52.
[47] Dunixi 1934: 465. See also Llano 1977: 35
[48] Kaperotxipi 1934: 462–3

what became a standard text on Basque art: *Arte Vasco, pintura, escultura, dibujo, grabado.*

Kaperotxipi's success is indicative of what most art-loving nationalists then wanted: dulcified representations of a recent but mythical past in a style that acknowledged the importance of modernism but ignored the avant-garde.[49] They wanted to be entertained, not visually challenged. Perhaps then, it is not so surprising that in the mid-1940s the Basque Government in exile turned down Picasso's offer of his *Guernica.*

The postwar period

The consequences of defeat in the Civil War were immediate. Artistic associations which trod an independent path were closed down; their bulletins were censored. Shortly after the fall of Bilbao, the extensive murals painted by members of the Association in the local Home for Military Orphans were totally destroyed. Those artists who had aligned openly with the nationalist forces, whether designing stamps, posters and banknotes, or decorating schools for the Basque Government, went into exile. Those artists who remained did not portray urban social conditions but tended to concentrate on landscapes, often empty of humanity.[50]

The new line was firmly stated in the official programme to an exhibition staged in Bilbao at the end of the war:

> Bilbao and Basque painters have contributed to the national pictorial renaissance. When young painters in Paris were obsessed by what was then called *la pintura clara* (i.e. impressionism), Manuel Losada turned his eyes to the extremely nuanced severities of the great tradition of Spanish painting. Zuloaga also let himself be won over by it; via Whistler and Manet, he reached Velázquez. The retinas of Basque painters are perhaps those which have tried to root the modern in El Greco's plays of colour . . . And because these painters, their eyes full of the national pictorial tradition, looked compassionately at the landscape around and enlivened their canvases with scenes of popular life, attempts were made with stupid and twisted political intention, to assign them to distant and regressive movements. But there already was, as the anecdote shows, the lesson of centuries of Spanish painting, without which they would not have succeeded in looking at things nor in seeing with an aesthetic intention. Bilbao, shaking itself free of the false ruralisms which wished to diminish it and to make it foolish, always looked at the world through Spain . . . There is no Bilbao without Spain. For this reason in the Bilbao made sullen by Internationals and stupified by petty regionalism, the spirit languished and the arts faded.
>
> Franco returned to it its true inspiration. It has been said that civilization only flourishes in the circle of peace that the sword traces. Within the circle of peace which Franco's sword has traced are reborn the arts in Bilbao.[51]

For all the fascists' bluster, the reality of their practice was a little less stark. Unlike its counterparts in Italy and Germany, Franco's regime did not

[49] Moya 1986: 151–2; Mur Pastor 1988: 25
[50] Sáenz de Gorbea 1986: 267-71; 1990: 257; Llorente 1995
[51] OJPP 1939

propagate a clear artistic line but a somewhat confused eclecticism. Classicism was openly embraced but recent avant-gardes were also tolerable if the resulting product was either patently supportive of the dictatorship or at the very least totally shorn of anti-fascist connotations. Zuloaga and Maeztu, for example, produced portraits of the new political elite and glorificatory scenes of military triumphs.[52] Furthermore, while the regime's politics of culture left no room for openly espoused nationalists who wished to portray the imagined virtues of their supposed homeland, it was prepared on occasion to allow local artists to produce posters in a *costumbrista* style which celebrated regionality and an apolitical folklorism.[53]

The regime's repressive ways and its ideologically motivated reinterpretation of recent art history had, however, an unforeseen consequence. In postwar Europe many artists no longer portrayed their political creed, if they had any, in their works. In Spain however the continuing constraints on one's freedom of expression would stimulate among some a rebel spirit which 'contributed to the identification of social and artistic revolution, between the political left and artistic vanguard'.[54] Thus, in the coming decades, the idea of 'Basque Art' was to take on a rather different tone to that of its earlier era. Instead of being merely an aesthetic taxon manipulated primarily by politicians, it would become above all a political category exploited by artists themselves for explicitly political ends. Unlike many of their predecessors, these new generations of artists cared, and cared passionately, about the origin, nature, and future of their ethnicity.

Brushes against Franco

The most significant figure in Basque art during much of the dictatorship was the sculptor Jorge Oteiza. Reacting against the sentimentalism of earlier Basque art and influenced by the socially committed art of the Russian constructivists, Oteiza tried to renovate local approaches by producing abstract works of an almost geometric nature, often enclosing a central space. But in the late 1950s, after gaining a certain degree of international prestige, he effectively stopped sculpting. Instead he dedicated himself to the promotion of artistic activity in his homeland and to the elaboration of his own particular theories about the place and point of humans in the world, viewed through a Basque prism. Putting aside his profound Catholicism for a blend of other creeds, such as marxism and existentialism, Oteiza proclaimed a 'utopian anthropology' grounded on his intuitive understanding of regional prehistory. It was, in other words, a new primitivism, one which proved popular for his place and times. And, like many of his primitivist predecessors in Britain or France, Oteiza saw his endeavours in almost shamanic terms, as helping to heal the ills of his society.[55]

---

[52] Alonso 2001: 75–96; Novo González 2006
[53] Gómez Gómez 2006
[54] Alonso Pimentel 2006: 112
[55] Maraña 1999; MacClancy 2003; Zulaika 2004

Oteiza argued that since the Basques were the only survivors of the pre-Indoeuropean peoples, Basque art was at root autochthonous and independent of Classical, Phoenician and Arab influence. According to him, Basque art started with the construction of the first local cromlech. By constructing it, its Neolithic shepherd-creator had dominated Nature and, by providing himself with an object of contemplation, had placed himself outside himself. This original cromlech was not intended to seal a funerary space but to create an internal emptiness, a place of silence where one could have direct contact with God or the Absolute. Only by emptying space could the shepherd-creator vanquish death and find true Life, the essential and imperishable. At the same time the cromlech was also a statue, an aesthetic construction offering spiritual protection.

The erection of this object had not just individual significance. It had lasting ethnic significance as well, for Oteiza regarded its raising as the primordial moment of the constitution of Basque society. Oteiza's notion of ethnicity was a deeply subjective one, based on a belief in a culturally constituting spirit or soul. The precise nature of this quasi-mystical concept was to be regarded as a mystery, on a par with Catholic ones such as that of the Trinity. Inaccessible to reason, it was apprehensible only by faith. To him, the cromlech-statue was the original way of simultaneously providing and expressing the Basque mode of being. It supplied an existential structure for Basque culture and, since psychosocial configurations persisted over time, the Basque people of the present day continued to maintain themselves spiritually within the same structure. However, over time, the Basques had become spiritually impoverished. Therefore there was a pressing contemporary need to reaffirm the autochthonous by recuperating the essence of the style – best exemplified in the cromlech-statue and the Basque language – which fitted the Basques as individuals and as a people. Following the train of this argument, Oteiza saw aesthetics as the expression of a mode of being, as an unveiling of the occult spirit enclosed in materiality. Politics was thus to be viewed as an applied aesthetics, enabling the Basques to cure themselves existentially.[56] Oteiza's interpretive excursions into the prehistory and culture of his own people might appear deeply idiosyncratic, yet they were to prove inspirational to a broad swathe of educated Basques. It is perhaps thus only fitting that when in 1957 a local learned society, the Grupo de Ciencias Naturales Aranzadi required a sculptor to carve a decorated stela in memory of the Basque ethnologist Fr. Donostia, they chose the leading popular anthropologist of the day, Oteiza.[57] On top of that, a significant number of urban-born artists, influenced by his almost ecological approach to an essential Basqueness, went to live in rural settings, often renovating old farmhouses to serve as both home and studio.[58]

Another key activist-artist of this period is the Biscayan painter Agustín

[56] Besides my own reading of Oteiza's works (especially 1963) my summary of Oteiza's approach is indebted to Pelay Orozco 1978; Azcona 1984: 173–224; Guasch 1985: 196–214; Ugarte 1996. Oteiza's *Ejercicios...* was not finally published until 1983.

[57] Arnaiz 2006

[58] Fernández de Larrinoa forthcoming

Ibarrola who, like Oteiza, wished to re-energize the regional production of art and to politicize it in the process. His first attempts had restricted aspirations. In 1955 he put together a touring exhibition around a series of Biscayan villages of paintings by himself and other Basque artists. At each village, poets would recite their verse, painters would discuss their works, and communist intellectuals would debate issues of the day. In 1962 on his return after a protracted residence outside the region, he organized a group of fellow Basque artists into Estampa Popular Vizcaina.[59] Its unifying aim was to produce a modern local art of clear opposition to the regime. For this reason they rejected both abstract formalism and rural *costumbrismo*, choosing instead to portray in a broadly realistic manner the social conditions of Basque industrial workers. But the group only managed to hold one exhibition before Ibarrola (the son of a communist forge worker) and another member, both active in the then illegal Basque Communist Party, were imprisoned.

On his release in 1965 Ibarrola worked together with Oteiza to stimulate the recovery of a national Basque art. To that end, they wanted to see established a 'cultural front' which would foment popular artistic activity in towns and villages and which would enable working classes to see that art was a key instrument in the creation of an autochthonous culture. At the same time they wished artists and others to organize themselves into professional bodies which would act as democratic institutions and as the harbingers of a form of self-government independent of the fascist state. Very often their more inclusive educational initiatives promoted an aesthetic style based on Oteiza's reading of constructivism and other contemporary movements within the Russian avant-garde. This style came to be seen as typical of what both artists termed the Movimiento De Escuela Vasca (Basque School Movement).[60]

Their first initiative, in 1965, was to create a region-wide network of artistic groups, with one in each of the four Basque provinces. However this bid to set up a loose but still co-operative association of artists failed within a year, above all, because of personal differences between members of the different bodies. A common desire to oppose Franco and to assist in the establishment of a modern Basque art was not enough to overcome the diversity especially of nationalist stances, and also of artistic styles, among the various members. Many of Oteiza and Ibarrola's persistent attempts to establish popular art academies from this time on were similarly unsuccessful and mostly shortlived.[61]

Their repeated failure, however, does not appear to have affected the local reputation of Oteiza, who was increasingly seen by his expanding band of followers in almost chiliastic terms. To them, he could be the prophet of a new Basque dawn, the visionary who would recover an otherwise lost

[59] Sáenz de Gorbea 1990: 260–1; García-Landarte 2006
[60] 'Conversación con Ibarrola', *Guadalimar* October 1977, pp. 37–9; Álvarez 1985
[61] A list of these initiatives is given in Martínez and Agirre 1995: 276. See also Itoiz 2005: 80–1

cultural identity. One former acolyte remembered him as venerable, defiant and deafening, as one who

> was capable of persuading us of our non-being. In relation to me, it was almost a relief. It occurred in this way because we preferred the most negative certainties, those which needed the greatest impulse of positivity to counteract them, and which conferred the greatest legitimacy. In truth the strongest factor was the impulse, the faith and the resolution, the passion, the action, the modernity of the wish for power.

Though Oteiza was a resolute and unbending anti-Franquist, who told several interviewers he had helped ETA formulate its cultural policy, he could still be used by the regime, for from the 1950s it allowed a small number of prestigious artists including himself, to exhibit abroad in order to advertise its supposedly increasing openness.[62]

During this period Oteiza was the most renowned artist within the Basque Country. But it was another local sculptor, Eduardo Chillida, who gained the greatest international reputation, and who became the most famous Basque artist yet. Unlike Oteiza, who adopted a primarily metaphysical approach to his ethnicity, Chillida was particularly drawn to the materials traditionally used by Basques: stone, clay, wood, iron. In a number of his sculptures he strove to exploit the aesthetic dimensions of indigenous agricultural instruments as a means to reconnect with his homeland and its customs. According to the Basque anthropologist Luxio Ugarte, Chillida worked in this way so as to show it was possible 'to immerse oneself in the deep meaning of a culture and of uneducated people's intuitive art in order to create a work of art, a Basque art, guided by these pilgrimages to the sources, where there is almost no intervention of the will, and where intuition signals the path to follow'. Chillida voiced a similar sentiment when he said that 'Luckily my work speaks Euskera. I do not speak it well, but my work does'. He wanted his works to have ethnic resonance. He wished them to look both at the present and the future, 'to make Basques remember what they were and what they should continue to be, a people with defined and differentiated cultural characteristics'.[63] Perhaps the comparison which should be made here is that while Oteiza created his own version of local prehistory, Chillida tended to focus on a much later but still pre-industrial past, eulogizing rural tools not yet made obsolete by the coming industrialization.[64] To this extent, if Oteiza was inspirational about a long distant Basque past, Chillida was nostalgic about a much more recent one.

Not a dedicated activist in the Oteizan mould, Chillida usually wished to modulate with care the significance for himself of his Basqueness. To a visiting English writer he might say that, as a young man, he had suddenly

---

[62] The quote is from Lizundia 2000: 144. According to an historian of ETA, in the mid-1960s Oteiza maintained close relations with the Echebarrieta brothers, then prominent members of the organization; in 1966, when ETA wished to regain popular support by making contact with Basque artists, among others, they started by contacting Oteiza (Garmendia 2000: 122, 128).

[63] Ugarte 1996: 63, 169; Chillida 2003: 46. Another local sculptor of the time, worthy of mention, who explored Basque themes in his work is Nestor Basterretxea, see Álvarez 2005.

[64] On Chillida's roots in a cultural mediaevalism, see Kortadi Olano 2003: ch. 15

decided to come home after several years in Paris because he had 'discovered the importance of being a Basque'. However, in discussions with colleagues and friends he liked to emphasize that he was 'a man before being Basque' while at the same time recognizing that he was 'totally conditioned by' his 'Basque identity'. For example, Chillida said light could be either white (as found in Greece) or black (as found in the Basque Country); he was therefore a sculptor who worked in black light. In these talks he stated that every man, because of his birth, came from somewhere, and he used to iterate the idea that the horizon should be seen as the patria of all men. This was one reason he gave why so many of his sculptures are positioned at seaviews.[65] As Martin Heidegger, who collaborated with Chillida on a book, said, his sculptures were rooted in his homeplace, but of universal dimension.[66]

One result of the activist efforts made by Oteiza, Ibarrola and like-minded local artists was that, from the late 1960s on, as ETA spearheaded armed reaction to the regime and as an extremely heavy-handed repression became the official order of the day, the sites of Basque art became increasingly conflictive arenas. The terms of these conflicts are very revealing of the almost utopic timbre of the times. In 1971 left-wing artists boycotted a large exhibition staged by the town hall of Baracaldo, a Bilbao suburb. They complained that the exhibition was selective, that the selectors were not Basque, and that it encouraged competitiveness by offering prizes. In response, a few months later, the municipality staged an open and successful exhibition of over 400 works by Basque artists. The following year a plutocratic Navarran family sponsored the Encuentros de Pamplona, a grand arts festival with international pretensions. But many Basque artists vigorously criticized its perceived elitism and, when a picture by a communist militant was removed from the exhibition, they denounced the act as a form of political manipulation. Public feeling against the organization of the Encuentros ran so high that ETA, for the first and only time in its history, came out on the side of the Basque arts and exploded bombs at strategic points of the city. The year after that, the town hall of Baracaldo attempted to stage another exhibition of contemporary art, this time with the selection committee composed solely of prominent Basque artists. But artists not on the committee argued against the discriminatory evaluation that any form of selection would entail. Also, they claimed that its members were choosing pictures by painters of their own particular political persuasion. Tired of this factional infighting, the municipality cancelled the proposed exhibition.[67]

Similarly, polemic and factionalism were the keynotes to exhibitions of Basque art held abroad. In 1970 Oteiza publicly damned the 'Exposición de pintura y escultura vasca contemporánea' mounted by the Basque Centre

---

[65] Elms 1992: 231; Chillida 2003: 37, 61, 119, 124, 168
[66] See Bozal 2006: 29; Rementería Arnaiz 2006
[67] Angulo 1978: 227–93; Guasch 1985: 162–71. For an incisive, highly personal account of the Pamplona Encuentros, see Sánchez-Ostiz 2002: 126–30; see also Díaz n.d.

of Mexico City. He had refused to participate because its organizers would not accede to his demand that the show tour all the South American cities where Basques were numerous. At the same time, a large group of Biscayan landscape painters stimulated a debate in the local press by crabbing the selection criteria of the organizer of the Exposition. In 1976 when Chillida, Oteiza and Ibarrola were invited to exhibit in the Venice Biennale, only the last agreed. Chillida, under pressure from nationalist artists, would only participate if the Basque representation at the exhibition were much broader in scope while Oteiza wanted a spectrum of Basque political forces to organize, in an extremely brief period of time, a special pavilion for artists from all seven of the Spanish and French provinces. In the end, the only Basques, other than Ibarrola, who did go to Venice were a group of left-wing nationalists who staged a concert of local music, organized the projection of Basque films, and held a round table discussion on their demand for an amnesty of all Basque political prisoners.[68] The sum consequences of all these actions was that, once Franco was dead and the transition to democracy had got under way, the majority of Basque artists were deeply politicized, and almost as deeply divided.

Most of them were united, however, by their commitment to a notion of 'Basque art'.[69] But many of them were also uniform in consistently failing to specify its content. For instance, Chillida usually refrained from being any more explicit than to say Basque art 'is a form of expressing oneself and of feeling the art and the universe that we Basques have'; 'I am a Basque and I understand things in a Basque way which I believe is a special way, this informs the way I see, my ideas of strength, force, materials, many things, this is natural'.[70] Ibarrola was even more unspecific, indeed he was as unspecific as it is possible to be, flatly stating that each artist could interpret 'Basque art' as they wished.

If these artists were unclear about what constitutes 'Basque art', they were almost as vague about what constituted 'Basqueness'. Oteiza's quasi-mystical utopian anthropology posits, as fundamental to his approach, the continued existence of a constituting (but seemingly unspecifiable) 'Basque spirit', which is supposed to have originated in prehistoric times. Chillida, when interviewed, was resolutely inexact about the nature of his ethnicity, which he frequently discussed in arboreal terms. He claimed that he was a Basque artist *because* his 'roots are sunk into the land and the men who are shaping the morning which is common to us all'. In another interview, he stated, 'When I arrived here [in 1950 after three years' residence in Paris] I had the feeling of a tree that has been transplanted and that suddenly has returned to its place'.[71] In contrast to the sort of biological metaphors which Chillida and some other local artists employed, Ibarrola's notion of Basque-

[68] Angulo 1978:300–15; Guasch 1985:171–3
[69] See the interviews with 30 Basque artists in 'Arte/Etnia/Cultura. Entorno en Euzkadi', *Guadalimar* October 1977, pp. 65–76
[70] Ugalde 1975: 174; Elms 1992: 233
[71] Ugalde 1975: 156; Dempsey 1990: 45. See also 'Conversación con Chillida', *Guadalimar* October 1977, pp. 50–51

ness was primarily political in motivation. Following the Basque Communist definition of 'Basque' as anyone who lived and sold their labour in the Basqueland (and thus not discriminating against migrants), Ibarrola argued that a painter of 'Basque art' did not need to have been born in the Basqueland. It was sufficient for them solely to reside there and to seek identification with Basque culture.

Of course, this persistent vagueness about 'Basqueness' and 'Basque art' is in many ways the whole point of the exercise. Both Oteiza and Chillida, by failing to substantiate to a significant degree the content of their key terms, enabled people who regarded themselves as 'Basques' to imagine that, in one way or another, their actions could exemplify 'Basque style' or 'Basque art'. Since these phrases were so empty, they could potentially be filled with almost any content. Ibarrola's definition of 'Basque art', the most candidly open-ended of them all, is simply the most extreme example of this strategy. For by refusing to limit his definition except in the very broadest of manners, he was both exploiting pervasive ambiguity for the sake of unifying Basqueland-based anti-Franquist artists, and attempting to justify the role of artists within the vanguard of the revolution. In this context, 'Basque art' was a political banner to be waved for rallying the troops, not an art historical term for isolating a particular style or painterly vision.

The demise of Franco, and of *'el arte vasco'*

For many activist artists, the death of the dictator was meant to usher in a revolutionary period in which the Basques would become independent on their own soil and art would take its rightfully prominent place in the new order. Instead they were united in their disappointment and their common opposition to the cultural policy of the new Basque Government. Despite having participated, in their own way, in the struggle against the regime, they felt cheated of what they considered to be the fruits deserved for their anti-fascist and pro-Basque labours.[72] In a satirical short story set in a Bilbao tax office, González de Durana caricatures the post-Franquist attitudes of a disgruntled activist-artist, clearly based on Oteiza:

> 'Hey!! Whatever next!! It is that I believe that we the artists of this country deserve to be treated with greater consideration. We are not just any kind of worker. We represent the notable and creative part of the Basque people, whom we have made universally famous. Can one say to me how much that is worth, 'eh? Of course, one does not know. It's certain that one also doesn't know how much we struggled against the dictatorship, how we were censored and our works destroyed, how we artists headed demonstrations showing the path to follow, with so many plans for the aesthetic construction of Euskadi. The vanguard, the people, all united in a single front, singing, reciting, painting, throughout the neighbourhoods, in the hamlets, wherever they called for us. Is that worth nothing? Is it that, now finally in a democracy – if we can call this miserable

[72] Barañano and González de Durana 1988: 8

situation that we are living as in some way remotely similar to one – they are going to send us the bill? This is inconceivable![73]

Since the majority of the Basque bourgeoisie remained indifferent to most local contemporary art (exceptionally few, for instance, of Chillida's sculptures were bought or commissioned by Basques), these artists were aggrieved that the new regional and provincial governments of the late 1970s through to the early 1990s supported only the work of a token number of living artists. In their eyes, the powers that be of the region (the governments, the major Basque banks and companies) were less concerned with stimulating contemporary artists than with promoting the now unthreatening kind of 'Basque art' created decades ago by Zuloaga, the Zubiaurres and their colleagues. For, as even supporters of the art of this period admit, the Basque pictures of the 1920s have been reproduced in prints and posters, in coffee-table books and magazines, on postcards, on television advertisments, and on calendars, to the level of saturation. These canvases were here being made to play the role of an easily recognizable 'Basque art', one which could serve to underline the cultural distinctiveness of the ethnic group both within the region and abroad.[74] In a phrase, these pictures were made to become ethnic icons.

What changed this scene was the revelation in 1991 by the Basque Government that a magnificent branch of the Guggenheim Museum was to be built, with Basque money, in the centre of Bilbao. In speedy reaction, over 300 Basque painters, writers, filmmakers, actors and singers formed a collective, 'Kultur Keska', to oppose the project. Since the Government, only a few months before, had refused to fund the construction of a Basque Cultural Centre, designed by Oteiza, in the centre of Bilbao, and since it had recently started to reduce its subsidies to a broad spectrum of regional cultural groups, Kultur Keska regarded the proposed (and highly expensive) museum as the central part of a shift in strategy from supporting local activities to sponsoring prestige projects imported from the United States. Oteiza, now in his mid-eighties though still very vigorous, called the signing of the agreement 'authentic double-dealing, something worthy of Disney, totally anti-Basque, and which will cause great damage to and paralysis of all the cultural activities which could be produced in our country'. Another critic worried about 'the great damage' it would do 'to our own culture': 'It is a way of entombing Basque identity'.[75]

The critic was wrong. The Museo did not bury Basque identity but, as the regional government had hoped, revitalized it (as discussed in the final chapter). Its success also led to a change of attitude towards contemporary art among local politicians. While a few of them, or their immediate predecessors, had already commissioned some contemporary public art in the 1980s, many more politicians now began to do so, at a much greater rate, and in a much more diverse manner. Today art by Oteiza, Chillida, their

---

[73] González de Durana 1992: 120
[74] See, e.g., Monahan 1992; Igartua and González 1993; Roberts 1994: 305
[75] M 24 i 1992; El País 5 ii 1992

colleagues and their imitators is commissioned for or reproduced in: the symbols of Basque public institutions and the programmes they organize; the prizes and commemorative statuettes they give out; the logos of political parties, pro-nationalist pressure groups, and even one newspaper (a nationalist one); monuments dedicated to political victims, whether killed by ETA, or by agents of the State; as a backdrop for parliamentary chambers and meeting-rooms of key Basque businesses; to dignify the interior of public buildings; to embellish city centres; to beautify otherwise anonymous estates; to break up the stark geometry of modern buildings; to decorate motorways; to heighten appreciation of the landscape; as keyrings and other souvenir trinkets; and so on.[76] One consequence of the prominence won by Oteiza and Chillida during the dictatorship had been the rise of '*el mimetismo vasco*' (Basque mimesis), where these artists' epigones, and their followers in turn, adopted the sculptural styles of their masters but within a different context and without the same sense of innovation.[77] At least one even tried to fuse the two styles. In the revealing words of a local critic, 'The work of Lertxundi possesses a strong Basque identity. The three basic materials which he uses, stone, iron, wood, are the three symbols of his origin which, moreover, he transforms into pure and *encastra* geometry, using an unmistakeable formula.'[78] The cumulative consequence of both this mimesis and, above all, the increasing public display of these styles was that contemporary Basque art in neo-Oteizan or Chillidesque modes started to become so common that its use threatened to turn these artists' visual vocabularies into a latter-day ethno-kitsch. They were, in other words, being made a contemporary supplement to the ethnic icons of their inter-war predecessors. The only important difference is that the earlier works are meant to give art historical depth to the cultural aspirations of *vasquismo*, while those by Chillida and his peers serve the role of giving a more modern edge to versions of Basque identity.

Despite these promotional efforts of Basque politicians, local public acceptance of these works remains low. In such a highly politicised society it is unsurprising that some open-air sculptures have been sprayed with graffiti, sometimes repeatedly. Chillida, for example, was particularly angry when one of his most loved pieces, the renowned *Peine de los Vientos* ('Comb of the Winds', see front cover), was painted with large 'anti-system' quotes.[79] What is more notable, however, is the number of works, in stone or wood, which have been gravely vandalized, partially or totally destroyed, chopped down, and in some cases physically removed to destinations unknown. In other cases neighbourhood groups have successfully protested against the placing of sculpture in their area. For instance, in 1991 a group of locals

[76] E.g. *M* 21 ix 1998: 9; 13 iii 1999: 3, 4; 15 iii 1999: 5; 28 iii 1999: 5; 26 v 1999: 10; 20 vi 1999: 8; 24 vi 1999: 15; 26 vi 1999: 12; 27 vii 1999: 5; 25 viii 1999: 8; 3 ix 1999: 3; 22 x 1999: 10; 17 xi 1999: 15; 28 iii 2000: 5; 1 iv 2000: 17; 25 v 2000: 19. The newspaper is the nationalist *Gara*.
[77] Ugarte 1996: 107; Urquijo 1998; Álvarez 2002: 889–90
[78] *M* 1 ii 2000: 7. See also *M* 7 iii 1999: 12; 7 xi 1999: 10
[79] Savater 2003: 378. On damage done to Oteiza's Works, see García Marcos 2004: 59

in a San Sebastian suburb publicly argued against the placing of a work by Ibarrola near their homes on the grounds that it was 'very ugly'.[80] At the same time, and as a further sign of public distance from contemporary art, it is important to underline that a market in modern versions of the earlier forms of Basque art continues to flourish in the region. Compared to their counterparts in other countries, very few members of the Basque bourgeoisie buy the contemporary works of their compatriots.[81]

It is very possible that the formation of Kultur Keska will turn out to be the last great unified act of Basque artist-activists.[82] At the turn of the century, Ibarrola became a committed leader of the Ermua Forum. Chillida died in 2002, Oteiza the next year. But many had left the ranks of his movement years before that, and, since the establishment of a post-Franquist social democracy, Basque commentators have become much more ready to criticize Oteiza's approach openly. They have disparaged as messianic and patriarchal his self-appointed role as standard-bearer of the cause, while they have assessed his teaching as overly dogmatic and narrow-visioned because he wished to marginalize everything which could not be brought under the banner of aesthetic nationalism. Moreover, his supposedly avant-garde educational initiatives were in fact but a version of constructivism which even by the 1960s had become a well-established part of the history of art. Barañano and González de Durana, attacking Oteizan 'nationalist stupidities' and its 'endogamic drive', condemned his historiography as 'autistic' and his aesthetic anthropology as more akin to a theology.[83] Jon Juaristi, in a series of vituperative passages, criticizes Oteiza for stirring up his followers against his local critics and against Ibarrola, and for organizing time-consuming campaigns against Chillida.[84] José María Lizundia, with all the fire of the righteous apostate, has crabbed his former camp-leader as a 'providential exegete of an imagined past, so constructed he could ignore all his predecessors'. In the name of freedom, he had propagated an impoverished vision of art which had turned its back on play, irony, sarcasm, parody, humour and irreverence. Instead Oteiza, according to Lizundia, had preferred 'politico-ideological skirmishes . . . which had led to nothing, absolutely nothing.'[85] Even such an otherwise sympathetic commentator as Joseba Zulaika has admitted how 'ideologically very patronizing' his mythologizing project was. Further-

---

[80] *Deia* 3 xi 1991: 59; *El País*, Babelia, supp. 16 i 1993: 8; *M* 2 iii 2000: 5; 20 v 2000: 7; 27 v 2000: 4–5; 29 v 2000: 14

[81] Alonso Pimentel 2006: 113, 115. On the market for neo-traditionalist art, see, for example, *M* 8 ix 1998: 14; 3 i 1999: 6; 11 vii 1999: 8; 10 i 2000, Vivir aquí (VA) supp., p. 10; *M* 25 iii 2000.

[82] The only organized collective act by Basque artists since 1991, of which I am aware, was the joint statement signed in 1998 by 143 of them, including Oteiza and Chillida, for the movement of imprisoned ETA members into local jails (*M* 29 xii 1998: 10).

[83] Barañano and González de Durana 1988: 14. Also, Martínez and Agirre 1995: 262, 275; Ugarte 1996: 25; Lizundia 2000: 36, 57, 112

[84] Juaristi 2006: 116–17, 211, 316–18. Juaristi does admit, however, his admiration for Oteiza's 'capacity to intimidate nationalists, who tried in vain to buy him, with large commissions and fiscal vacations' (ibid.: 116–17).

[85] Lizundia 2000: 35–6, 158. See also the criticisms of Oteiza mentioned in García Marcos 2004: 56 and Jimenez de Aberasturi Apraiz 2004: 74–5

more, one central problem of the pedagogical approach of Oteiza and Ibarrola was that it left completely open just who were to be considered 'artists'. As Ibarrola later confessed, when reminiscing about the open school for artists he and Oteiza ran in the early 1970s in the Biscayan village of Deba, a significant proportion of those who attended had a lot of patriotic spirit but very little talent. 'Quite frankly, it is one thing to have a sense of the Basque national personality; it is another thing to have a professional sense of concrete material with its specific and creative demands.'[86]

Today very few within the generations of local contemporary artists who have appeared since the late 1970s would wish their work to be labelled 'Basque'. To them, application of the ethnic epithet runs the real risk of being considered provincial, making one's work unsaleable on the international market, if one could even get an opening into it.[87] To these artists 'Basque art' is something they can see in museums. There is not even reference to it in the work they produce. The only artist with any renown today who dares to make reference to his Basqueness is the 'queer conceptualist' Txomin Badiola. And he is able to make this reference successfully precisely because he, at one and the same time, both playfully invokes and disavows national specificity. According to the Spanish cultural commentator Julian Smith, since Badiola's return in 1998 from New York to Bilbao, he has become both more explicit and typically ironic in his treatment of Basqueness. For example, visitors to his 1999 installation 'Gimme Shelter' had to pass through transversal bars in the colours of the *ikurriña* in order to enter an inner space where images were projected of a woman shooting a Basque *pelota* player and of an *ertzaina* (Basque policeman) grabbing a colleague by the neck. Photos in this space included one of an *ertzaina* reading a book entitled *Prehistoric Man in the Basque Country* and one of a traditional Basque dancer poring over a *Captain America* comic.[88]

'Basque art' was a banner raised by different people at different times for different reasons. Review of its history shows that its predominant uses over the last 120 years have been nationalistic in motivation.

Review also shows the remarkably central importance of one particular scholarly discipline throughout this chronicle. Various anthropologies, both academic and popular, have played a surprisingly influential role throughout the development of an idea of 'Basque art'. Sabino Arana set the terms of debate, by drawing on the physical anthropological vocabulary of his time. The work of Aranzadi, who was by chance both an academic anthropologist and a trained illustrator, served to legitimate Arana's approach to human classification as well as to ensure its extension into art criticism.

By the 1950s this physiometric approach was increasingly unfashionable because of the commonly recognized danger it ran of sliding into racism.

---

[86] Angulo 1978: 220; Zulaika 2003b: 144
[87] San Martín 2002: 904–5. For a now rare example of a contemporary Basque artist who makes explicit reference to Basque tradition, see *Deia* 30 vi 2006: 69
[88] Smith 2003: 86–112. On 'Gimme Shelter' see *Evasión. El Correo Digital*, 30 i 2001, http://canales.elcorreodigital.com/evasion/tendencias/ten300101badiola.html. Accessed 22 vi 04

Thus, to a certain extent, Oteiza was able to become so influential because he provided an alternative language and ideology for the new, emerging generation of Basque activists dissatisfied with cephalic indices and somatic measurement. This move can be seen as, in part, a shift from a nineteenth-century popular anthropology to a much more modern version. One key difference, however, was that the anthropology of early nationalism was based on supposedly scientific procedures while that of Oteiza was openly mystical. Secondly, the physiognomic approach of Arana and Aranzadi was predominantly concerned with the contemporary while the anthropology of Oteiza was grounded on a redirection to the most distant Basque past possible.

Chillida, unlike Oteiza, did not ground his approach in terms of an idiosyncratic anthropology. However Basque art critics have been quick to regard his sculptural investigations of anvils and other rural tools in ethnological terms, seeing his sculptures as an exploratory visual ethnography of material culture. Chillida, moreover, was quite prepared to use academic anthropology to legitimate his explorations. Commenting on Joseba Zulaika's *Tratado estético-ritual vasco*, an investigation by a Basque anthropologist into the symbolic keys of Basque life, he stated that he was very struck at how many of his own numerous prints were entitled with the same Euskera terms which Zulaika argued were culturally central. For Chillida, Zulaika's work tallied neatly with his intuitionist, almost structuralist belief that the intimate meaning of his work came from the very root of the Basque.[89]

Among the disciples of the Basque School Movement, the most anthropologically motivated is the sculptor José Ulibarrena who has established an ethnographic museum in northern Navarre which he has filled with both local material culture and his own sculptures. Besides holding discussion groups and roundtables at the museum, he has also published books on his 'investigations into the characteristic expressions of Euskara Aesthetics': 'All the pieces we present have, I repeat, an aspect, a rhythm, some strokes and some forms, all plainly autochthonous . . . Both Euskera and Basque aesthetics are as archaic as our ethnicity and give a clear idea of our identity.'[90]

Despite his efforts, Ulibarrena is today an isolated example. Almost all contemporary art in the Basque Country has no apparent need for an anthropologically based aesthetics, whether popular or academic, mystical or material. We should not, however, toll the bell for an ethnographically-grounded idea of 'Basque art' too soon, as it is easy to imagine novel, fresh encounters between anthropology and artistic practice. For instance, it is possible some locals may start to adapt the experimental approaches of those Western and non-Western artists who are self-consciously exploiting fieldwork methods and anthropological styles of representation to comment on both the present predicament and the ways they have been represented in the past.[91] In the Basque Country, anthropology has served several politico-artistic purposes. It may yet serve others.

[89] Ugarte 1995: 86–7; 1996: 54–5
[90] Ulibarrena 1990: 6. See also Ulibarrena 1992
[91] On the work of these artists see Schneider and Wright 2006

7
Political Graffiti
A Photo Essay

Travel writers emphasize the Basque Country's rural beauty, traditions, architecture, language and liveliness. They revel in the picturesque, the quaint and the distinctive. They like to dwell on the age of buildings, the narrowness of city streets and the general contours of townscapes. Yet almost none of the more contemporary visitors among this loose group makes any reference to a ubiquitous, modern, visually very striking feature of the landscape: political graffiti.

The sole exception is Robert Elms, a young British writer. Visiting Bilbao in 1990, he found

> The perpetual graffiti forms a street language of its own baffling complexity. The initials of this and that party and tendency running into the slogans of some splinter group or other. The kind of giant, full-scale murals which provide the only real colour to the streets of Belfast are also emblazoned on numerous walls here, singing the praises of some dead or imprisoned martyr to the all-consuming cause.

For him, San Sebastian was similar: 'It too is a town covered in graffiti screaming of hunger strikes and demonstrations.'[1]

Graffiti, like posters, command our attention. Whether witty or uninspired, visually sophisticated or crude, optically arresting or numbingly repetitive, they are very difficult to ignore. Casting our eyes as we proceed through city streets or rural landscapes, they fall unwantedly into our field of vision and clamour for sustained regard. However hard we try, we cannot avoid them. Despite these noteworthy similarities, there is of course the major difference. Posters, carrying legally tolerated messages, are stuck up in already-designated, rented-out spaces; they form an integral part of the regulated townscape and rural roadsides. They are where they are meant to be, and where town halls allow them to be. (And if they are put up anywhere else they are usually removed.) In contrast, graffiti is not planned by municipal authorities and cuts directly through any sense of a planned environment. That is their point. They are an unofficial means of redefining surfaces and turning public spaces into political ones.[2] A structural wall of a building is made into an advertisement for the far right; a fence separating a car-park from the street is turned into a defence of terrorism. In many cases, the painted site is chosen deliberately: a stridently

[1] Elms 1992: 221, 223
[2] Linstroth 2002: 212

151

7.1 The road side of a rural grain-store, Guenduláin, Navarre, overpainted at least four times by different groups.

anti-capitalist message goes up on the shutters of a bank; a protest against a judicial decision is placed near the court where the judgement was passed down. Thus, depending on where it is placed, the more clashing the message, the greater its force.[3]

The *grafiteros'* intent is not just spatio-political, at least not for the nationalists. For them, it is linguistico-political as well. Their slogans are painted in Euskera, as a further way of making their linguistic point that it is the language which should be spoken in the Basque area. It is also a way to reclaim public space for Euskera, otherwise often confined to the domestic realm. And if these nationalist *grafiteros* choose to reach a wider audience, they might condescend to Castilian, but Basquize it in the process, substituting tx for ch, b for v, etc.

In the Basque Country, political graffiti is doubly ubiquitous. First, unlike most styles of the art, Basque political graffiti is not confined to the towns, but transcends any supposed urban/rural divide. The *grafiteros* go to work wherever they wish to make their mark. Second, Basque political graffiti is not restricted to the usual surfaces (walls, road signs) but is painted wherever it is considered worth putting up: a cliff face, a dam, a hillside, along an aqueduct.

In fact the more inaccessible the graffito the better, for two main reasons.

[3] Del Valle 1990: 55, 57

7.2 The inaccessible. This dam-face graffiti, Alloz, Navarre, has been left untouched for at least fifteen years.

First, what is difficult to access is troublesome and expensive to remove. Thus the more inaccessible graffiti tend to last as long as their paint. Second, the difficulty of access to the painted area dramatically demonstrates the climbing skills of the *grafiteros* and may serve to remind its viewers of the historic and positive association between Basque nationalism and Basque mountaineering, which has long been both a common pursuit and a prestigious one for its elite climbers.[4] As one of their number put it, 'You have to take into account that in the Basque Country there has always been great interest in mountaineering. It seems almost consubstantial with the Basque people, who live surrounded by mountains'.[5] In 1908 members of 'Juventud Vasca' (the Basque Youth movement) founded Mendigoitzale Bazkuna (Mountaineering Association), which was to play key roles in regional history and contribute to the development of a nationalist mystique. During the Second Republic, its members became a section of the most intransigent of nationalist political forces and acted as the shock troops of radical nationalism; in the Civil War they constituted a major share of the Basque militias; throughout the repressive period following, they organized the local resistance and the clandestine escorting of exiles across the Pyrenees into France.[6] During the later decades of the dictator's regime, mountaineering was one of the rare ways by which concerned locals could meet and discuss their predicament in an unpoliced setting. Today, the sustained successes of the best Basque climbers at scaling the most difficult and highest peaks around the world continue to fill the front pages of the regional press. Thus a graffito on the face of a cliff or a dam is redolent of nationalist connotations; it becomes a daring, lasting reminder of Basque skill, endeavour and politics, a further statement of the achievement of local climbers. In these cases the medium really is the message.

Scholars of graffiti underline the extent to which the activity is a source of individual pride.[7] Stressing that fact in the Basque case would be to miss the main point. Though colouring a public surface might puff up the painter's chest, the key reason for the exercise is not personal advertisement but furthering the collective cause. For Basque activists, writing graffiti is at one and the same time an individual achievement and, much more importantly, a contribution to the partisan effort. Unlike the subsequent fame garnered by subway artists in New York, no accolades, even informally, have been bestowed on Basque *grafiteros*, even decades after the event. They retain their anonymity.

The sociologist Nancy Macdonald argues that the writing of graffiti may be viewed as a rite de passage for modern urban youth.[8] In the Basque Country this is no figure of speech. Putting up pro-ETA graffiti is quite literally an initiation into the organization. Among certain sections of ETA one of the first tasks for recent recruits is putting up the group's symbols and latest messages in the locality. It is a preliminary training at nocturnal,

[4] Elorza 2000: 50–1
[5] Quote from Pérez-Agote 1987: 187
[6] Larronde 1977: 323; Heiberg 1989: 71
[7] Cooper and Chalfant 1984; Philips 1999; Macdonald 2001
[8] Macdonald 2001: 101–2

7.3 The traditional symbol of the armed organization, a snake entwining around an axe, with the slogan 'In ETA Jarrai' (the youth wing of the radical nationalists), Alloz, Navarre. It is almost a test of local feelings to see how long this sort of graffiti remains unblemished.

illegal practice. It is also, of course, a training in evasion, as a fledgling *grafitero* caught by the police painting pro-ETA messages will be both fined and registered. A person filed by the police for this kind of activity is no longer an unknown participant in the radical struggle and so is a much less valuable recruit to a clandestine organization.

Putting up these messages and images is, by definition, a secret activity. Active *grafiteros*, those who have not yet left their brushes to dry or their paintcans to rust, must remain anonymous to the general public, or else give up their role. Unsurprising, then, that the only time I ever saw the writing going straight on to the wall was at a mass demonstration in Pamplona by radical nationalists, which the paramilitary National Police was trying hard to suppress with baton charges, tear gas and rubber bullets. As the crowd held the street, nervously awaiting the next charge, an agitated youth broke ranks, turned around and scribbled a rapid message across the wall of the city's main bank. He just found time to finish it.

As this example suggests, putting up graffiti is primarily an activity for local youth, rather than middle-aged stalwarts. To my knowledge, the police have yet to arrest a *grafitero* over the age of 25. In 1997, while interviewing the leader of a local minuscule political party, I asked why so much graffiti for his organization had recently appeared in the city. He candidly replied, with a smile, 'But we are recruiting so many young people these days. And they go out together at night.'

A significant proportion of these graffiti state the illegal, for example, support of political violence. Some state what cannot be legally said. One summer's day in 1995, while in Bilbao, I heard the mid-day news on the radio that ETA had just released X, a Basque industrialist they had kidnapped several weeks previously. It was presumed his family had paid the ransom. That night on a wall in the city's Old Quarter I saw the comment, 'Thanks X. The money will be useful.' Some state feelings too raw, too pitiless, to be fit for the mass media. When a policeman was shot by ETA, one repeated graffiti which went up was 'Hard-head, give us back the bullet.'[9]

Some Basque political graffiti is put up by centrist groups, whether leaning towards the right or the left. But the majority is painted in the name of radical groups, whether on the Basque nationalist far left or the Spanish nationalist far right. Scholars of the phenomenon frequently like to argue that graffiti is a way for the unvoiced to express themselves.[10] This generalization only holds good here in a partial manner: for the radical nationalists, whose graffiti are the most common of all, had for over two decades their own, highly successful newspaper, *Egin*, and several associated magazines. To this extent, the work of their *grafiteros* should be seen as but another mode of radical nationalist expression. Perhaps we could state that it is a preferred activity of those who favour 'direct action'.

In the Basque Country graffiti is taken very seriously as a mode of communication. Local newspapers will give critical coverage to the recent appearance of threatening graffiti against local businesses, while political parties will openly denounce intimidating signs.[11] For instance, in December 2000 the PNV publicly complained in a forthright manner when radical nationalists put up graffiti threatening one of its members, the mayor of a Navarran town.[12] The local courts and town halls are prepared to go further.[13] In 2000 the town hall of Portugalete, a traditionally working-class district on the Left Bank of the river which flows through Bilbao, spent months promoting an anti-graffiti publicity campaign and then levied many fines of between 100,000 and 150,000 pesetas.[14] At the same time the Alavan wing of PSOE petitioned the provincial Deputation to budget 10,000,000 pesetas to fund the removal of all graffiti in the province which made 'fascist' allusions or went against 'fundamental values such as life and liberty'. Under the rubric of 'Recuperation of spaces for peace', the socialists' general aim was

> To rub out from the environment in which we daily move, all the messages which attack peaceful coexistence or encourage violent actions. It is unacceptable that the streets are drowned in threats against the most basic principles because in the end one creates a culture of violence.[15]

[9] Tremlett 2006: 293

[10] E.g. Phillips 1999

[11] E.g. *M Euskadi* supp. 3 v 1999: 8; 17 vii 1999: 15; 22 v 2001: 13

[12] *M Euskadi* supp., 2 xii 2000: 11

[13] E.g. the two-year sentence passed down to a local for painting a series of pro-terrorist and threatening graffiti (*El País* 12 I 2005: 24)

[14] *M Gran Bilbao* supp., 22 i 2001: 2. See also *M Gran Bilbao* supp., 18 x 2000: 16

[15] *M Euskadi* supp., 21 i 2001: 14

7.4 An unwanted image of the area, Alloz, Navarre ('Euskal Herria Askatu', 'The free Basque people'). As I took this photo, several passing drivers hooted and waved their fists at me.

This proposal appeared so viable because the city hall of Vitoria, capital of Alava, had several years before established the precedent of dedicating a section of its own annual budget to the removal of graffiti. Judges are also prepared to act strongly against *grafiteros*, on occasion handing down stiff sentences. In early 2000, however, moderate nationalists thought things had gone too far and they publicly criticized the public prosecutor who, on the grounds they had committed an 'apology of terrorism', sought to give a pair of radical *grafiteros* eight years apiece.[16]

As well as legal and economic dimensions to the practice of graffiti, there is also an important civic dimension, above all in cities whose image increasingly effects their market. In 1999 in Bilbao, then beginning to re-launch itself as a home of culture and high-quality services, a columnist complained of the way graffiti sullied the new, gleaming image of the city. This 'counter-aesthetic', with its own algebra of party acronyms, ruffled his refined sensibility. That same year in San Sebastian the mayor condemned the 'anti-civic', 'anti-ecological' messages put up by radical nationalists, whose effect was to dirty this tourist-centred town.[17] To this extent the continuing contest between *grafiteros* and their would-be suppressors is at root a clash of aesthetics, a battle over style or notions of spatial order, fought

16 *M Euskadi supp.*, 25 i 2000: 12
17 *M Vivir aquí supp.*, 3 v 1999: 8; *Euskadi supp.*, 25 v 1999: 24

with spray-cans and water-blasters, one where the antagonists never phys-ically meet. The degree to which graffiti may provide an unwanted image of the area was plainly revealed to me in 2001 when I stopped by a rural roadside to photograph a message painted along the side of an aqueduct. As I brought out my camera and tried to work out the best position from which to take my shots, several passers-by hooted their horns and waved their fists at me. Their hostility was patent.

Of course, all these different reactionary moves only serve to legitimate *grafiteros'* activity. For if their graffiti were unimportant, why would legal, political and police forces go to such efforts to suppress the practice? Obviously, whitening a wall does not get rid of graffiti. It simply provides a new blank surface on which to paint fresh graffiti. In this sense *grafiteros* and their activist opponents are unspeaking partners in an odd duet of the criminalized and the enforcers of the common norm.[18]

In the Basque Country, we cannot make any simplistic generalization that graffiti are visual blots on the townscape, unwanted and disliked by the great majority. For there is evidence to the contrary. In 1987 the mayor of Bilbao (then a still very contaminated city) proclaimed to 'clean up' the urban area by getting his employees to remove all green-painted graffiti. In response, a libertarian collective argued the opposite in the pages of *Egin*:

> For those of us who do not have control over or frequent access to the 'hard' media of communication, there are not many other ways for us to reach the people. In this way, besides squashing a rich and beautiful street-art, it violates a basic right which is that of the freedom of expression of minority groups, and which condemns us to ostracism.[19]

In the decaying Bilbao neighbourhood they came from, they did not see why the town hall was so keen to rid the place of graffiti yet did nothing to clean the river or purify the air. At this rate it is difficult not to agree with the Pamplonan writer Miguel Sánchez-Ostiz, who sees graffiti as almost con-substantial with his hometown, as virtually a traditional part of the land-scape: 'A city is also its graffiti, its murals and Pamplona has both, in abundance, like it or not.'[20] Many of those I knew in that city would have regarded it as a sterile, alienating environment if it were suddenly shorn of all its graffiti.

Graffiti appears so much the exemplar of the ephemeral statement (painted today, washed out tomorrow) that it is easy to forget its histori-cal dimension. Marginalia in political histories of the area attest to the repeated appearance of writings on the wall during times of agitation.[21] But much of this disappeared during the early, most heavy-handed years of the dictatorship. Some locals, who were teenagers at the time, remember the revolutionizing effect of its reappearance in the mid-1960s. After so many years of imposed silence, the nationalist message was being openly re-stated in public, to their excitement and joy. Today the historical dimension

---

[18] On this point see Ferrell 1996: 159
[19] *Egin* 10 viii 1987: 2, quoted in Del Valle 1990: 56
[20] Sánchez-Ostiz 2002: 190
[21] E.g. Elorza 2000: 51

7.5 Any language so long as it is not Castilian. The *only* words painted out in this multilingual sign are 'Bienvenidos' and 'Navarra'.

7.6 No Euskera here. The Basque terms for both towns are painted out, while the added 'NAVARRA' is to remind onlookers that they are not in the Basque Country.

7.7 A midnight dialogue. The name for this Navarran town during the Francoist era was 'Leiza'. Since the death of the dictator and the revival of nationalism in the area, it has been re-Basquized 'Leitza'. The original 'Leiza' on this sign is faintly evident. It has been officially repainted 'Leitza'. A nocturnal *navarrista* then whited out the 'T'. An anonymous radical nationalist later replaced it, in red.

7.8 The monument to Germán Rodríguez, in the place where he was shot during the Sanfermines of 1978. The first two monuments to him on this spot were removed by nocturnal anti-nationalists. This third version is made of solid metal with a shaft penetrating more than a metre underground, set in concrete. Since anti-nationalists cannot remove or destroy this monument easily, they daub it with paint instead.

(All photographs taken Summer 2001 © Jeremy MacClancy)

is noticeable by default, as graffiti styles are constantly evolving. According to one of its theorists, graffiti is 'an art form that celebrates change and feeds on new ideas'; at present, internationally, there is no one dominant style; instead, 'anything goes'.[22] In most Western metropoli today, one can find tags, stick-ups, stencils and logos, besides the more traditional formats. Yet, as far as I can judge, political graffiti in the Basque Country has not fundamentally changed in style, since its mushrooming in the 1970s. In 1983 one group of activists vaguely associated with the Comandos Autonomos Anticapitalistas (a short-lived armed group which operated independently of ETA) deliberately chose a different style to that of HB, which they perceived as always the same, ideologically hardline. In contrast, they saw their work as more romantic, as aimed straight at the heart. But they soon put their brushes aside, and left the walls for the *grafiteros* to cover in their standard manner.[23] To this extent, the great majority of Basque political graffiti, even if freshly daubed, is of a piece with its most active time: the last years of Franco and the first decade and a half after his death.

There are two variants left to consider. For at the very edge of graffiti is the plainly gestural: painting out signs, or throwing paint at a concrete object of dislike. Obscuring the unwanted language, whether it be Castilian or Euskera, in a bilingual sign is a particularly common form of roadside protest. The less common, competitive succession of obscuring and repainting a sign quickly becomes a midnight dialogue between activists of opposed camps. The second variant, throwing paint, is an unworded, imageless, but still crudely articulate form of protest. Particularly attractive to these paintpot-carrying activists are political monuments, whether they be to Franquist leaders (e.g. the statue to General Mola in the centre of Pamplona) or to those killed by the forces of reaction (e.g. that to Germán Rodríguez, the *abertzale* shot during the Sanfermines of 1978, again in the centre of Pamplona), Others aim their paint at specific buildings. In 1985, in the Casco Viejo of Pamplona, a newly restored and prominent corner-building was splattered with paint-bombs in a harshly contrastive colour the day the scaffolding was taken down. The general impression I gathered from the crowd inspecting the damage was that it was a rejection by unemployed youths of this early attempt by the socialist-run town hall to gentrify the increasingly dilapidated Old Quarter. Sixteen years later persons unknown threw 'a great quantity of paint', primarily yellows and greens, at the central headquarters of the PNV in Navarre. Its occupants blamed 'certain sectors of the *abertzale* left'.[24] In May 2005 radical gesturalists used their paint-bombs to make a colour-coded message. In a co-ordinated attack on PNV club-premises in two cities, they daubed in Euskera, 'PNV Fascists! *Españolistas!*', on the walls and then threw yellow and red paint: the colours of the Spanish flag.[25]

---

[22] Manco 2004: 7
[23] In Espinosa and López 1993: 61
[24] M 12 v 2001: 19. For paint-throwing at overhead motorway signs, see *Gara* 13 v 2006: 23
[25] *El Diario Vasco* 20 v 2006: 35; *M* 20 v 06: 14

8
Art Museum

Museums are just a lot of lies, and the people who make art their business are mostly impostors . . . We have infected the pictures in our museums with all our stupidities, all our mistakes, all our poverty of spirit. We have turned them into petty and ridiculous things.
Pablo Picasso (quoted in Barr 1946: 274)

In October 1997 the Museo Guggenheim Bilbao opened in Bilbao to a blaze of fireworks and publicity. The fireworks died down but the publicity has persisted and, from its very first day, visitors have continued to pour in, in unforeseen numbers. Almost on its own, the Museo has radically changed the image of the city, modified the regional economy, and opened up important debates about Basque identity and the place of art within it. These debates show no signs of dying down. The local effects of the Museo have been so wide-ranging and, to a great extent, so unexpected that the people of Bilbao are still accommodating themselves to the transformations it has initiated. Globally, the Museo's triumph has been so widely acknowledged and so broadly advertised that a variety of city authorities in America, Europe and Asia have considered imitating the Basque initiative.

In this chapter, I examine this, the world's first franchise art museum. I choose the Museo as my topic of study because it is a revolutionary type of art museum, because it has been such a great international success since its opening, because it has generated broad, prolonged polemic (especially about its effects on Basque identity), and because it threatens to become a model for future museums around the world. As a new kind of phenomenon within the Westernized worlds of museums, art and public planning, it raises fundamental questions both about our understanding and the uses of art, and about the nature of and roles of museums, especially in relation to regional identity and urban revitalization.[1]

The project

In December 1991 the Basque Government and the Guggenheim Foundation of New York officially agreed to the establishment of a Guggenheim Museum in Bilbao. The Museo would be a world-class building designed by

[1] MacClancy 1997 is a first report on the Museo, prior to its opening.

8.1 Guggenheim Museum, Bilbao, 2001, designed by Frank O. Gehry
(© Jeremy MacClancy)

an architect of great international repute, Frank O. Gehry, and sited on disused land on the waterfront in the centre of the city. Over the thirty years the agreement would run (with an option to extend it for a further seventy-five years), the Foundation would supply the Museo with a continuous series of exhibitions, all of high quality, while the Government would gradually assemble its own permanent collection.[2]

The Basque politicians had three main arguments to justify their large but risky investment. First, given that the Foundation is generally regarded as having the best (in terms of quality, size and scope) private collection in the world of twentieth-century art, the agreement was the most effective way to establish a museum of modern and contemporary art in the area. In recent decades the work of most Basque artists had suffered because of the lack of such a museum in the peninsula. The building of the Museo would rectify that.

Second, for over twenty years the Bilbao area had suffered the decay of its heavy industries, high unemployment and the armed violence occasioned by the continuing activity of ETA. The Basque Government thus saw the Museo as a central component of their strategy to improve the image of the country. It would become an emblematic building for Bilbao, in the same way that Sydney Opera House had become for that city. On this argument, the Museo was an exercise (albeit an extremely costly one) in public relations.

Third, the Government planned to revitalize Bilbao generally, by commissioning the construction of a series of impressive buildings: a business centre, a grand and visually striking convention and performing arts centre (to be called the Euskalduna), a large transport interchange, a metro system, a new terminal for the city's airport, and new bridges over its river. As a deliberate marketing strategy, the Basque Government chose architects of the greatest renown to design these buildings: Sir Norman Foster, Sir James Stirling, Santiago Calatrava, Cesar Pelli. Astutely, Basque leaders realized that world-class practitioners would 'sell' the city abroad far more effectively than if they themselves did it. The overall strategy behind all these projects was to establish Bilbao as a European centre for service industries, modern technologies and upmarket tourism. The Museo was meant to be a key part of this strategy, attracting businessmen with cultural aspirations and cultivated tourists with deep pockets.[3]

To the Foundation, the agreement was in part a way out of its current economic difficulties. As a totally private body which receives no public subsidy, the Foundation had gone deeply into debt in the early 1990s to pay for the renovation of their famous Frank Lloyd Wright building which overlooks Central Park. A newly appointed director, the art historian-cum-

---

[2] The building would cost 10,000 million pesetas and 5,000 million would be dedicated to the purchase of pictures and sculptures for the collection. The course of the lengthy negotiations leading to the construction of the museum is detailed in Tellitu, Esteban and González 1997; see also Zulaika 1997

[3] Information for this section was drawn from promotional literature produced by the Consorcio del Proyecto Guggenheim Bilbao.

institutional entrepreneur Thomas Krens, decided that the most effective way to balance its books was to exploit its under-used resources. Since only 3 per cent of its collection could be exhibited at any one time, he argued that the Foundation should embark on an 'economics of scale'. The first part of this plan was the opening of an extension in Soho, the artistic quarter of New York. The second part was to reach agreements with foreign governments or city halls for the construction of new Guggenheim Museums, designed by famous architects, in which a travelling series of exhibitions selected from the Foundation's collection would be shown. In return, the Foundation would receive, in each case, a large fee for lending its name, pictures and expertise.[4] The agreement with the Basque Government was the first it had signed.

Success

Ever since its opening in the autumn of 1997 the Gugu (as it rapidly became known) has been a resounding success, at a level much greater than either its promoters or critics expected. In its first year it received 1,360,000 visitors, almost double the number predicted; in its second year it received over a million visitors, once again many more than expected; the following year, staff had several times to close the doors when one exhibition proved too popular.[5] These promising results have allowed the Museo to be much more self-financing than originally forecast, at the level of 70 per cent, one of the highest such figures among European museums. It has also won a surprisingly broad array of prizes: not just for its architecture and construction but for its management, restaurant, image and website as well.[6] Most importantly to some, in its first three years its direct economic impact in the Basque Country was calculated as just over 1,000 million Euros. In other words, the initial investment in the Museo by the Basque Government was paid back within three years.[7]

The building is not just much visited and much garlanded, it is also much used, for a surprising plethora of purposes: as a platform for prize-giving ceremonies, a setting for rock videos, a home of launch-parties for luxury products, an auditorium for concerts of contemporary classical music, a catwalk for fashion shows, a cinema for art movies. It is a frequent venue for receptions, parties and dinners hosted by the Basque Government, its departments, regional political parties, and local, national and international businesses. Its futuristic exterior is used as background in the fashion features of newspapers, as well as in advertments for airlines, perfume

[4] Durieux 1995. The payment by the Government to the Foundation was fixed at 2,000 million pesetas.
[5] *M* 28 xi 1999: 7
[6] *M* 5 xii 1998: 58; 18 iii 1999: 11; 14 viii 1999: 5; 24 xii 1999, Vivir aquí (VA) supp., p. 8; 30 iii 2000:11; 25 iv 2000, Gran Bilbao (GB) supp., p. 4; 29 iv 2000, GB supp., p. 8; 5 v 2000, GB supp., p. 6
[7] Azua 2004

(Cerruti), cars (Audi, Seat), wine (Biscayan txakoli, Catalan cava), and a host of other products whose style is key to their sales.[8] At times it seems as though no part of the Museo is left unused. Its riverbank has become a site for rock bands; its esplanade a stage for modern dance, Scots bagpipers, or circus troupes; its shiny titanium sheathing a suitably reflective surface for city firework displays.[9] Political protestors have exploited its prominence by demonstrating at its entrance, jamming the cash-tills, occupying its pool, catapulting stones at the sheath, chaining themselves to its fences, or climbing the tower to hang banners from its top.[10] Even the car park adjacent to the Museo has been taken advantage of: as the meeting-place for associations of vintage, veteran and classic cars or motorbikes, as well being a stopping-point for a transnational rally of luxury cars.[11] To some locals, the Museo's greatest public moment came in February 1999 when a section of the latest James Bond movie was filmed there. Contingents of police had to be called out, to keep the crowds back.[12]

Its success can also be calibrated in terms of, and, in local eyes, is legitimated by, the level of international, especially American, interest. *The Washington Post* called it 'the great building of our time'; *Time* news magazine, 'one of the five best buildings of the century'; *The Times*, London, 'the world's most attractive modern building', *The Evening Standard*, London, 'the most talked-about new building for decades'.[13] In international terms, the building immediately set an architectural standard, included in histories of the subject as a supreme example of what architects were capable of at the end of the century.[14] In the course of 1998, over ninety television crews shot footage of the building and foreign journalists wrote over 4,000 articles on it. The free publicity generated by this continuing international media activity has been calculated as equivalent to 20 million Euros

[8] *Evening Standard*, London, 16 iv 1998: 24–5; *Gastronomika*, Bilbao, 1999, No. 39: 37; *M* 1 iv 1998: 12; 14 vi 1998: 21; 17 vi 1998: 13, 15; 23 vi 1998: 1, 9; 19 vii 1998: 15; 22 vii 1998: 16; 11 viii 1998: 1, 11; 12 viii 1998: 16; 5 ix 1998: 11; 14 ix 1998: 8; 21 ix 1998: 4; 22 ix 1998: 6; 7 x 1998: 1, 6; 31 x 1998: 10; 15 xi 1998: 20; 10 i 1999: 22-3; 15 i 1999: 8; 25 xi 1999: 73; *El País* (Edición Internacional) 9 vi 1997: 20

[9] *M* 23 iii 1998: 4; 31 v 1998: 6; 15 iv 1999: 14; 18 iv 1999: 1; 29 xi 1999: 8, 27 xii 1999, VA supp., p. 1, 6. A further example of the Museo's use was provided by the Basque tourist office, which shot a promotional television advertisement there, projecting images on the metallic walls to the accompaniment of an avant-garde theatre group acting as dragons, contortionists, mountebanks and clowns on stilts, see *M* 22 iii 1998: 14

[10] *M* 2 xii 1999, VA supp., p. 11; 9 xii 1999, VA supp., p. 1; 23 i 2000, GB supp., p. 8; 11 ii 2000, GB supp., p. 3; 10 iii 2000, GB supp., p. 6; 12 iii 2000, GB supp., p. 1, 4, 5; 26 iii 2000: 16

[11] *M* 31 v 1998: 1, 7; 20 ii 2000, GB supp., p. 1; 1 v 2000, GB supp., p. 7; 21 v 2000, GB supp, p.1

[12] *M* 17 ii 1999: 1

[13] *Evening Standard*, London, 20 x 1997: 54; *The Washington Post* 31 iii 1999; *The Times* quote in *M* 1 iv 1999: 3. See also, for example, *Art in America* vii 1997: 48–55; *The Independent on Sunday*, London, 13 vii 1997: 15; *The European*, London, 2–8 x 1997: 50–1. For further British reactions to the building, see *The Guardian* 4 x 1997: 6; *The Guardian* Weekend 25 x 1997: 58- -61; *The Independent on Sunday* Magazine 24 viii 1997: 14–15; *The Observer* Life 12 x 1997: 14–20

[14] *The Guardian* Weekend, London, 9 i 1999: 62; *The Independent on Sunday* Real Life, London, 24 i 1999: 12. Harvard architecture students, experiencing '*bilbomanía*', now treat Bilbao as an urban site worthy of their postgraduate projects, see *M* 25 iii 1998: 16.

annually.[15] In many ways that figure is irrelevant, as the key points are that the Basque Government did not pay for the publicity, that the panegyrics of the journalists were opinions offered for free. 2,500 million pesetas' worth of purchased publicity would not have had the same worldwide effect. As the city's mayor put it, without exaggeration, 'Bilbao is now on the Mapamundi.'[16]

In this context, the selection of Gehry was inspired, for he is a very successful architect both of buildings and of the reception of his own work. In the words of Beatriz Colombina, he is the creator of his own aura, his own media effect, who usefully provided journalists with many of the metaphors which were subsequently used to describe the Museo, that is. he provided his commentators with their narrative lines.[17]

Additional publicity is locally generated, as Basque newspapers consistently trumpet the visits to the Gugu of famous actors, dancers, industrialists, film producers, Nobel laureates, rock musicians, politicians, princes, painters, sculptors.[18] These are photo-opportunities of mutual benefit to the Museo and its celebrated visitors, a chance for both to reflect their glory, off the polish of the other. Even the visit of a renowned but reserved philosopher to the building was given feet of column inches. Paul Ricoeur thought the Gugu a 'vertiginous synthesis of chaos and cosmos'.[19]

'El efecto "Guggy"'

Within months of its opening, and the emerging scale of its success already discernible, journalists and locals started to become aware of a broad range of effects, caused by the Museo, on the society and economy of Bilbao in particular and the Basque Country in general.

Perhaps the most unforeseen consequence of the Museo's success has been the wave-like effect on local museums generally. In the words of one Basque commentator, 'What is surprising is not that the citizenship has now discovered a museum, but that it has discovered museums.'[20] The most striking case is that of the Museo de Bellas Artes, a few hundred yards from the Guggenheim itself. Its number of visitors has increased markedly, despite the fact that, since the opening of the Gugu, it started charging for entrance. During 1997 its number of visitors rose by 22 per cent, and all its major special exhibitions had to be extended.[21] Between 1997 and 2004, the number of its 'Friends' quintupled.

[15] *M* 2 iii 1999: 10; Azua 2004
[16] *M* 26 ix 1998: 15
[17] Colombina 2004
[18] *M* 18 iv 1998: 11; 24 iv 1998: 12; 7 vi 1998: 15; 24 viii 1998: 16; 22 xii 1998: 8; 31 i 1999: 11; 13 ii 1999: 9; 25 ii 1999: 19; 4 v 1999; 1, 10, 66; 8 iv 2000, GB supp., p. 7; 29 iv 2000, GB supp., p. 18
[19] *M* 25 I 1999: 10
[20] Goméz Nazabal 1998
[21] *M* 19 ii 1999: 16. For example, the special exhibition it held from December 1997 to March 1998, comparing the artistic visions of Sorolla and Zuloaga proved so popular, it was extended

Some have wished to capitalize on the success of the Gugu by creating a Basque network of contemporary art museums. A medium-sized one has been planned in the northeast of the area, in Irun, based on the long-standing tradition of artists who have resided alongside or visited the nearby River Bidasoa.[22] Another, much larger, has been built in the south of the area, in the administrative capital of the Basque Country, Vitoria; it re-houses the collection assembled by the Deputation of Alava since 1975.[23] The Deputation of Navarre, with the agreement of Oteiza, paid for the construction of a special museum a few kilometres outside of Pamplona dedicated to his work; the Deputation of Guipuzcoa helped Chillida with the costs of a museum (which has become highly successful) dedicated to his work just outside San Sebastian. The town hall of Bilbao even agreed to support a group of local businessmen who wished to create a museum to Dalí, though the Catalan surrealist had no connections with the city.[24] The general idea behind these specific initiatives was to persuade visitors to the Gugu to stay in the region a little longer, touring its cultural attractions.

At the same time, the lesson that 'architecture sells' has been well learnt by the owners of Basque vineyards, three of which have commissioned famed architects (including Gehry) to design futuristic wineries for them.[25] The Museo has also set a new standard of architectural audacity for the city. An architect charged with renovating a key building on one of Bilbao's central squares explicitly rose to the challenge by having its façade repainted a bold pink and white.[26]

As hoped, the Gugu is having a major effect on tourism and, to a certain extent, on the regional economy generally. Tourism generates 4 per cent of the Gross National Product of the Basque Country, and is its seventh most important sector of activity in terms of Gross Added Value. In 1998 tourism to the Basque Country rose by 28 per cent, with most of the increase due to the Museo.[27] In its first year, 79 per cent of the Gugu's visitors had journeyed to Bilbao especially to see the Museo. Spaniards made up 32 per cent of its visitors coming from outside the Basque Country and 26 per cent came from outside Spain. So many North Americans were prepared to make the flight over to see the Museo that, to the great surprise of the Basque Department of Tourism, tourists from the USA constituted the second greatest number, by nation, of foreign visitors to the city.[28] Visitors to the Gugu in its first year spent, in total, over 30,000 million pesetas during

[21] (cont.) for a further period and its accompanying catalogue had to be re-printed. The final tally was 127,000 visitors, see M 14 iii 1998: 11

[22] M 6 vii 1998: 3. On the 'School' of Bidasoa, see Zubiaur 1986

[23] M 12 xi 1998: 3; 29 xii 1998: 11

[24] M 3 x 99: 2, 11

[25] M 20 xi 1998: 4; 23 v 1999: 1, 3; 29 v 2000: 15; 2 vi 2000: 15

[26] 'The Guggenheim is daring,' he stated. 'The city needs new airs.' See M 8 viii 1999: 19.

[27] M 4 i 1999: 3

[28] M 15 x 1998: 6. The Gugu is also having an effect on the companies which participated in its construction. The managing director of the local business which manufactured and erected its metal structures claims that doing the job has given it an international reach and image. See M 20 iv 1998: 8

their stay. The generation of added value and wealth caused by this influx was calculated as 0.47 per cent of the Gross National Product of the Basque Country. The Museo was thus considered, in its first year, to have maintained 3,816 jobs, or 0.51 per cent of the employed population of the area.[29]

Since the opening of the Gugu, the rate of occupancy of Bilbao hotels has increased remarkably. In festive periods it has become difficult to find any accommodation in the city – as economic commentators admit, a phenomenon unimaginable before September 1997.[30] With the opening, in 1998 and 1999 respectively, of the Euskalduna in Bilbao and of the Kursaal (an equally grand conference and performing arts centre) in San Sebastian, it was hoped to maintain the rate of increase by the stimulation of 'convention tourism'.[31] Even rural tourism is benefiting, with an observable rise since 1997 in 'agrotourism'.[32]

'Society'

The Museo is also having a direct effect on a certain sector of Bilbao's population. Several commentators have observed that, since its opening, the Gugu has very rapidly become highly fashionable and so, by extension, has the city itself. Regional newspapers note with approval the recent opening of modish boutiques by internationally recognized firms.[33] Some of these shops do not do enough business to justify their presence: they are only there because of the image Bilbao now has.[34] 'Society' gatherings, staged above all in the Museo, but also elsewhere in the city, have suddenly become popular. The inaugural party for a new exhibition, a Basque Government reception, a prestigious firm's launch of its latest product, the pre-debut of an international film: all become the excuse for local gossip columnists to list and comment on the more noteworthy guests whom the event has been able to attract. One enthused journalist thought his catalogue of the prominent at one party so internationally glittering, so stellar, that he ended his piece with 'Bilbao is now in the universe.' [35]

If we follow Duncan's idea that state museums are designed as spaces for the enactment of civic rituals, then the soirées held in the Gugu may be regarded as secular ceremonies enabling and consolidating the formation of

[29] These data come from the KPMG Peat Marwick report on the Museo's first year, quoted in *M* 24 x 1998: B1
[30] *M* 7 xii 1998: 6
[31] *M* 4 i 1999: 3
[32] *M* 22 v 2000, GB supp., p. 3
[33] *M* 14 x 1998: 6; 20 xi 1998: 12; 5 iv 1999: 7; 14 ii 2000, GB supp., p. 1, 3; 26 ii 2000, GB supp., p. 10
[34] *M* 6 iii 2000, GB supp., p. 2
[35] *M* 7 vi 1998: 7. See also *M* 21 vi 1998: 10; 18 vii 1998: 4; 19 vii 1998: 15; 19 x 1998: 10; 4 ii 1999: 9; 21 xi 1999: 8; 22 xi 1999: 6, 7, 56; 23 xi 1999: 14; 16 ii 2000: 27, GB supp., p. 7; 17 ii 2000, GB supp., p. 8; 27 ii 2000, GB supp., p. 7; 30 iii 2000, GB supp., p. 9; 18 iv 2000, GB supp., p. 10

a new Bilbao-based elite.[36] In the late nineteenth century, the rapid indus-trialization of the area had stimulated the rise of a newly enriched elite. Many of these industrialists were ennobled and, in the first decades of this century, patronized the cultural renaissance of the city. But the Civil War, its immediate Franquist aftermath, and the subsequent decline of heavy industry devastated old fortunes and disturbed established hierarchies. Thus this renovated sense of 'Bilbao Society' is an essentially recent phenomenon, one based on the newly grounded elites of hegemonic nationalist politicians, their mandarins, captains of contemporary industries and various creative artists who like to bask under the bright lights. The transition to democracy now effected, the days of constant demonstration and popular calls for radical change now past, these latter-day elitists can afford to parade them-selves (and so be defined) at the Gugu's gala events. Their bid for status, stimulated by the opening of the Gugu, has been strengthened by the opening of the Euskalduna, with a concert hall large enough to stage the operas so beloved by a certain section of affluent *bilbaínos*. The final piece in this socio-architectural scenario will be the construction of a series of high-rise buildings of great luxury and prestige, on the spare land along the riverbank between the Gugu and the Euskalduna. One Bilbao journalist has already proudly compared this future neighbourhood with Marbella's 'Diamond Mile' or London's Belgravia; it is what the new Bilbao 'lacked'.[37]

Within this context of art and architecture being deployed to sharpen social distinctions, it is noteworthy that, within a year of opening, the Gugu already had more 'Friends of the Museum', who are automatically invited to special events there, than either the Prado or the Reina Sofía Museo de Arte Contemporanea, the two leading national art galleries in Madrid. Yet, if the Gugu is to set a novel, *civilizing* standard for a newly re-discovered 'Society', then members of that elite have to behave, and dress, according-ly. The soirées thus become key occasions for the nonchalant parading of a vested sophistication and the nocturnal creation of *glamour* (the English word is used in the local press). This striving for an effortless, but all too evanescent, style by those aspiring to high status is a game of high stakes. For, as some *bilbaínos* are only too well aware, they run the risk of looking like a group of provincials out of place in a world-class building; their attempt at sparkle is outshone by the titanium, their desire to enchant laid bare by the lack of magic. All too easy, in these circumstances, for even the smartest gown to look like the Emperor's New Clothes. (Perhaps it is for this reason that the opening of the Museo has revitalized the local lingerie sector.)[38] In the words of one local commentator, assessing in 1998 the opening party for the Robert Rauschenberg retrospective, 'It is very true that Bilbao society, in order to stage glittering events (to which it should become accustomed) needs information and social recycling. A gala night needs elegance, glamour and even a touch of extravagance. Thanks to the

[36] Duncan 1995
[37] *M* 4 vii 1999: 2
[38] *M* 25 i 2000, GB supp., p. 10

importation of celebrities it was possible to find all these key aspects.'[39] A year later, at another Gugu gala, one society columnist finally felt able to congratulate the self-garlanded: listing the best-dressed women, he pronounced, 'A display of ladies *de couché*, the elegance of a summer Bilbao caught in sultry weather. Bilbao, at last, can show itself off.'[40]

Image, icon, exemplar

The social and cultural stakes set by the rise of the Gugu are high because of what the building represents on a broader scale. For, despite the academic popularity of the 'invention-of-tradition' argument, many ethnic nationalists in Europe are in fact as much concerned with the development of local modernities as with the re-polishing of local pasts.[41] Thus, if the continuing Basque subcultures maintaining Athletic Club de Bilbao or '*el arte vasco*' can be considered processes for the fabrication of Basque modernities, then the rise of the Gugu could be termed the creation of a Basque 'super-modernity'.

What is distinctive, however, about this latest cultural form is that, for the first time ever in their history, Basques are not proclaiming that they are different but still just as modern as others. This time, thanks to the Museo, Basques can proclaim that they are both different and *more modern* than others. And more modern in a way recognized and valued by prestigious others. The examples of Athletic and '*el arte vasco*' showed that Basques were able to fabricate a form of modernity comparable to that already established by foreigners of high status. In contrast, the success of the Gugu shows that they are capable of establishing a new worldwide standard, one highly praised by culturally powerful onlookers and worthy of emulation by them. Thus the Gugu is not just a unique building; it has had a truly innovative impact: turning Basques, on the global scale, from bandwagon-followers to the leading standard-bearers of the new. It might be argued that the 'Basqueness' of the building should be cast in doubt since it was designed by an American. But it could just as easily be counter-argued that it took the vision of leading Basques to commission such a revolutionary architect. The point remains: the idea of the Gugu is not an imitation of others but an exemplar to be imitated by them.

In this sense, the Gugu does indeed appear to be fulfilling its function of changing the external image of Bilbao, with Spanish and foreign journalists alike seeing the building as a major contribution towards the successful establishment, for the city and the Basque Country as a whole, of a new identity: non-terrorist, cultured, creative, modern and cosmopolitan. In late 1998 Gehry, in gratitude for the construction of the building he had designed, commissioned a symphony dedicated to the Basques, to be called 'Atrium', in reference to the inner space of the Museo. Local papers emphasized the fame of the composer (Esa-Pekka Salonen) and the fact that the symphony would

[39] *M* 20 x 1998: 12
[40] *M* 6 vii 1999: 12
[41] On this point see MacClancy 1988, 1996b; Urla 1993

once again turn outsiders' attention to the Basque Country: 'The challenge is . . . to offer something interesting to those who observe us.'[42]

Of course raising the city's external image goes hand in hand with changing its internal one as well. In the words of the Director of the Euskalduna, 'The Guggenheim has stimulated our self-esteem in those things in which we thought ourselves weak.'[43] Local writers echo the sentiment: the building has brought the city's inhabitants 'a good dose of optimism and self-esteem'; thanks to the Gugu, 'we have come to believe the miracle . . . We are the best.'[44]

Much of this re-evaluation is due to the tourist gaze. For, to their great surprise, locals have had to become accustomed to their city, its events, and themselves becoming the objects of visitors' scrutiny.[45] Prior to October 1997, the only postcards available were a miserable clutch of tired city portraits lying almost forgotten in the corners of newsagents' kiosks. Now 'tourist shops' (hitherto unknown) sell a colourful variety of wide-angle and telephoto shots artfully depicting the Gugu, the Euskalduna, and rediscovered 'sites' of the Bilbao townscape. One journalist noted that Bilbao has become 'an open and admirable space which tourists photograph with passion, as if dealing with a recently discovered treasure'. Even *Euskadi Information*, the then daily newspaper of the radical nationalists, did not criticize the coming of tourists but detailed their activity in wondrous terms: a Rolls Royce with foreign number-plates becomes stuck in the narrow streets of the Old Quarter; a horde of American millionaires disembarks from a luxury cruiser. 'What things! What things!' was the radical reporter's only comment.[46]

The building itself has gained, within a remarkably short space of time, iconic status within the Basque Country. It is not simply that government departments include its silhouette in their publicity. Its use is much more widespread and popular than that. In 1998 the annual group photograph of the Athletic squad had the Museo as its backdrop; the next year the annual poster for the city's bullfights backgrounded the Gugu against a bull, with the surfaces of both stylized in the same manner.[47] At the 1998 International Competition of Paellas held in the area, the Gugu and Puppy (the giant dog sculpture at its entrance, see Photo 8.4, p. 177) were two of the four most popular themes for culinary sculptures atop the paellas.[48] Even the term 'Guggenheim' has itself become a phonetic standard, and is used in the rewriting of cliches.[49] Perhaps the most telling example, because

---

[42] *M* 18 xii 1998: 10

[43] *M* 17 ii 1999: 9

[44] *M* 15 x 1999: 2

[45] *M* 10 viii 1999: 19; 22 viii 1999: 9

[46] *M* 15 x 1999: 2

[47] *M* 9 viii 1999: 13

[48] *M* 26 vii 1998: 5. 'Guggenheim' was also the name given to a local designer *pintxo* (Basque bar snack); see *M* 7 vi 2000: 8

[49] *M* 16 x 1999: 7. For an example of a rewritten cliché ('a truth like the Guggenheim' instead of 'a truth like a temple') see *M* 1 vi 1999: 2. The status of the Gugu has also brought with it an unwanted association with terrorist violence. The day before its official inauguration by

8.2 The arrival of the 'Guggenheim Impact' in the main plaza, Cirauqui fiestas, September 1998 (© Jeremy MacClancy)

8.3 The Cirauqui Guggenheim unveiled (© Jeremy MacClancy)

it reveals how '*el efecto "Guggy"*' has reached even the more distant Basque villages, is the following: in 1998, at the annual fiestas of Cirauqui, the small Navarran village where I do my fieldwork, a prize-winning entry in the Competition for Fancy-Dress Performances was 'The Guggenheim Impact'. Watched by a packed crowd, into the village's main plaza wobbled a large silver-sheathed shape with pointy upper edges. As it reached centre-stage, smartly uniformed hostesses toured the crowd, distributing a stylish, explicatory pamphlet. The points of the structure were then slowly lowered, revealing, to the applause of the crowd, nine silver-dressed and silver-painted statues: local women representing Greco-Roman goddesses. According to the pamphlet, 'The titanium-scale lamination of the Guggenheim has created a School. In this festive week we bring you a very special interpretation of the Guggenheim.'

The Museo has also had an international effect. Since its success became apparent, the representatives of more than ninety cities from around the globe have approached the Guggenheim Foundation, to see if it could work with them. Among other places, the Foundation has since established franchises in St Petersburg, Berlin, Las Vegas, and one is planned for Rio de Janeiro.

Critics

Basque reaction to the initial agreement between their government and the Guggenheim Foundation was immediate, and much of it negative. The more enduring criticisms of these sceptical journalists and creative artists (who organized themselves into Kultur Kezka, a some 300-strong anti-Gugu collective) were threefold. First, they queried their government's economic forecasts for the Museo as wildly over-optimistic. They feared the 'pharaonic' pretensions of their elected leaders would end, not as monument to their politicians' aspirations, but – like the pyramids – as a tomb to them. Second, they were deeply angered that the Basque Government was so ready to end subsidies to local cultural activities for the sake of importing prestige projects. As one critic put it, 'The powers that be do not concern themselves with the state of Culture if the Culture is not of the State'.[50] Third, they feared the project as a threatening example of the 'Coca-colonization' of indigenous culture by American forces. To them, the Foundation was hawking its prestige like a common brand-name and dealing with the pictures in its collection as though they were stock in an ordinary financial market. In the eyes of the critics, art was special and was to be treated as such.[51]

---

[49] (cont.) the King of Spain, Juan Carlos I, a local policeman was shot dead when he surprised two ETA gunmen laying bombs in the flower-pots of the Museo's esplanade. The area has now been named after him; a ceremony of remembrance was held there on the first anniversary of his slaying (M 14 x 1998; 12 v 1999: 20).

[50] Araluze 1992

[51] For further details of the early critics' position and of American criticism of the Foundation's approach, see MacClancy 1997: 93–5. In a reply to Basque critics who viewed the Museo

Despite the trumpeting of the Museo's subsequent success and the emergence of its broad range of effects, many former critics remain unconvinced while a number of new ones have come on board. For expository convenience I group their criticisms into two main headings: the Guggenheim as neo-Disney and the building itself as the main piece of art on display.

Gugu/Disney

Some local commentators question people's use of the Gugu. They have observed that few visitors concentrate on the pictures and objects exhibited, the great majority just choosing to stroll through, and pleasure in, the interior of this complex building. Others have spoken of people queueing for an exhibition of an artist whom they don't understand, and of visitors astonished by the walls and the space but walking past, as though on tiptoes, the works exhibited. It is revealing that even by 2000, the presence of the Museo did not appear to have boosted sales in the local contemporary art galleries.[52] One commentator has spoken of 'the ritualization of taste for the Museo' where some people feel almost obliged to visit the building for social or architectural rather than artistic reasons, and against which they pose to be photographed.[53] For this group of visitors, the common local phrase 'the cathedral of titanium' is not a mere metaphor for the Museo but the designation of a mysterious reality, promising access to higher values, to be respected, and tiptoed through.

Other critics have taken a somewhat different tack. Instead of wondering whether some of its visitors regard the Museo as a new kind of sacred space, they find a comparison of the Gugu with Disney far more telling and they worry that the new museum is more theme park than cultural centre.[54] As one visitor complained,

> This is like Disneyland. You can't enjoy the works exhibited because immediately you are pushed by a group of pensioners or the typical Anglosaxon tourist with sandals and the skin of a crab. This museum has turned into just another tourist attraction. One sees pictures or works of art in the same way that one would visit a souvenir shop in Salamanca.[55]

There is much to recommend this identificiation, for if we follow Bryman's analysis of Disney, many suggestive parallels between the entertainment corporation and the Gugu quickly become evident.[56] Like the Disney parks, though not quite to the same degree, the Museo represents a holistic

---

[51] (cont.) as a form of 'Coca-colonization', the Director of the Bilbao Museo de Bellas Artes, Javier Viar, has pointed out that in fact the influence of American styles was already evident in the 1950s and '60s in the work, for example, of Oteiza and Chillida (Viar 2004).
[52] *M* 18 i 2000, GB supp., p. 2
[53] Goméz Nazabal 1998; *M* 24 xi 1998: 10; 4 iii 1999: 20
[54] *M* 26 iii 1999: 20
[55] *M* 13 v 1998: 4
[56] Bryman 1999. See also Alofsin 2001

approach to urban planning.[57] Furthermore, in both the parks and the Museo, there is a clear breach between production and consumption, achieved by visually removing all hint of production. In both, 'it is only residents' capacity to consume that is viewed as in any sense significant or important'. Some local critics are well aware of all this. The Basque painter Fernando Illana, for example, disparaged the project because it sanctioned consumption over production, turning potentially active producers into passive clients. It is revealing that the Gugu has as yet no plans to exhibit the work of such major artists as Marcel Broodthaers or Hans Haacke, both of whom have striven to lay bare the social and material conditions of art's production, the very conditions 'that it has been the museum's function to dissemble'.[58] Just as Disneyland presents an unthreatening and sanitized vision of other cultures in particular and of the world in general, so the Museo puts forward a safe and relatively uncontroversial view of twentieth-century art. Its staff wish to entertain, maybe even to educate, its visitors; they are not attempting to make them ask searching questions about art, its modes of production, its places in society.[59]

Both Disney and the Gugu also exemplify the tendency towards 'the dedifferentiation of consumption' whereby the separable activities of shopping, eating and park/museum visiting become inextricably interwoven. The prize-winning restaurant of the Museo is prominently sited and usually full; its cafeteria has become a place to meet; the Museo's quarterly *Guia* ('Guide') advertises the impressive range of goods and gifts, 'in which design and quality of material come first', offered by the Museo shop (so large it is on two levels). Fjellman has observed that the merchandise associated with the Disney films has become part of 'an endless round of self-referential co-advertisments'.[60] One can see something of the same process in the Museo bookstore where the bestselling postcard is not a reproduction of a famous painting but a photograph of the building itself. Similarly, during the Rauschenberg retrospective, one well-displayed picture (commissioned by the Museo and now part of its permanent collection) was *Bilbao Scraps 1997*; its main components were vegetable-dye transfers of images of the building. And, perhaps most revealingly, in the spring of 2000 the Art Institute of Chicago staged an exhibition on the 'Gugu effect' in Bilbao. In other words, widening the closed circle of self-reference, this American art museum has chosen to mount an exhibition, not about art, but about another art museum. At this rate, it could easily be argued that what some visitors are buying when they pay for their ticket is not so much a

[57] The distinguished art critic and historian John Richardson has criticized Gehry for his 'establishment of potentially lucrative links (shades of Disneyworld) with hotel and tourist interests' (Richardson 1992: 22).

[58] Crimp 1993: 287. It is of course possible to argue, drawing on modern work in consumer studies, that the passivity of consumers is here being greatly exaggerated. Whether or not we would wish to accept this argument, the main point still strongly holds: that the processes underlying and structuring visitors' experiences of both Disneyland and the Gugu are remarkably similar in a variety of dimensions.

[59] See the criticism of the painter José Ibarrola, son of Agustín, M 8 ii 2000, GB supp., p. 7

[60] Fjellman 1992

8.4 Tourists being photographed against the backdrop of 'Puppy', 2001

(© Jeremy MacClancy)

culturally enriching occasion, rather 'the Guggenheim Experience'. What they are purchasing is more the sign value of the goods and their connection to ideas of a cultivated life-style and a rounded personal identity. The danger in all this process is, as one wag put it, 'If Gugu is Disney, are all we visitors Mickey Mouse?'

Like Disney to a certain extent, the Gugu now has its own emblematic, rather jokey animal: '*Puppy*'. This ten-metre high, terrier-shaped sculpture, completely covered with flowering plants and created by the American artist Jeff Koons, is strategically placed between the Museo's entrance and the road which runs by it. It has very quickly became a popular favorite: many visitors choose to be photographed alongside it, local children make models of it in art classes, its biannual replanting is given prominent treatment in the regional press. The mutt is now also the butt of jokes. For example: on first sighting it, a tourist gasps; the local standing next to him says, 'You think that impressive? Look at its kennel.' The joke might be weak but its point is strong. This 'very silly but very funny' sculpture serves as an imposing yet unthreatening introduction to the art within the doghouse.[61] Just like a Disney creation, it is meant to charm potential customers, not to scare them away. And, just like so many Disney creations, it seems to be a great success.

A further mode common to the Gugu and Disney parks is their equal reliance on the spectacular as a hook to draw punters in, where both the buildings themselves and what they do are meant to be gawped at. It is not by chance that Gehry has designed buildings for both the Guggenheim Foundation and the Disney Corporation. While the production of spectacle for the primary sake of profit has been a relatively uncontroversial success for a commercial organization such as Disney, its exploitation by the Guggenheim Foundation, whose original aim was to edify, has proved far more polemical. Some Basque critics have seen the Gugu as an all too good exemplar of this economically motivated 'culture of spectacle'. To them, the Museo appears part of *el negocio del ocio* (the business of pleasure), where culture is treated not as source of creativity and dynamism, but as a profitable commodity meant to lend tone and lustre to its commodifier, the Basque Government. It is important here to remember just what the spectacular scale of the Gugu enables. As Gehry boasted,

> The galleries give the opportunity to have three blockbuster shows on a big scale at once. You could have Serra, Rosenquist and Baselitz inside the building, a giant retrospective of each, concurrent in that museum, and I can't think of any other museum in the world where you can do that.

Staging blockbuster exhibitions in the Museo might keep numbers up but it does not satisfy the sceptical. Thus, one called the Gugu 'a circus' where the spectacular predominated, while Hilton Kramer has complained that the Guggenheim's production of spectacle goes hand in hand with a drop in the level of public discourse about art.[62] The director of the Pompidou Centre in Paris openly railed against what he called the 'guggenheimization of culture': particularly over-reliance on patrons, who only help fund spectacular exhibitions and fail to assist those for less well-known artists. Many of these patrons, he pointed out, are linked to the world of fashion: 'the sale of perfume and such things. Something passing which contrasts with the concept of a museum to look after things eternally.'[63] To all these critics, spectacle is suspect and Mickey Mouse not even in the picture. Better to hold fast to traditional methods of display.

Container vs. contained

Bertrand Russell liked to exemplify his Theory of Logical Types by asking whether the complete catalogue to a library included a reference to itself. Something like the same categorical confusion occurs with the Gugu. For, unlike most other museums which stage blockbuster exhibitions, the Gugu generates a sense of spectacle as much because of the building as because

[61] The quote comes from Glancey 1997: 61
[62] Kramer 1992: 7
[63] M 3 x 1998: 53

of what it shows. The obvious question here is whether the building itself is the best piece of art it puts on display.

There is no doubt the Museo is widely recognized as an outstanding architectural work of art, a marvel of engineering. Depending on the architectural critic one chooses, the Gugu can be classed as 'postmodernist', 'deconstructivist' or 'cosmogenic'. The idea of Gehry, influenced by celebrated contemporary artists, many of whom are his personal friends, was to break down barriers, and stimulate dialogues, between architecture and art, and architecture and the people. He said he did not want to put up a cold and intimidating building, but a populist, non-elitist one: 'I want people to go along and feel part of it.'[64] Thus his building does away with the conventional notion of a museum as a large box, composed of smaller boxes organized in a hierarchic manner. Instead its structure relies on skewed, irregular geometries. There is a variety of internal spaces, many of which flow into and out of one another yet which, together, cohere as a unified whole. There are different sorts of rooms for art of different scales and only some conform to the 'white cubes' so beloved of modernist art galleries. Gehry wanted to provide the new kinds of space needed for the newer, sometimes enormous kinds of art produced by his contemporaries. The most striking example of this is the Gugu's 'Fish' gallery: longer than a football pitch, it can contain not one, but several oversize pieces of sculpture.[65] No commentator has doubted how visually striking the Museo is, but many have gone on to argue that the building is in fact so visually powerful that it competes for attention with the objects exhibited, a competition the objects often lose. The official audio-guide only reinforces this tendency: its forty-minute tour of the architecture does not guide listeners to a single work of art, other than the Museo itself. That the architectural style of a museum building is an integral part of the museum itself is nothing new. Let us take two unexceptional examples. The Oxford University Museum of Natural History, built in the 1850s, is a celebration of the Neo-Gothic, structured throughout with decorative art 'conveying truthful statements about natural facts'; its walls are literally part of the lessons visiting students were meant to learn.[66] The Horniman Museum of Ethnographica, London, opened in 1901, was constructed in the then avant-garde Arts and Crafts style in order to provoke thoughtful comparison between the *fin de*

[64] Quoted in Tellitu, Esteban and González 1997: 182. For critiques of Gehry's claim to have produced a democratic architecture, see Alofsin 2001, Foster 2001.
[65] The building may be revolutionary and highly popular but not all are swayed. Some think it more pretty than radical and pandering to impoverished tastes. While many observers have likened it to a 'metal flower', as evocative of sailing ships or a fish, Guipuzcoan intellectual Alvaro Bermejo belittled it as 'chocolate box', Oteiza damned it as a 'cheese factory', and leading Basque critic Jon Juaristi compared it to 'a gigantic soufflé deflating over the river' (Juaristi 1997: 36; *M* 19 x 1998: 10). Leading Spanish architect Luis Peña Ganchegui has classed the Gugu as an example of an architectural style which comes from the culture of camp (a style influenced by kitsch and pop), because it is based on increasing and varying the scale and context of things in order to attract attention. In his words, 'The Museo ... is kitsch, but it is produced by a dandy, hence its richness. Gehry is the Oscar Wilde of architecture'(*M* 7 iii 1999: 68). For further criticisms, see *M* Universitaria Vasco y Educacíon (UVE) supplement 18 viii 1999: 4
[66] Haward 1991

siècle modernism of the building and its non-Western exhibits.[67] But in both these cases the architecture of the container, unlike that of the Gugu, was intended to gently complement and contrast the contents, not to vie aggressively for visitors' attention.

In this sense the Gugu is identical to its New York counterpart, whose wondrous architectural style has long been attacked for impeding the view of its contents. Thomas Krens is well aware of the tension: 'My objective is to make the building take second stage to what we put in it, and I think we're going to come very close to that. The perfect thing would be to come very close to that. Meanwhile you work towards that.' Artists whose works are displayed in the Museo are just as conscious of the problem. The American sculptor Richard Serra, commissioned to make a particularly large piece for the 'Fish' gallery, stated frankly that his intention was to compete with, and to eclipse, the building itself: 'And I believe, sincerely, that I have achieved that. I wanted people to pay attention to the objects exhibited, not to the building. Now the protagonists are the sculptures, not the gallery – a space capable of consuming and converting into a simple object everything exhibited there.'[68]

The price paid for creating a spectacle is not just aesthetic. Gehry had wanted the atrium to have flat walls in order to be able to hang paintings more easily. Krens, who imposed his will, wanted the walls to lean, so as to create a greater effect.[69] In 2003, however, one of the leaning large glass panels in the atrium fell in, narrowly missing a visitor. It then transpired it was known this was likely to happen; the risk had been calculated, and thought worth running.[70]

Some critics have also been very taken aback by the dramatically varied uses to which the building is being put. It is as though commercial exploitation of this prestigious site affronts their notion of what a museum is and should be doing, as though renting out the atrium to a perfume-manufacturer or *haute couturier* prostituted its edifying ideals. One critic complained that the outside companies which hired the Gugu for its shows were treating the Museo like a 'duty-free zone', which happened to be in the Basque Country.[71] In the words of another: 'Soon some rich kid will hold his birthday party there. In time. Money is money.'[72] One cartoon in a local newspaper showed a rural Basque male complaining, 'Museum?!! Anyone would say the pictures are mere decorative elements on the walls of a gigantic cultural "whorehouse".'

[67] Teague 1993
[68] *M* 26 iii 1999: 9. A local art critic, Pedro Txillida (1999) assessing the Chillida retrospective there stated that it had managed 'to make a spectacular museum as unspectacular as possible on the basis of making it almost disappear. In principle, it does not seem to me logical that the container should compete with the contained, but in this case it is resolved in an extremely brilliant manner.'
[69] Gilbert-Rolfe 2004
[70] Rodríguez 2004
[71] *M* 18 ii 2000: 6
[72] *M* 12 x 1998: 4

Some think the revival of Bilbao is already so radical that they can now afford to be nostalgic for what has been lost. These critics liked the dirt, the rust, the hard edge to the city. They mistrust what they see as the false glamour of the shiny, and they disparage the rise of a Basque version of the 'beautiful people' (the English phrase is used in the local press).[73] They are also very well aware that the coming of the Guggenheim to Bilbao has not (or not yet) benefited all sectors of local society. If anything, the plight of the poorest has been made worse because they are being forced to live within sight of a conspicuous, flaunted affluence.[74]

Some critics continue to complain that the subsidies for the Gugu prevent the Basque Government from stimulating local cultural initiatives, and that the Gugu itself has yet to fulfill some of its important original functions. Two years after its opening, critics could pointedly remark that the Museo still lacked the solid establishment of its own collection and its own programme of artistic activities. By the end of 1998, only two shows had been held there which even featured the work of Basque artitsts. Even at the time of writing (2007), the Museo's series of exhibitions continues to be managed from New York; an Artistic Director for the Museo has yet to be appointed. It is true that the Gugu has bought the work of a few Basque artists. But, with the exception of Chillida and belatedly of Oteiza, all of those artists lived in New York and, as one complained, the money he had been paid for his works was 'pocket change'. For these reasons, critics of the project feel their charge of 'American imperialism' still sticks.[75]

Not surprising, then, that in his futurist satire on regional life *Si Sabino viviría*, the local academic Iban Zaldua portrays the Guggenheim as an American military outpost, heavily defended against attacks from the wild characters left inhabiting the devastated remains of the Basque Country.[76]

Of cultural identities, economics and the nature of art

I would like to conclude this chapter by looking a little more closely at the coherence and power of the central arguments employed by the protagonists of both sides. For doing so may reveal just how stubbornly traditionalist is the ideology of the artists (supposed leaders of the avant-garde) and just how radical the programme of the political conservatives who supported the project.

Cultural identities

The PNV has been the major party in all the coalitions which have formed the successive Basque Governments since the death of Franco. Firmly

---

[73] *M* 13 i 2000, VA supp., p. 6; 12 v 2000, GB supp., p. 16
[74] *M* 18 ii 2000, GB supp., p. 9; 5 iii 2000, GB supp., p. 2
[75] It is revealing that, ever since its opening, the argument that the Museo would benefit the work of most Basque artists has not even been mentioned by any of its promoters or supporters. The 'pocket change' quote comes from Zulaika 2004.
[76] Zaldua 2005

situated on the centre-right, it was one of the founders of the European Christian Democratic Movement. While its nationalist claims may at times move towards the radical, its social and economic policies never stray into the left. As card-carrying nationalists, its members constantly strive to stimulate and reinforce Basque identity. Given that critics claimed the Gugu would 'entomb' or do 'great damage to our own culture',[77] it is at first glance paradoxical that the impetus for the project came exclusively from the Party's deputies and representatives.

The paradox is only apparent, as the Party's politicians are merely upholding the evaluation of aesthetics propounded by Sabino Arana: art was only important to the extent it could be put to nationalist ends.[78] Similarly, the PNV only backed the Gugu project, not because they were bedazzled by the art, but because they could foresee some of its benefits for Basque society. The key difference between the contemporary PNV and that of Arana's time is that Arana had a narrowly racist and essentially backward-looking ideology aimed at retaining the prominence of Basques within their homeland, against the changes caused by the massive influx of non-Basque migrants seeking jobs in the new industries. In marked contrast, his Party has today a much more broadly based vision of nationalism.

Both the PNV and radical nationalists are concerned to generate locally a Basque cultural plurality. Thus, as well as subsidising marked aspects of 'customary' Basque culture (improvisational troubadours, Basque folk music and dance groups, Basque rural sports, etc.) the PNV, with the tacit support of its radical counterparts, at the same time promotes an essentially urban-based culture which looks to the innovation of recent decades and the present as much as to the traditions of the pre-industrial past. Examples here would include modern Basque musics, 'Eusko-rap', and urban bobsleigh races. However, while the radical nationalists direct almost all their cultural efforts towards encouraging and publicizing locally based, popular initiatives (especially ones which appeal to their predominantly younger share of the electorate), unlike the PNV they are not prepared to support 'top-down' initiatives, particularly ones such as the Gugu which involve paying outsiders to enter the country, bringing their work with them. To them, the idea of a high cultural project such as the Museo runs too strongly counter to their ideology of Basque socialism. Quite simply, it is too foreign, insufficiently 'bottom-up' for their political beliefs.

In sharp contrast, PNV politicians regard the Museo as a way for Basques to transcend the geographical restrictiveness of the present form of their ethnic identity, by producing an emblematic building which, to be appreciated appropriately, needs to be compared with others *outside* the Basqueland. To them the project demonstrates that Bilbao is not closed in upon itself but open to international currents, as the Museo is an integral part of a transatlantic axis, linked to New York and Venice, the homes of the two

[77] M 24 I 1992
[78] On Arana's ideas about art see the previous chapter.

oldest Guggenheim Museums. As two leading members of the PNV have stated, the project is a way of overcoming 'our smallness, our provincialism, the sadness of our reality, and the narrowness of our horizons'; it is to be a 'means of augmenting the values of plurality, tolerance and openness'.[79] These politicians do not want to support a decaying Basque society, where 'culture' is defined in purely populist terms, but a prosperous Basque Country, where the encounter between an imported initiative and local ways may stimulate and revitalize Basque culture in new, perhaps unexpected manners. Unlike their political opponents within the radical camp, they want to foment an open-ended Basque society where the local intermeshes with the global, the high with the low, and the modern with the antique. Krens is emphatic on this point: 'When the Basque authorities put themselves in contact with me, I asked, precisely, that if cultural identity were so important, why bring the Guggenheim, and they explained to me that they needed a challenge'.[80]

At the same time, Krens has tried to play down the charge of 'American imperialism' by emphasizing that the Guggenheim Foundation wants 'to encourage interchange'. He wishes to portray it as an international organization of co-ordinating museums, as (in his own phrase) 'a United Nations of art': 'The nineteenth-century model of the museum as a closed encyclopaedia is an idea of the past . . . I don't believe there is a confrontation of America against Spain. That is an argument based on a concept of the museum from the last century.'[81] Krens's conception of a transcontinental, decentralized art foundation dovetails neatly with the Basque Government's idea of strengthening overseas connections and introducing its citizenry to a broader range of interests. If this is 'American imperialism' then it is of a kind which does not perturb PNV politicians.[82]

---

[79] Laskurain 1991; Arregi 1992

[80] M 18 x 1998: 3. The exploitation of the Abandoibarra site itself can also be put to nationalistic ends: built over a former Carlist graveyard, it can be seen to symbolize the final victory of nationalism (Ros 2002). Also, the site was within the former pueblo of Abando which, because of expanding industrialization, was incorporated into Bilbao. Since the father of Sabino Arana was mayor of Abando and since the PNV was so antagonistic to industrialization, placing the Museo there could be viewed as the ultimate revenge of Basque nationalism (K. Fernández de Larrinoa, pers. comm.)

[81] M 18 x 1998: 3. Krens has stated that not all its exhibitions will originate in New York and then be exported to its overseas franchises; some will originate, for example, in Bilbao and then travel to New York. He has also questioned the idea of the New York branch 'owning' visiting exhibitions; some visiting shows will go directly to Bilbao, and not end up there after first being shown in New York.

[82] When a critic of the project suggested that 'Bilbao' come before 'Guggenheim' in the name of the museum, the member of the Basque Government responsible for Culture smartly replied, 'None of that. We have bought the Coca-Cola brandname, which is going to be a bigger attraction than Basqueness and we want it seen clearly that it is Coca-Cola and not Eusko-Cola or something like that' (quoted in Tellitu, Esteban and González 1997: 23).

Also, Krens might have a vision but the economic dimensions of his policies have lost much of their lustre: of the two Guggenheim branches he opened in Las Vegas in 2001, one had to close within 18 months; the planned massive Gehry-designed branch to be built along the Hudson River in New York has had to be cancelled, and the Soho branch he created early in his tenure has had to close its doors.

Economics

The idea of the Museo might be attractively challenging to the PNV but it is still possible to worry whether members of the Party, in their rush to reinvigorate Bilbao, have not blinded themselves by the brightness of their civic vision. For there are two main arguments against their dream of the revitalized city.

First, the economic grounds for the project are not quite as firm as they would like to proclaim. The idea that boosting the arts persuades businesses to relocate is not in fact borne out by studies of how and why firms choose to site their offices and factories. Furthermore, according to the 'economics of agglomeration', the co-residence in large cities of a significant number and varied range of high cultural producers has synergistic effects.[83] But this logic only makes much sense for metropoli the size of London; its relevance for a city the size of Bilbao, with just over a million inhabitants, is much less clear.

Since its opening, it is true, many have visited the Museo; many have visited other Basque museums as well; hotels are regularly full. But there are no reports from the Basque Government about any further economic consequences of the Gugu. Basque politicians might like to boast of the number of jobs the Museo has helped to maintain (4,547 in 2003) but they tend not to talk about the kinds of jobs on that list. Within the Museo itself, the tours are given by freelancers, the information staff are student interns, the security guards are sub-contracted, and those who prepare the exhibitions are hired for only one show at a time.[84] As one curator complained, 'We are told what to do by emails. Yet our salaries are low given our qualifications.'[85] This is an economic universe where terms such as 'casualization' and 'flexibilization' loom large, and short-term contracts appear to be the order of the day. Furthermore, the Museo does not appear to have fulfilled its promise of helping to establish the city as an European centre for service industries and high-technology companies. Even the boost it gave to an emerging 'museum mode of production' has failed to convince all. The proposal in December 1998 by the local branch of Partido Popular (the then ruling party of national government) to revitalize the Left Bank of the Bilbao estuary, home of decaying heavy industry, by creating a 'Museum of the Iron and Steel Industry', was greeted as a joke in bad taste, especially given the high level of the jobless in the area.[86] In sum, the Gugu is a great popular success, but the broader commercial consequences of that success remain to be realized.

Secondly, economic development, to be effective, needs to be co-ordinated centrally. If not, the economic development of one area brings in its train the decline of another. On top of that, if the bid of one city to shine by erect-

---

[83] Heilbrun and Gray 1993: 302–23
[84] Fraser 2004
[85] Camara 2004
[86] *M* 11 xii 1998: 2, 4

ing an emblematic building is quickly imitated by others, any possibility of co-ordination is replaced by a spiral of expensive competition, of ultimate benefit only to architects and construction companies. It is indicative that the threatening examples of the Gugu and the Euskalduna led the municipal authorities of neighbouring San Sebastian to help fund the building of the Kursaal, the visually daring convention centre designed by the renowned, Navarran architect Rafael Moneo, even though the city hall was already deeply in debt.[87] In October 1999, in Vitoria, the third city of the Basque Country, the newly elected city government proposed, at great cost, to throw out the already well-advanced plans for a new museum of art and to replace it with a much more striking, much more innovative building, *in order* to rival the Gugu.[88] Exactly the same game was being played beyond the Basque Country. For instance the Valencian Government commissioned an enormous, futuristic 'City of Arts and Sciences', designed by one of the architects involved in the Bilbao project, Santiago Calatrava, and which, in the words of one commentator, would make the Gugu look like just 'an ice cream stall'.[89] If the end-result of this tournament of civic rivalry is that every major Spanish city has its own emblematic building dedicated to *el negocio del ocio*, then the Museo Guggenheim will end up as no longer distinctive, merely as one (albeit a very good one) of a nation-wide urban series.

Art/money

Two questions which have run throughout the debate over the Gugu are the nature of art and how it is to be understood. Both Basque sceptics and American art critics have censured the Foundation for its policy of franchising because, in their eyes, it amounts to 'an almost total rejection of the traditional museum as a fixed place where art is collected and preserved and studied'. Criticizing Krens's idea of a 'galaxy of museums', Hilton Kramer has argued that,

> The collection . . . is now downgraded to the status of support system – a circulating 'asset' to be exploited and deployed and, when convenient, depleted through deaccessioning. No longer considered a cultural treasure in its own right, it is to be put at the disposal of the accelerating requirements of the new 'galaxy' and the director's acquisitory appetite.[90]

To him, Krens's influential role in the museum world manifests the degree to which 'the marketing mentality' has triumphed in the museum profession. Comments such as Kramer's expose artists' and art critics' urge to regard economics as alien to the cultural domain of great paintings. They

[87] For the opinions of the mayor of San Sebastian on the economic-cultural 'battle' between his city and the Gugu (and all it represents), see *M* 5 vi 1999: 18. For further information on the Kursaal, see the special '*Kursaal*' edition of the *Documentos* supplement of *M* 2 vi 1999
[88] *M* 20 x 1999: 6; 21 x 1999: 14; 24 x 1999: 10; 26 x 1999: 2, 8; 27 x 1999: 4–5; 28 iii 1999: 3
[89] Barnatan 1998
[90] Kramer 1992: 4

wish to help create a sharply bounded social space where art is produced autonomously and is impervious to assessment in anything other than purely (supposedly timeless) aesthetic terms. They want, in other words, for art to retain its aura, its supposedly original aura.

Despite these protestations to exclude economics from art, work by art historians consistently demonstrates that many artists have been, or are, well aware of the financial workings of artworlds and how to increase their own share of it. As Jean Gimpel, who ran his family's famed art-dealership for many years, put it:

> Artists have a reputation for detachment from the goods of this world. They profess not to be interested in money. For the most part this is humbug. As soon as contemporary painters achieve success, past promises and debts of gratitude seem to have no further currency. They will abandon overnight, for a better contract, dealers who have served their course over many years. The dealers who drive the hardest bargains are often the artists themselves. This behaviour results from their firm conviction of belonging to a superior order of beings. They look upon themselves as the high priests or demi-gods of art. They are not accountable to simple mortals.[91]

It is relatively easy, using the works of art historians, to compile a long historical list of artists acutely conscious of the mechanisms of the market.[92] For example, Rembrandt (and Italian artists of the same period) would bid up their pictures at auction to maintain their value; Renoir thought there only one indicator of the value of paintings: the sale-room; Picasso was almost as good at selling his pictures as he was at painting them.[93]

Artists might strive for autonomy, but they have still to enter the appropriate networks in order to sell their paintings. Studies by historians and sociologists have repeatedly shown that the artworlds and art markets of Western Europe and North America are best viewed as complex arenas in which a variety of participants (academicians, artists, curators, collectors, critics, historians, dealers, etc.) struggle to control the definition, appreciation and evalution of works of art.[94] Despite artists' claims to the uniqueness of their products, this market is, in economic terms, a relatively standard, competitive one, where price is determined mainly by supply and demand.[95] At least from the seventeenth century on, dealers and collectors have consistently played the market, treating it as but another form of speculative investment.[96]

[91] Gimpel 1991: 3
[92] Watson 1992: xxiv
[93] Haskell 1980: 17; Alpers 1988; Renoir quote from Duret-Robert 1977: 249
[94] E.g., Green 1987; Moulin 1987; Marquis 1991; Bourdieu 1993, 1996; Fitzgerald 1995; Plattner 1996; Brewer 1997; Cowen 1998: 83–128. The Basque art historian González de Durana's fictional work (1992) suggests that the Basque artworld and art market is just as constituted by greed, mendacity and double-dealing as its larger counterparts in London and New York.
[95] Frey and Pommerehne 1989
[96] In 1675 the Paris market was so buoyant that one aristocrat could write to a friend, 'Pictures are as good as gold bars, there has never been a better investment. You will always get double for them if you want to sell.' In the late eighteenth century Diderot wrote indignant articles about the way nobles and bourgeoisie were exploiting arists and speculating in works of art. Zola in his novel *L'Oeuvre* showed how in the Paris of the 1880s pictures, especially

Dealers do not just sell paintings, they may also participate (sometimes very actively) in the creation of styles in order to sell their paintings. Indeed much of the history of art is more the history of successful dealers than of visionary artists. Our understandings of Impressionism, Post-Impressionism, Cubism and postwar American art would be very different if it had not been for the astute interventions into the market of, respectively, Paul Durand-Ruel, Paul Rosenberg, Ambroise Vollard, Daniel-Henry Kahnweiler and Leo Castelli. Crane argues that so many new styles of art (Abstract Expressionism, Pop, Minimalism, Photorealism, Figurative) proliferated in New York in the postwar decades because, in a highly competitive and expanding market, different galleries established niches with each promoting a particular style. Without the continual opening of new galleries, she contends, the history of these styles would have been substantially different.[97] This handling of art as but another marketable item is, moreover, a common worldwide strategy, one not limited to developed Western economies. Many societies throughout the globe treat art as a commodity which can be bought and sold like any other.[98]

Artists may wish to exclude economics from art but others have been happy to celebrate their conjunction. Reitlinger, in his economic history of taste, argues that the 'peculiar fascination' in the price of pictures has existed since the early sixteenth century and that by the middle of the eighteenth century art prices had the same interest for a certain section of the educated public as they do today.[99] There is a major tension at play here. Some openly delight in the high value of famed paintings, yet others (dedicated art lovers and art critics) remain vehemently opposed to the monetary ranking of art.[100] In the words of Frey and Pommerehne, 'While the international art market may function efficiently and relative quantities may systematically react to changes in relative prices in the way predicted by economic theory, people resent the operation of the market. The market is considered a public bad in the case of art.'[101] This tension remains unresolved.

If the point of this brief excursus into the history and nature of the Western art market has been to show that art can be easily regarded and

---

[96] (cont.) ones by Impressionists, were looked upon in stock-market terms, with bankers intervening at critical moments in order to maintain the elevated pricing of the paintings (Gimpel 1991: 75, 81, 122–3, 144–5). Pisarro complained that collectors only regarded paintings like shares: 'It is disgusting to be part of such a degenerate business' (Pisarro 1925: 39).

[97] Crane 1987: 110–18

[98] Becker 1982: 167

[99] Reitlinger 1961: ix. Popular relish in art auctions is evidenced by the following quote, from an English periodical of the late 1880s: 'The moment the picture comes upon the easel it is received with loud clapping of hands, repeated as often as the bidders outvie one another in their advances of perhaps a thousand guineas, and when the hammer falls at last for a lumping sum, there is a perfect uproar, just as the crowd roars its delight when the Derby is run, for the Christie audience revels in high prices simply for money's sake, though of course some of the applause is meant for the picture' (*The Graphic* 10 ix 1887, quoted in Reitlinger 1961: frontispiece).

[100] See, for example, 'The Anti-Market Mentality' in Grampp 1989: 24–8

[101] Frey and Pommerehne 1989: 126

studied as merely another commodity, it has also served to underline its residual distinctiveness: the *claims* made by some artists, art critics and art lovers that economics should be alien to art. These claims ultimately derive from the official academies of art and agencies of state patronage which emerged in the later seventeenth and eighteenth centuries, and which regarded worldliness in artists 'as detrimental to the standing of the profession'.[102] There is good reason for the continued existence of these claims. Though the interests of players in the art market may diverge (there is, for instance, usually a great degree of mutual mistrust between artists and dealers), most have sufficient in common to collaborate in the maintenance of a mystifying ideology separating art from other forms of economic activity.[103] For instance the supposedly original 'aura', whose loss Walter Benjamin prematurely lamented in the 1920s, has a much, much later origin than the Neolithic date which some have tried to give it. As a quick perusal of any critical review of rock art will show, as far as we can judge, prehistoric painters had a host of other priorities than the production of a postulated 'aura'.[104] 'Aura' should be seen as a modern idea, produced to differentiate artists from others, and which has been given a bogus antiquity to mask its modernity. Among other functions, artists' mystifying ideology serves to legitimate and bolster their own positions within this culturally prestigious sphere of activity. To use Bourdieu's terms,[105] they seek to retain the cultural capital on which their status rests and so resist strongly any easy conversion of that into economic capital. To maintain their privileged rank within society, they wish to see maintained the fictive separation of these spheres.

For these reasons, it is difficult not to see the comments by critics of the Gugu about the culture of spectacle as special pleading, as claims by hegemons to maintain supremacy, to retain their particular vision of art and of its display, and to shore up the elitist nature of their own positions. For though some people may be drawn in by the sense of spectacle that does not mean they are necessarily impervious to the power of the paintings. Just because very large numbers attend blockbuster exhibitions that does not mean they are all sheep. Some might come for the spectacle but stay, or come back, for the art. At times it is hard not to think that what these critics are in fact crabbing is the threatened popularization of their hitherto select pursuit.[106]

---

[102] Fitzgerald 1995: 6

[103] Becker 1982: 117, 167. In a similar vein, Jensen (2002) argues for an expressive view of art rather than an instrumental one, which tends all too easily to defend the positions of the art elite.

[104] See, for example, Bahn 1998

[105] Bourdieu 1977

[106] The arguments employed by critics of the Gugu also rely on the common conceptions of money as inherently subversive of the moral economy, and of commoditization as a singular, irrevocable process. On the highly cultural specificity of these notions and their lack of applicability outside modern Western contexts, see MacClancy 1997.

The Gugu stands for many things. To its supporters, it represents an open-ended cultural plurality, economic revitalization, a refiguring of the social landscape, a creative recategorization of 'art' and 'museum'. To its opponents, it is a top-down imposition, a threatening importation from an over-powerful nation, a dangerous blurring of the lines between art and economics, and between art and entertainment.

Perhaps that last point is the most suggestive one, for while the brash commercialism of Disney may appear much more muted in the Gugu, the fact that broadly similar principles are involved in the running of both the corporation and the franchise museum is almost indisputable. Moreover, in their own times, both have been new products for new contexts: contexts they have helped to create. Thus if Disney can be seen as one of the brightest icons of global capitalism in the late twentieth century, could the Gugu be regarded as the herald for a redrawn sense of 'culture' in the coming millennium? What price a people's palace?

There is no neat end to a discussion of this nature, no tidy conclusion tying together its various threads. There is no foreseeable end to the continuing debate on the Museo. In fact, it is easy to argue that this is the way things should be: a national museum serving as a permanent site of open discourse, as both a source of high cultural satisfaction and a stimulus to constant discussion on what it is and should be doing. At this rate the erection of the Museo Guggenheim Bilbao may act as a greater jolt to the culture and identity of the Basque Country than either its politicians or its artists imagined.

No End

Our partial survey done we can ask, to what effect? What light can a fieldwork-grounded anthropology shed on contemporary nationalisms?

The first point should have been repeatedly demonstrated to all those who have read the text, rather than skipped straight to this endnote, i.e. that we impoverish our understanding of nationalism if we are not prepared to study its lived reality. If one definition of anthropology is to take people seriously, then it behoves us to listen to what locals are saying and to attend to what they are doing. After all, the much-vaunted strength of social anthropology is to learn, through intensive fieldwork, the ways locals understand and act in the world, to delineate the connections they may make between seemingly unrelated contexts. Perhaps the most revealing example here is the homology made by Pamplonan activists between bull-running and demonstrations, underpinned by the performative understanding of nationalism. Other examples might be the appearance of the Gugu in a small Navarran village, the role of gastronomic societies within Basque society, the importance of skull shape in Basque public sculpture of the 1920s, the value of mountaineers to radical political parties, the particular intermeshing of interests between nationalist politicians and genetic anthropologists, and so on. Though, like Deutsch, Kedourie, Gellner and Anderson, I have studied respectively and in my own way social dimensions of communication, intellectual genealogies, modes of modernization, and newspapers, I like to think the insights I have produced are a direct consequence of a fieldwork-based approach, broadly conceived. The grand theories of those four academic greats have widened our understanding of nationalism; that does not mean there is not space and great value for an anthropological broadening of the limits to studies of nationalism. Far from it, for ethnographic studies can illuminate both the strengths and the blind spots of theories produced from within allied disciplines.

There is no reason why lived reality should be contained by analysts' categories, so it is no surprise that each chapter-theme is not discreet, but intertwines with others: several commentators see local food and football as equally unifying; some regard both football and old bones as bodily manifestations of Basque 'breeding' ('raza'), which is after all fuelled by Basque appetites cultivated through the consumption of Basque cuisine, and portrayed as such in 'el arte vasco'; the connections between local art and the Gugu are obvious. It is also worthwhile to highlight the ways certain themes resurface repeatedly throughout the chapters: the importance of landscape (in the appreciation of local cuisine, prehistoric monuments, graffiti and art); the masculine bias which underlies so much of Basque nationalist representation (the lauding of male appetites and male football-players, and the absence of female artists from the local canon); the tendency, mentioned in the introduction, for anthropologists and their work to be deployed for nationalist ends in, for instance, the representation of the Basque people, their genes, their art and their museums. Of course, what is significant is not just that this intertwining occurs, but that it carries evocative power with it. In this manner, each aspect of a marked Basque culture can be made redolent or suggestive of several others, and thus that much more forceful.

Similarly local notions of identity themselves can rise to the surface within a particular arena, and then sink, only to reappear later in a slightly different guise. For example, the way a marked Basque art emerged in the first decades of the last century, to then disappear, only to be revived in a transmogrified form decades later by Oteiza, his acolytes, and his contemporaries. The same could easily be stated for Basque cuisine (first seen as honestly traditional, then as radically innovative, now as the standard-bearer of the authentic and the autochthonous), or for Basque biology (first cranial, then haematological, next genetic, now genomic). We already well know that neither identity or modes of identification are stable; these examples underline just how labile they can be, shifting and slipping according to context and time.

It is true that some chapters make only relatively brief mention of nationalism, e.g. those on football or the Guggenheim. Yet this slighting reference may be regarded as one of the points I wish to make: that there are other, still significant modes of social identity in the Basque Country than purely nationalist ones. Just because a local institution has been strongly associated with the nationalist project at any one or for some time does not mean that it cannot be viewed independently of nationalism. So, even though Athletic is seen as indisputably, even magnificently Basque, and even though the Gugu is memorably part of the Basque townscape and iconic imagery, what is important is when and how the club or the museum is seen (or made) to complement (or clash) with nationalist approaches of the moment. For instance, at times Athletic has been deeply politicized, on occasion to the pleasure of many *socios*, on other occasions to their displeasure. Similarly, the Gugu project was conceived by moderate nationalists, criticized by their radical brethren, and yet may come to serve general *vasquista* interests. Basque nationalism does not exhaust the meanings, even the predominant meanings, potentially borne by either.

Too many accounts of nationalism revisit the same topics of land, language and party politics. My list is different and serves to highlight the diversity of themes which might be touched by nationalism. At the same time it is, to an important extent, an arbitrary listing. While all the topics I investigated are important social arenas with the Basque Country, there are others deserving of attention which would be equally illuminating of present-day nationalism: dance, adult comics, classical music, modern urban sports, armed violence, the annual nationalist gathering of Aberri Eguna ('The Day of the Basques'), Basque ethnographic museums, Basque television, local exploitation of the internet, and so on. The fact I have not studied those arenas is not a value judgement, rather a consequence of serendipitous circumstances in the course of my fieldwork and subsequent academic opportunities.[1]

One implication of this book is that we cannot speak of the 'nationalism of the X', but of the multiple nationalisms, at times complementary, at other times competing, given voice within any one nationalist arena. This point was reinforced for me in February 2006 when I gave a class on nationalism at the Universidad de Alicante in southeastern Spain. In their questions, the (mostly mature) students repeatedly asked why do the Basques do A if they have stated B? My response on each occasion was that many of their queries mixed the actions and statements of different Basque, and Basque nationalist groupings. I think the evidence and arguments of this book show that we can make informative generalizations about life in the Basque Country. But those generalizations have to be carefully formulated and cognizant of the contemporary nationalisms competing for attention. For these reasons, I have chosen to speak of the Basque arena, a mixed space of multiple voices, each clamouring at different degrees of intensity, with differing rates of success at wooing listeners, and gaining adherents, at least for a while.

What will be of interest is the extent to which further work by other anthropologists of European nationalisms will confirm, question, refine or extend any of my comments, both the more general and the more ethnographic. It is in this way that we can hope to construct a comparative anthropology of nationalisms in Europe, whether at the regional, nation-state or EU level.

My last comment, though veering towards the trite, is of course that there is no end. Some nationalists continue to struggle for an independent Basque nation-state; others accept an uneasy cohabitation with the central administration of Madrid; some Basques want to have done with the whole business and get on with the rest of their lives. My job, as an ethnographer, is to follow them, analysing as we go.

---

[1] In an effort not to reproduce the obfuscations of my predecessors, I confess the personal reasons for my choice. Chapter Two, on Navarran activist sub-culture is a direct product of the year I spent in Pamplona learning Castilian: the friends I made were all on the margins of that culture or very well-acquainted with it; the chapter on food was the belated result of a visit by a Madrid-based old friend, a food journalist, who, during lunch with my landlords, urged me to study what was under my nose; those on football, bones and art were all the eventual consequence of academic invitations to give papers. As an anthropologist who has published on art, the topics of political graffiti and the Gugu naturally interested me.

Bibliography

Abad Alegría, Francisco 1999 *Tradiciones en el fogón. Usos y recetas culinarios desaparecidos o en trance de acabar olvidados.* Pamplona: Pamiela

Abad Alegría, Francisco and Ruíz Ruíz, R. 1986 *Cocinar en Navarra.* Pamplona: Pamiela

Actes. Premier congres mondial de gastronomie basque 1994 and 1995

Agirre Arriaga, Imanol 1993 'Presencia de la antropología en la genesis de una estética vasca', *bi Tarte I*, no. 1, pp. 45–61

Aguirre, A. L., Pancorbo, M. M. de, Perez Elortondo, P., Albisu, L., and Lostao, C. M. 1985 'Estudio de los marcadores geneticos haptoglobina, transferrina y Gc en Vizcaya y Navarra', *Actas del IV Congreso Español de Antropología Biológica*, (Barcelona), pp. 613–22

Aguirre, A. L, Vicario, A., Mazon, L. L., de Pancorbo, M. M., Arizti, P., Estomba, A., and C. M. Lostao, 1989 'AK1, PGD, GC and HP frequencies in the Basque population: a review', *Gene Geography*, 3, pp. 41–51

Aguirre Franco, Rafael 1983 *Las Sociedades Populares.* San Sebastian: Caja de Ahorros Provincial de Guipúzcoa

—— 1995 *El Turismo en el País Vasco. Vida e Historia.* San Sebastian: Txertoa

Aguirre Sorondo, Antxon 1996 *La sidra. Sagardoa.* Donostia–San Sebastian: R & B

—— 2003 'Primeros datos sobre la sidra', *Euskonews and Media*, 205, http://www.euskonews.com/10203zbk/20301es.html. Accessed 28 March 2003

Aguirreazkuenaga, Joseba 1998 'Génesis de la sociabilidad moderna en Bilbao: (1800-1850) II: Tabernas y cafés', *Bidebarrieta III*, pp. 349–61

Aiestaran Álvarez, Carlos 2001 *Echevarría. Guardameta del Athletic Club 1938–1942.* Bilbao: Beta III milenio

Alofsin, Anthony 2001 'Putting a shine on things', *Times Literary Supplement*, 2 November, pp. 16, 18

Alonso, José Manuel 1998 *Athletic for ever!* Vol. 1 Crónica. Temas Vizcainos, no. 281. Bilbao: Bilbao Bizkaia Kutxa

Alonso, de Errasti, Ignacio 2001 *El Pintor José Sarriegui.* Bilbao: Temas Vizcainos-Bizkaiko Gaiak, nos 313–14.

Alonso, Santos and Armour, John A.L. 1998 'MS205 minisatellite diversity in Basques: evidence for a pre-neolithic component', *Genome Research* 8, pp. 1289–98

Alonso Pimentel, Carmen 2006 'La pintura y las artes gráficas en el País Vasco entre 1939 y 1975', *Ondare*, 25, pp. 103–47

Alpers, Svetlana 1988 *Rembrandt's enterprise. The studio and the market.* London: Thames and Hudson

Altuna, Jesús 1990 'La caza de herbívoros durante el Paleolítico y Mesolítico del País Vasco', *Munibe (Antropólogia –Arkeólogia)* 42, pp. 229–40

Altuna, Jesús and Mariezkurrena, Koro 2001 'El problema de la domesticación en el País Vasco y resto de la Región Cantábrica', in *XV Congreso de Estudios Vascos*, I, Donosti: Eusko-Ikaskuntza, pp. 123–7

Álvarez Junco, José 1998 'La nación en duda' in J. Pan-Montojo (ed.) *Más se perdió en Cuba. España, 1898 y la crisis de fin de siglo.* Madrid: Alianza Editorial

Álvarez, María Soledad 1985 'Corrientes y Estilos del grupo Guipuzcoano de la Escuela Vasca de Escultura', *Muga*, April, no. 42, pp. 4–21

—— 2002 'De las señas de la identidad al multiculturalismo. Una revisión de la escultura vasca en 2000', *XV Congreso de Estudios Vascos vol. II.* Donostia: Eusko-Ikaskuntza, pp. 875–901

—— 2005 'Análisis, discurso y expresividad en la escultura de Basterretxea', *Euskonews and Media* 318, http://www.euskonews.com/0318zbk/gaia31801es.html. Accessed 18 October 2005

193

Alzualde, A., Izagirre, N., Alonso, S., Alonso, A. and de la Rúa, C. 2005 'Temporal mitochondrial DNA variation in the Basque Country: influence of post-Neolithic events', *Annals of Human Genetics*, 69, no. 6, pp. 665–79

Alzualde, A., Izagirre, N., Alonso, S., Alonso, A., Albarrán C., Azkarate, A. and de la Rúa, C. 2006 'Insights into the "isolation of the Basques: mtDNA lineages from the historical site of Aldaieta (6th–7th centuries AD), *American journal of physical anthropology*, 130, no. 3, pp. 394–404

Alzuri Milanés, Miriam 1998 'Juan de la Encina, crítico de arte' in F. Chueca, M. Alzuri, M-D. Jiménez and L. Gutiérrez (eds), *Juan de la Encina (1883–1963) y el arte de su tiempo*. Bilbao: Museo de Bellas Artes de Bilbao, pp. 21–41

Amezaga, Ibone 2006 'El futuro de las razas autóctonas de Euskal Herria', *Asmoz ta jakitez*, no. 164, February, p. 4

Ammermann, A.J. and Cavalli-Sforza, L.L. 1984 *The Neolithic transition and the genetics of populations in Europe*. Princeton: Princeton University Press

Anasagasti, A. 1987 'Estacionalidad de los matrimonios en una población pescadora (1882–1906)', *Eusko-Ikaskuntza. Sociedad de Estudios Vascos. Homenaje al Dr. José Maria Basabe. Cuadernos de sección Antropología-Etnografía*, vol. 4, pp. 57–70

Anderson, Benedict 1983 *Imagined communities: Reflections on the origin and spread of nationalism*. London: Verso.

Anderson, J.M. 1988 *Ancient languages of the Hispanic peninsula*. Lanham, MD: University Press of America

Anderson, Perry 1992 'Science, politics, enchantment', in Hall and Jarvie (eds) *Transition to modernity: essays on power, wealth and belief*, pp. 187–212

Andrés Ruperez, María Teresa 1990 'El fenómeno dolménico en el País Vasco', *Munibe (Antropólogia-Arkeólogia)* 42, pp. 141–52

Angulo Barturen, Javier 1978 *Ibarrola ¿Un pintor maldito? (Arte vasco de postguerra. 1950–1977)*. San Sebastian: Haranburu

Anon 1897 'Sirimiri', *Euskalduna*, no. 69, 25 December, p. 547–8

—— 1900 'Exposición de Arte Modernista en Bilbao', *Euskalduna*, no. 162, 12 August, p. 317

—— 1906a 'Un cuadro de Ugarte', *La Baskonia*, no. 455, 20 May, p. 370

—— 1906b 'El pintor Berrueta', *La Baskonia*, no. 471, 30 October, p. 38

—— 1910 'Campeonato de Foot-ball', *Bizkaitarra*, 26 March

—— 1918 '¡Adios al "Amparo"!', *La Belle Epoque Bilbaina*. [Reprinted in 1964 *La Belle Epoque Bilbaina 1917–1922*.] Bilbao, pp. 91–2

Anthias, Floya 2002 'Where do I belong? Narrating collective identity and translocational positionality', *Ethnicities*, 2, no. 4, pp. 491–514

Apalategi, J. 1985 *Los vascos, de la autonomía a la independencia*. Txertoa: San Sebastian

Appadurai, Arjun 1996 *Modernity at large. Cultural dimensions in globalization*. Minneapolis: University of Minnesota Press

Appiah, A. 1986 'The uncompleted argument: Du Bois and the illusion of race', in H.L.Gates, jun. (ed.) *"Race", writing, and difference*. Chicago: University of Chicago Press, pp. 21–37

Araluze, Julio 1992 'Cultura del prestigio, desprestigio de la Cultura', *Egin* 20 January, p. 11

Aramburu, Fernando 1996 *Fuegos con Limon*. Barcelona: Tusquets

Arana Goiri, Sabino 1894 'La exposición artístico', *Bizkaitarra* no. 14, 31 August

—— 1895 'Juicio critico de "La historia general del señorio de Bizcaya" escrita por D. E. J. Labayru', *Bizkaitarra*, no. 28, 16 June

—— 1897 'La politica y el arte en Euskeria', *Baseritarra*, 22 August, p. 1

—— 1931 *La Nación Vasca*. Bilbao: Veroes

—— 1980 *Obras completas*. San Sebastian: Sendoa

Aranzadi, Juan 2000 *Milenarismo Vasco. Edad de Oro, etnia y nativismo*. Madrid: Taurus. 2nd ed. [orig pub. 1982]

—— 2001 *El escudo de Arquíloco. Sobre mesías, mártires y terroristas. Vol. 1, Sangre Vasca*. Madrid: A. Machado Libros

Aranzadi, Telesforo de 1889 *El pueblo euskalduna. Estudio de Antropología*. San Sebastian

—— 1901 'Los escultores mediterraneos y la raza vasca', *Euskal Erria XLV*, pp. 129–31

—— 1918 'Nuestra postura y el ideal ajeno', *Hermes*, no. 20, pp. 25–30

—— 1919 *Tipo y Raza en los Vascos*. Bilbao: Bilbaína de Artes Gráficas

—— 1928 'De algunas fantasias de dibujante', *Euskalerriaren Alde*, no. 291, pp. 116–18

—— 1933 'Lo típico y lo hermoso en la raza', *Yakintza*, no. 6, pp. 459–63

Ardanza, José Antonio 1987 'Prólogo' in *La Cocina Moderna en Euzkadi* by Juan José Lapitz. Madrid: Espasa-Calpe, pp. 13–14

Aretxaga, Begoña 1999 'A hall of mirrors: on the spectral character of Basque violence', in W.A. Douglass, C. Urza, L. White, and J. Zulaika (eds) *Basque politics and nationalism on the eve of the millennium*. Reno: University of Nevada Press, pp. 115–26

Arias de Apraiz, Elvira 1912 *Libro de Cocina o pequeña recopilación de recetas culinarias*. Vitoria: Egaña

Arnaiz Gómez, Ana 2006 'Entre escultura y monumento. La estela del Padre Donosita para Agiña del escultor Jorge Oteiza', *Ondare*, 25, pp. 305–25

Arnaiz Villena, Antonio and Alonso García, Jorge 1998 *El origen de los vascos y otros pueblos mediterráneos*. Madrid: Editorial Complutense

Arpal, Jesús 1985 'Solidaridades elementales y organizaciones colectivas en el País Vasco: cuadrillas, txokos, asociaciones' in Pierre Bidart (ed.) *Processus sociaux, ideologies et pratiques culturelles dans la société basque*. Pau: Université de Pau and CNRS, pp. 129–54

Arraiza, Francisco 1930 *La cocina navarra*. Pamplona

Arribas, José Luis 1990 'El Magdaleniense Superior/Final en el País Vasco', *Munibe (Antropólogia–Arkeólogia)* 42, pp. 55–63

Arrizabalaga, Álvaro 2001 'Aquellos primeros cromañes …', *Euskonews and Media*, 13, 9 July

Arrizabalaga, Álvaro and Iriarte, María José 2001 'El yacimiento arqueológico de Irikaitz (Zestoa, Gipuzkoa). Aportación al conocimiento del Paleolítico antiguo en Euskal Herria', in *XV Congreso de Estudios Vascos*, I, Donosti: Eusko-Ikaskuntza, pp. 115–22

Athletic Club Bilbao (1986), *Historia del Athletic Club Bilbao*. 6 vols. Bilbao: Athletic Club

Azcona, Jesus 1984 *Etnia y nacionalismo vasco. Una aproximación desde la antropología*. Barcelona: Anthropos

Azkarate Garai-Olaun, Agustín 1990 'Algunas consideraciones sobre la Arqueología de Epoca Germánica en Euskal Herria', *Munibe (Antropólogia–Arkeólogia)* 42, pp. 345–55

Azkue, Dionisio de 1915 'Arte. Opiniones', *La Tarde*, 3 December

Azua, Jon 2005, 'Guggenheim Bilbao: competitive strategies for the new culture-economy spaces' in Guasch and Zulaika (eds), *Learning from the Guggenheim*, pp. 73–95.

Azurmendi, Mikel 2000 *Y se limpie aquella tierra. Limpieza étnica y de sangre en el País Vasco (siglos XVI–XVIII)*. Madrid: Taurus

Bacigalupe, Antonio 1986, 'De la critica constructiva' in Athletic Club 1986, vol. 1, pp. 136–7

Bacigalupe, Carlos 1995 *Cafés parlantes de Bilbao. Del Romanticismo a la Belle Epoque*. Bilbao: Caffé Baqué

Bahn, Paul G. 1998 *Cambridge illustrated history of prehistoric art*. Cambridge: Cambridge University Press

Balakrishnan, Gopal 1996a 'Introduction' in Balakrishnan (ed.) 1996b, pp. 1–16

—— (ed.) 1996b *Mapping the Nation*. London: Verso

Ball, Phil 2001 *Morbo. The story of Spanish football*. London: WSC Books

Barandiarián, José Miguel de 1972 *Obras completas*, Tomo no. 1. Bilbao: La Gran Enciclopedia Vasca

Barañano, Kosme de and González de Durana, Javier 1988 'Arte vasco: cuatro reflexiones y un epílogo', *Cuadernos de Alzate* 8, pp. 3–18

Barañano, Kosme de, González de Durana, Javier and Juaristi, Jon 1987 *Arte en el País Vasco*. Cuadernos Arte. Madrid: Catedra

Barbujani, Guido 2000 'Geographic patterns: how to identify them and why', *Human biology* 72, pp. 133–53

—— 2001 'Geographical patterns of nuclear and mitochondrial DNA variation in Europe', in *XV Congreso de Estudios Vascos*, I, Donosti: Eusko-Ikaskuntza, pp. 161–9

Barnatan, Marcos-Ricardo 1998 'Una ciudad en marcha' *El Mundo (del País Vasco)* 2 March p. 47

Barr, Ann and Levy, Paul 1984 *The official foodie handbook*. London: Ebury

Barth, Fredrik 1969 'Introduction' in F. Barth (ed.) *Ethnic groups and boundaries: the social organization of culture difference*. Oslo: Universitetsforlaget

Basabe Prado, José Maria 1985 'Identidad vasca y biología de la población', *Euskaldunak. La etnia vasca*, vol. 5. San Sebastian: Ekor

Bauman, Zygmunt 1992 'Soil, blood and identity', *Sociological Review*, 40, pp. 675–701

Bayangel, Barón de 1944 'Elogio de la cocina vasca', *Vida Vasca XXI*, p. 96

Becker, Howard 1982 *Art worlds*. Berkeley: University of California Press

Beguiristain, María Amor 1990 'El Habitat del Eneolítico a la Edad del Bronce en Àlava y Navarra', *Munibe (Antropólogia–Arkeólogia)* 42, pp. 125–33

Belarmo, E. 1986 'Al Athletic de le quiere por lo que es' in Athletic Club 1986, vol. 1, pp. 156–7

Beltran, Juan Mari 1998 'La Txalaparta', *Euskonews and Media*, 1–100, 10. Bilbao: Eusko Ikaskuntza (CD)

Bengoa, José Maria n.d. (c.1990) *Las raices de la alimentación vasca*. San Sebastian: C.O. de Farmacéuticos de Guipuzcoa

Bennasar, I. 1987 'Dossier biográfico del Dr. José Maria Basabe Prado, SJ, Catedrático de antropología de la facultad de ciencias de la Universidad del País Vasco', *Eusko-Ikaskuntza*.

Sociedad de Estudios Vascos. Homenaje al Dr. José Maria Basabe. Cuadernos de sección Antropología-Etnografía, 4, pp. 15–45

Berganza, Eduardo 1990 'El Epipaleolítico en el País Vasco', *Munibe (Antropólogia –Arkeólogia)* 42, pp. 81–9

Bertranpetit, J. and Cavalli-Sforza, Luca L. 1991 'A genetic reconstruction of the history of the population of the Iberian peninsula', *Annals of human genetics*, 55, pp. 51–67

Billig, Michael 1995 *Banal nationalism*. London: Sage

Bloch, Maurice and Parry, Jonathan (eds) 1989 *Money and the morality of exchange*. Cambridge: Cambridge University Press

Bolland, Gonzalo 1999 'Un mundo uniforme', *El Mundo. Edición del País Vasco*. Vivir Aqui supplement, 20 October, p. 2

Bourdieu, Pierre 1977 *Outline of a theory of practice*. Cambridge: Cambridge University Press

—— 1993 *The field of cultural production. Essays on art and literature*. Cambridge: Polity Press

—— 1996 *The rules of art. Genesis and structure of a literary field*. Cambridge: Polity Press

Boyd, W. C. 1950 *Genetics and the races of man*. Oxford: Blackwell

Bozal, Valeriano 2006 'Arte, ideología e identidad en los años del franquismo', *Ondare*, 25, pp. 17–31

Breuilly, John 1996 'Approaches to Nationalism' in G. Balakrishnan (ed.) *Mapping the Nation*. 1996b, pp. 146–66

Brewer, John 1997 *The pleasures of the imagination. English culture in the eighteenth century*. London: HarperCollins

Brubaker, Rogers, and Cooper, Frederick 2000 'Beyond "identity"', *Theory and Society*, 29, no. 1, pp. 1–47

Bryman, Alan 1999 'The Disneyization of society', *Sociological Review*, 47, no. 1, pp. 24–47

Busca Isusi, José María 1971 'Los progresos tecnicos (¿) de la cocina vasca', *Boletín de la Cofradia Vasca de Gastronomía V*, pp. 74–8

—— 1987 *Traditional Basque cooking. History and preparation*. Reno: University of Nevada Press (orig. pub. in Castilian 1983)

Calera, Ana-María 1976 *La cocina vasca*. Bilbao: La Gran Enciclopedia Vasca

Camara, Ely 2005 'The franchise museum – an instrument of cultural colonization?' in Guasch and Zulaika (eds)

Campión, Arturo 1919 'La raza baska, ¿es fea o hermosa?' *Hermes*, no. 41, pp. 197–202

Caraballo, C., Rebato, E. and Basabe, J.M. 1985 'Estudio comparativo de la sensibilidad gustativa a la fenitiltiocarbamida (P.T.C.) en las poblaciones vasca autóctona, mixta y foránea', *Eusko-Ikaskuntza. Sociedad de Estudios Vascos. Cuadernos de sección Antropología-Etnografía*, 2, pp. 313–18

Castañer López, Xesqui 1993 *La imagen de la mujer en la plastica vasca contemporanea (s.xviii-xx). Aproximación a una metodología del género*. Bilbao: Universidad del País Vasco

Castillo, José 1968 *Manual de la cocina economica vasca*. San Sebastian: Icharopena

—— 1983 'Las Verduras' in *Cocina vasca. Nuestra cocina por nuestros mejores cocineros*. San Sebastian: Sendoa, pp. 23–5

Castresana, Luis de 1966 *El otro árbol de Guernica*. Madrid: Prensa Española

—— 1968 'Aliron', *Elogios, asperezas y nostalgias del País Vasco*. Bilbao: La Gran Enciclopedia

Cava, Ana 1990 'El Neolítico en el País vasco', *Munibe (Antropólogia –Arkeólogia)* 42, pp. 97–106

Cavalli-Sforza, Luca L. 1988 'The Basque population and ancient migrations in Europe', *Munibe*, Suplemento, no. 6, pp. 129–37

Cerrato, J. 1986 'Historia en paginas de oro' in Athletic Club Bilbao 1986, vol. 2, pp. 216–17

Chapman, Malcolm 1992 *The Celts: the construction of a myth*. London: Palgrave Macmillan

—— (ed.) 1993 *Social and biological aspects of ethnicity*. Oxford: Oxford University Press

Chillida, Susanna (ed.) 2003 *Elogio del horizonte. Conversaciones con Eduardo Chillida*. Barcelona: Destino

Clifford, James 2003 *On the edges of anthropology*. Chicago: Prickly Paradigm Press

Cohen, Abner 1974a 'Introduction: The lesson of ethnicity' in Abner Cohen (ed.) *Urban Ethnicity*, ASA Monographs, no. 12, London: Tavistock, pp. ix–xxiv

1974b *Two-dimensional man. An essay on the anthropology of power and symbolism in complex society*. London: Routledge and Kegan Paul

Cohen, Anthony P. 1987 *Whalsay. Symbol, segment and boundary in a Shetland Island community*. Manchester: Manchester University Press

Cole, Jeffrey 1997 *The new racism in Europe. A Sicilian ethnography*. Cambridge: Cambridge University Press

Collins, Roger 1986 *The Basques*. Oxford: Blackwell

—— 1990 'The ethnogenesis of the Basques' in H. Wolfram and W. Pohl (eds), *Typen der Ethnogenese unter besonderer Berücksichtigung der Bayern*, Teil 1, Veröffentlichungen der Kommission für Frühmittelalterforschung, Bd. 12, Vienna: Verlag der Österreichischen Akademie der Wissenschaften, pp. 35–44

Colomina, Beatriz 2005 'Media architect' in Zulaika and Guasch (eds), *Learning from the Guggenheim*, pp. 259–72

Connor, Walker 1972 'Nation-building or nation-destroying?', *World politics* 24, pp. 319–55

Cooper, Martha and Chalfant, Henry 1984 *Subway art*. London: Thames and Hudson

Corcuera Atienza, Javier 1979 *Orígenes, ideología y organización del nacionalismo vasco 1876–1904*. Madrid: Siglo Veintiuno

Cornell, Stephen 1996 'The variable ties that bind: content and circumstance in ethnic processes', *Ethnic and Racial Studies*, 19, no. 2, April, pp. 265–89

Cornell, Stephen, and Hartmann, Douglas 1998 *Ethnicity and race. Making identities in a changing world*. Thousand Oaks: Pine Forge

Cosmos 1915a 'Ante una exposición, los hermanos Zubiaurre y el renacimiento vasco. Intimidades', *El Pueblo Vasco* 8 November

—— 1915b 'Ante una exposición arte y sentimiento. Mi replica', *El Pueblo Vasco* 16 November

Coulon, Christian 2000 'La cocina como objeto político' in F. Letamendía and C. Coulon (eds), *Cocinas del mundo. La política en la mesa*. Madrid: Fundamentos, pp. 19–28

Cowen, Tyler 1998 *In praise of commercial culture*. Cambridge, MA: Harvard University Press

Crane, Diane 1987 *The transformation of the avant-garde. The New York artworld, 1940–1985*. Chicago: University of Chicago Press

Crimp, Douglas 1993 *On the museum's ruins*. Cambridge, MA: MIT

Danforth, Loring 1997 *The Macedonian conflict. Ethnic nationalism in a transnational world*. Princeton: Princeton University Press

De La Iglesia, Àlex 1998 *Payasos en la lavadora* [Clowns in the Laundrette]. Barcelona: Planeta

De La Rúa, Concepción 1985 *El craneo vasco: morfología y factores craneofaciales*. Diputación Foral de Vizcaya, Bilbao

—— 1988 'Revisión de los craneos prehistoricos de Urtiaga (Pais Vasco)', *Munibe*, Suplemento no. 6, pp. 269–80.

—— 1990 'Los estudios de paleoantropología en el País Vasco', *Munibe*, 42, pp. 199–219

—— 1995 'La historia del poblamiento del País Vasco desde una perspectiva antropológica' in Jaume Bertranpetit and Elisenda Vives (eds), *Muntayes I Població. El passat dels Pirineus des d'una perspective multidisciplinària*. Andorra La Vella: Centre de Trobada de la Cultures Pirinenques, pp. 301–15

Delgado, Manolo 1986 'Cuando los sueños se hacen realidad' in Athletic Club 1986, vol. 3, pp. 206–7

de Lope, Manuel 2001 *La sangre ajena*. Barcelona: Debate

Del Valle, Teresa 1990 'La violencia de las mujeres en la ciudad. Lecturas desde la marginalidad' in V.Maquieira and C.Sánchez (eds) *Violencia y sociedad patriarcal*. Madrid: Pablo Iglesias, pp. 47–65

—— 1988 *Korrika. Rituales de la lengua en el espacio*. Barcelona: Anthropos. Eng trans. 1994 *Korrika. Basque ritual for ethnic identity*. Reno: University of Nevada Press

Dempsey, Andrew 1990 'Chillida in conversation' in *Chillida*. London: South Bank Centre, pp. 37–50

De Pablo, Santiago, Mees, Ludger, and Rodríguez Ranz, Jose A. 1999 *El péndulo patriótico. Historia del Partido Nacionalista Vasco*. Barcelona: Crítica

Deutsch, Karl 1963 *Nationalism and social communication. An inquiry into the foundations of nationality*. Cambridge, MA: MIT

Díaz Cuyás, José (with Carmen Pardo) n.d. 'Caso de estudio: Pamplona era una fiesta', http://www.desacuerdos.org/segundaext.jsp?SECCION=15&ID1=1105. Accessed 4 March 2005

Díaz Herrera, José and Durán, Isabel 2001 *Arzalluz. La dictadura del miedo*. Barcelona: Planeta

Díaz Noci, Javier 1999 'The creation of the Basque identity through cultural symbols in modern times', http://www.ehu.es/diaz-noci/Conf/C17.pdf. Accessed 14 March 2005

—— 2000 'Los nacionalistas van al fútbol. Deporte, ideología y periodismo en los años 20 y 30', *Zer. Revista de estudios de comunicación*, no. 9, November, s.p., http://www.ehu.es/zer/zer9/9noci.html. Accessed 15 June 2004

Douglass, William 1969 *Death in Murélaga*. Seattle: University of Washington Press

Duncan, Carol 1995 *Civilizing rituals. Inside public art museums*. London: Routledge

Dunixi (pseud. José de Arteche) 1915a 'Exposición Zuloaga-Uranga', *Euzkadi* 12 February

—— 1915b 'Hablemos de arte', *Euzkadi* 23 February

—— 1915c 'Algo mas sobre arte', *Euzkadi* 29 March

—— 1915d 'Algo mas sobre arte II', *Euzkadi* 6 April

—— 1934 'El pintor Flores Kaperotxipi', *Yakintza*, 12, pp. 463–6

Duret-Robert, François 1977 'The verdict of the sale-room' in *Phaidon encyclopedia of Impressio-*

nism, ed. Maurice Serullaz. New York: Phaidon

Durieux, Isabelle 1995 'Guggenheim. Le musée qui veut devenir une multinationale' *L'Expansion*. Paris, no. 504, 26 June

Eagleton, Terry 1990 *The ideology of the aesthetic*. Oxford: Basil Blackwell

Echegaray, Fernando de 1948 'Del buen comer y beber de los Bilbaínos', *Vida Vasca XXV*, pp. 198–200

Echevarria, Juan D. de 1999 'Comais, bebais, pagueis. Pequeña historia de un gran restaurante', *Boletín de la Cofradía Vasca de Gastronomía*, no. 45, May, pp. 71–7

Edensor, Tim 2002 *National identity, popular culture and everyday life*. Oxford: Berg

Eleizalde, Luis de 1919 'Arana-Goiri, Poeta' in *Hermes*, nos. 51–2 [orig. pub. 1906 in *Euskadi*]

Ellingson, Ter 2001 *The myth of the noble savage*. Berkeley: University of Califorina Press

Elms, Robert 1992 *Spain, a portrait after the general*. London: Heinemann

Elorza, Antonio 2000 'Vascos guerreros' in A. Elorza (ed.) *La historia de ETA*. Madrid: Temas de hoy. Historia, pp. 13–75

Encina, Juan de la 1919 *La Trama del Arte Vasco*. Bilbao: Vasca

Ergoyen, Antonio de Ergoyen 1953 'Angulas a la Bilbaina', *Vida Vasca*, pp. 196–7

Eriksen, Thomas Hylland 1993a *Ethnicity and nationalism. Anthropological perspectives*. London: Pluto

—— 1993b 'Formal and informal nationalism', *Ethnic and Racial Studies*, 16, no. 1, January, pp. 1–25

Escartin, P. 1986, 'Athletic de Bilbao, Un estilo de juego y una linea de conducta' in Athletic Club 1986, vol. 2, pp. 156–7

Escribano, Maria n.d. 'La Txalaparta a traves del tiempo. Un análisis etnomusicológico'

Espinosa, Pedro and López, Elena 1993 *Hertzainak. La confesión radical*. Vitoria: Aianai.

Esteban Delgado, Milagros 1990 'Aproximación a la Guipúzcoa de los primeros siglos de nuestra Era', *Munibe (Antropólogia –Arkeólogia)* 42, pp. 337–44

Estévez, A. (1986), 'El Athletic, un sentimiento' in Athletic Club 1986, vol. 2, pp. 116–17

Estornes Zubizarreta, I. 1983 *La Sociedad de Estudios Vascos. Aportación de Eusko Ikaskuntza a la Cultura Vasca (1918–1936)*. San Sebastian: Eusko Ikaskuntza

ETA (Euskadi ta askatasuna) 1979 *Documentos*. 18 vols. San Sebastian: Hordago

Etcheverry, M.A. 1959 'Grupos sanguineos y factor Rh en los Vascos' in T. de Aranzadi, de Barandiarán, J.M., and Etcheverry, M.A, *La raza vasca*. San Sebastian: Auñamendi, pp. 49–69

Ezkerra, Iñaki 2002 *ETA pro nobis. El pecado original de la Iglesia vasca*. Barcelona: Planeta

Ferembach, D. 1988 'Préhistoire et peuplement ancien du Pays Basque' *Munibe*, Suplemento, no. 6, pp. 139–48

Ferguson, Priscilla Parkhurst 2004 *Accounting for taste. The triumph of French cuisine*. Chicago: University of Chicago Press

Fernández de Larrinoa, Kepa (forthcoming) 'Farms, flats and villas: senses of country living in a Basque-speaking village', in J. MacClancy (ed.), *Alternative countrysides: anthropological approaches to contemporary rural West Europe*. Oxford: Berghahn.

Ferrell, Jeff 1996 *Crimes of style. Urban graffiti and the politics of criminality*. Boston: Northeastern University Press

Fitzgerald, Michael F. 1995 *Making Modernism. Picasso and the creation of the market for twentieth-century art*. Berkeley: University of California Press

Fjellman, S. M. 1992 *Vinyl leaves: Walt Disney world and America*. Boulder: Westview

Foster, Hal 2001 'Why all the hoopla?', *London Review of Books*, 23 August, pp. 24–6

Foster, Robert J. 2002 *Materializing the nation. Commodities, consumption, and media in Papua New Guinea*. Bloomington: Indiana University Press

Frade, K-tono 1986, *La salsa de San Mames*. Colección 'temas vizcainos', no. 162. Bilbao: Caja de Ahorros Vizcaina

Fraser, Andrea 2005 'Isn't this a wonderful place? (A tour of the tour of the Guggenheim Bilbao)' in Guasch and Zulaika (eds) *Learning from the Guggenheim*, pp. 37–58

Frey, Bruno S. and Werner W. Pommerehne 1989 *Muses and markets. Explorations in the economics of the arts*. Oxford: Basil Blackwell

Gabaccia, Donna R. 1998 *We are what we eat. Ethnic food and the making of Americans*. Cambridge, MA: Harvard University Press

Ganeko 1998 'Guggenheim, un museo donde la pela es la pela', *El Mundo*, 13 October 1998, p. 4

García García, María Luisa 1997 'El poblamiento en época romana en Navarra: sistemas de distribución y modelos de asentamientos', *Isturitz*, 8, pp. 85–110

García Marcos, Juan Antonio 2004 'Jorge Oteiza y la critica. Un antes y después a 1957' in Estabaliz Jiménez de Aberasturi Apraiz (ed.) *Acercarse a Jorge Oteiza*. San Sebastián: Txertoa, pp. 39–66

García Santos, Rafael 1986 *La cocina vasca de ayer, hoy y mañana*. San Sebastian: Haranburu

—— 1989 'Introducción' to *El Amparo* by Ursula, Sira and Vicenta Azcaray y Eguileor. Donostia: Kriselu

García-Landarte Puertas, Valeria 2006 'Estampa Popular de Vizcaya. El realismo social de los años 60 del País Vasco', *Ondare* 25, pp. 393–404

Garmendía, José María 2002 'ETA: nacimiento, desarollo y crisis (1959–1978)' in A. Elorza (ed.) *La historia de ETA*. Madrid: Temas de hoy. Historia

Geertz, Clifford 1973 *The interpretation of cultures*. New York: Basic Books

Gellner, David 1997 'Preface' in E. Gellner *Nationalism*, pp. vii–x

Gellner, Ernest 1983 *Nations and nationalism*. Oxford: Basil Blackwell

—— 1996 'Reply to my Critics' in Hall and Jarvie (eds) *The social philosophy of Ernest Gellner*, pp. 625–87.

—— 1997 *Nationalism*. London: Phoenix

Genders, Elaine and Player, Elaine 1989 *Race relations in prisons*. Oxford: Oxford University Press

Gilbert-Rolfe, Jeremy 2005 'Frank Gehry is not Andy Warhol: a choice between life and death', in Guasch and Zulaika (eds) *Learning from the Guggenheim*, pp. 219–33

Gimpel, Jean 1991 *Against art and artists*, Revised ed. [orig. pub. 1968]. Edinburgh: Polygon

Glancey, Jonathan 1997 'Basque in glory', *The Guardian* Weekend, London, 25 October, pp. 58–61

Goicoetxea Marcaida, A. 1985 *Telesforo de Aranzadi. Vida y obra*. San Sebastian: Sociedad de Ciencias Aranzadi

Gómez Gómez, Agustín 2006 'Semiótica del cartel vasco durante los primeros años de la dictadura', *Ondare*, 25, pp. 403–11

Gómez Nazabal, José Ramon 1998 'El efecto "Guggy"', *El Mundo* 9 March, p. 4

Gómez Prieto, Julia and Darricau, Joëlle 1997 *Descubriendo la Prehistoria Vasca. Guía de Turismo Cultural*. Donostia-San Sebastian: Elkarlanean

González de Durana, Javier 1983 *Ideologias artisticas en el País Vasco de 1900. Arte y política en los orígenes de la modernidad*. Coleccion Abiatu. Bilbao: Ekin

—— 1984 *Adolfo Guiard. Estudio Biográfico, Analisis Estético. Catalogación de su Obra*. Bilbao: Museo de Bellas Artes

—— 1992 *Relatos y Arrebatos*. Bilbao: Haizegoa

—— 1993 'La invención de la pintura vasca' in C. Pena (ed.) *Centro y Periferia en la Modernización de la Pintura Española (1880–1918)* Madrid: Ministerio de Cultura, pp. 394–402

—— 2004 'Los orígenes de la modernidad en el arte vasco: Arte Vasco y compromiso político', *Ondare*, Sp. Issue 'Revisión del arte vasco entre 1875–1939', no. 23, pp. 15–34

Gorrochategui, Javier and Yarritu, María José 1990 'El Complejo Cultural del Neolíticao Final-Edad del Bronce en el País Vasco Cantábrico', *Munibe (Antropólogia–Arkeólogia)* 42, pp. 107–23

Gorrochategui, Joaquín 2001 'Planteamientos de la lingüística histórica en la datación del Euskera', in *XV Congreso de Estudios Vascos, I*, Donosti: Eusko-Ikaskuntza, pp. 103–14

Grampp, William 1989 *Pricing the priceless. art, artists and economics*. New York: Basic Books

Green, Nicholas 1987 'Dealing in temperaments: economic transformation of the artistic field in France during the second half of the nineteenth century' *Art History*, 10, no. 1, pp. 59–78

Guasch, Ana María 1985 *Arte y ideología en el País Vasco: 1940–1980*. Madrid: Akal

Guasch, Ana María and Zulaika, Joseba (eds) 2005 *Learning from the Guggenheim*. Reno: Center for Basque Studies, University of Nevada, Reno

Guevara Aguirresarobe, J. I. 1988 *Estructura genética de la Rioja alavesa. Analisis de la consanguinidad y otros factores demogenéticos asociados (siglo XIX)*, Memoria de Licenciatura, Universidad del País Vasco (Unpublished)

Gullestad, M. 2005 'Normalizing racial boundaries. The Norwegian dispute about the term neger', *Social Anthropology, 13*, Part 1, February, pp. 27–46

Gurruchaga, A. 1985 *El código nacionalista durante el franquismo*. Barcelona: Anthropos

Gutiérrez, Navidad 1997 'Ethnic revivals with nation-states? The theories of E. Gellner and A.D. Smith revisited' in H-R. Wicker (ed.) *Rethinking ethnicity and nationalism. The struggle for meaning and order in Europe*. Oxford: Berg, pp. 163–74

Hall, John A. 1998a 'Introduction' in Hall 1998b, pp. 1–20

—— (ed.) 1998b *The state of the nation. Ernest Gellner and the theory of nationalism*. Cambridge: Cambridge University Press

Hall, John A. and I. Jarvie (eds) 1996 *The social philosophy of Ernest Gellner*, Poznan Studies in the Philosophy of Sciences and the Humanities 48. Amsterdam: Rodopi

Haranburu Altuna, Luis 2000 *Historia de la alimentación y de la cocina en el País Vasco*. Alegia, Gipuzkoa: Hiria

Harris, Rosemary 1972 *Prejudice and tolerance in Ulster: a study of neighbours and 'strangers' in a border county*. Manchester: Manchester University Press

Harrison, Faye V. 2002 'Unravelling "race" for the 21st century' in J. MacClancy (ed.) *Exotic no more. Anthropology on the front lines.* Chicago: University of Chicago Press, pp. 145–66

Haskell, Francis 1980 *Patrons and painters. Art and society in Baroque Italy.* New Haven: Yale University Press

Haward, Birkin 1991 *Oxford University Museum. Its architecture and art.* Oxford: Oxford University Museum

Hayward, Victoria 1997 'The Guggenheim-Bilbao: A museum for the 21st century'. Unpublished MS.

Heiberg, Marianne 1989 *The making of the Basque nation.* Cambridge: Cambridge University Presss

Heilbrun, James and Gray, Charles M. 1993 *The Economics of art and culture. An American perspective.* Cambridge: Cambridge University Press

Herzfeld, Michael 1982 *Ours once more: folklore, ideology and the making of modern Greece.* Austin: University of Texas Press

Hobsbawm, E.J. and Ranger, T.O. (eds) 1983 *The invention of tradition.* Cambridge: Cambridge University Press

Hroch, Miroslav 1996 'From National Movement to the Fully-Formed Nation: The Nation-Building Process in Europe' in Balakrishnan 1996b, *Mapping the Nation*, pp. 78–97

Hualde Alfaro, José María, Pagola Lorente, Javier, and Torre Hernández, Paloma 1989 *Quesos de Navarra.* Pamplona: Gobierno de Navarra

Huizinga, Johan 1949 *Homo ludens. A study of the play-element in culture.* London: Routledge and Kegan Paul [orig pub in Dutch, 1938].

Igartua, Conchi and González de Aspuru, Sara 1993 *Costumbrismo vasco. Arte para leer 3.* Vitoria: Museo de Bellas Artes de Alava

Imanol 1915 'Arte. Opiniones', *La Tarde* 30 November

Iriarte Chiapusso, María José 2002 'La dinámica del paisaje litoral y la intervención humana sobre el mismo durante el inicio del Holoceno', *Euskonews and Media*, 172, http://suse00.su.ehu.es/euskonews/0172zbk/gaia017203es.html. Accessed 21 June 2002

Iribarren, José Maria 1956 'El comer, el vestir y la vida de los navarros de 1817 a través de un "memorial de ratonera"', *Príncipe de Viana*, 17, pp. 473–86

Iriondo, M., Manzano, C., and de la Rúa, C. 1996 'HLA-DQA1 in autochthonous Basques: description of a genocline for the DQA1*0201 allele in Europe', *International Journal of Legal Medicine*, 109, pp. 181–5

Iriondo, Mikel, de la Rúa, Concepción, del Carmen Barbero, María, Aguirre, Ana and Manzano, Carmen 1999 'Analysis of 6 Short Tandem Repeat Loci in Navarre (Northern Spain)', *Human Biology*, 71, 1, pp. 43–54

Isasi Urdangarin, José Mari 1998 *Variaciones Julen Guerrero.* Vitoria: Bassari

Ispizua, Segundo de 1915 'Arte. Opiniones', *La Tarde* 2 December

Itoiz, Julia 2005 *La otra experiencia. El libro que nadie quiso publicar sobre Jorge Oteiza.* Gasteiz: Arabera

Iturbe, José Angel and Letamendía, Francisco 2000 'Culture, política y gastronomía en el País Vasco' in Letamendía and Coulon, pp. 79–101

Iturrieta, José Luis 1997 'Introducción' to *La Cocina Vasca en Vizcaya* by Roberto Asúa. Oria: Alegia, Guipuzcoa

Iturrioz, R. 1987 'Estudio sobre la identidad vasca y serología de su población', *Eusko-Ikaskuntza. Sociedad de Estudios Vascos. Homenaje al Dr. José Maria Basabe. Cuadernos de sección Antropología-Etnografía*, vol. 4, pp. 299–314.

Izagirre, Koldo 1997 *Incursiones en territorio enemigo.* Pamplona: Pamiela

Izagirre, Neskuts and de la Rúa, Concepción 1999 'An mtDNA analysis in ancient Basque populations: implications for Haplogroup V as a market for a major Paleolithic expansion from southwestern Europe', *American Journal of Human Genetics* 65, pp. 199–207

Izagirre, Neskuts, Alonso, Santos and de la Rúa, Concepción 2001 'DNA analysis and the evolutionary history of the Basque population: a review', *Journal of Anthropological Research*, 57, pp. 325–44

Izagirre, Neskuts, Alonso, Santos, Alzualde, Ainhoa and de la Rúa, Concepción 2003 '¿Qué es el ADN antiguo? Aplicaciones y límites', *Euskonews and Media*, 229, 7 November

Jackes, Mary, Lubell, David and Meiklejohn, Christopher 1997 'On physical anthropological aspects of the Mesolithic-Neolithic transition in the Iberian Peninsula', *Current Anthropology*, 38, 5, pp. 839–46

Jacob, James E. 1994 *Hills of conflict. Basque nationalism in France.* Reno: University of Nevada Press

—— 1999 'The future of Basque nationalism in France', in W.A. Douglass, C. Urza, L. White, and J. Zulaika (eds) *Basque politics and nationalism on the eve of the millennium.* Reno: University of Nevada Press, pp. 155–74

Jacobs, Michael 1994, *Between hopes and memories. A Spanish journey.* London: Picador

Jacobsen, William H. Jr 1999 'Basque language origin theories' in W.A. Douglass, C. Urza, L. White and J. Zulaika (eds) *Basque cultural studies*. Reno: Basque Studies Program, University of Nevada Press, pp. 27–43

Jaffrelot, Christophe 2005 'For a theory of nationalism' in Alain Dieckhoff and Christophe Jaffrelot (eds) *Revisiting nationalism. Theories and processes*. London: Hurst, pp. 10–61

James, Paul 1996 *Nation formation. Towards a theory of abstract community*. London: Sage

Jenkins, Richard 1997 *Rethinking ethnicity. Arguments and explorations* London: Sage

—— 2002 'Imagine but not imaginary: ethnicity and nationalism in the modern world', in J. MacClancy (ed.) *Exotic no more. Anthropology on the front lines*. Chicago: University of Chicago Press, pp. 114–28

Jensen, Joli 2002 *Is art good for us? Beliefs about high culture in American life*. Lanham: Rowman and Littlefield

Jiménez de Aberasturi Apraiz, Estibaliz 2004 'Jorge Oteiza: promoter de la actualización del arte vasco' 1957' in Estabaliz Jiménez de Aberasturi Apraiz (ed.) *Acercarse a Jorge Oteiza*. San Sebastián: Txertoa, pp. 67–80

Jobling, Mark 2001 'European Y chromosome diversity: population movement, geography and language', in *XV Congreso de Estudios Vascos, I*, Donosti: Eusko-Ikaskuntza, pp. 171–6

Juaristi, Jon 1997 *El buck melancólico. Historias de nacionalistas vascos*. Madrid: Espasa

—— 1999 *Sacra némesis. Nuevas historias de nacionalismo vascos*. Madrid: Espasa

—— 2006 *Cambio de destino. Memorias*. Barcelona: Seix Barral

Kaperotxipi, Flores 1934 'Mis modelos, mis cuadros y yo', *Yakintza*, 12, pp. 461–3

—— 1954 *Arte Vasco, pintura, escultura, dibujo, grabado*. Biblioteca de cultura vasca. Buenos Aires: Ekin

Kapferer, Bruce 1988 *Legends of people, myths of state. violence, intolerance and political culture in Sri Lanka and Australia*. Washington: Smithsonian Institution Press

Karakisadou, Anastasia 1997 *Fields of wheat, hills of blood. Passages to nationhood in Greek Macedonia 1870–1990*. Chicago: University of Chicago Press

Kasmir, Sharryn 1999 'From the margins: punk rock and the repositioning of ethnicity and gender in Basque identity', in W.A. Douglass, C. Urza, L. White, and J. Zulaika (eds) *Basque cultural studies*. Reno: University of Nevada Press, pp. 178–204

Kedourie, Elie 1960 *Nationalism*. London: Hutchinson.

Kizkitza (pseud. of Engracio de Aranzadi) 1910 *La Patria de los Vascos*. San Sebastian: Gipuzhoarra

Kortadi-Olano, Edorta 1978 'Relexiones en torno a la Escuela Vasca de Pintura; sus raices y desarollo', *Cultura Vasca II*. San Sebastian: Erein, pp. 319–30

—— 2003 *Una mirada sobre Eduardo Chillida. Vida y obra de un artista universal*. Madrid: Síntesis

Kramer, Hilton 1992 'Dispersing a museum collection', *The New Criterion II*, no. 1, September, pp. 4–7

Kurlansky, Mark 1997 *Cod. A biography of the fish that changed the world*. London: Jonathan Cape

—— 1999 *The Basque history of the world*. London: Jonathan Cape

Labayen, Francisco M. 1951 'Pot-pourri Vasco. Alimentación, laboriosidad, bailes y danzas', *Vida Vasca XXVIII*, pp. 98–101

Lafuente Ferrari, Enrique 1981 'Prólogo' in *La Trama del Arte Vasco y selección de articulos publicados en Hermes* by Juan de la Encina, edited by Enrique Lafuente Ferrari. Madrid: Espasa-Calpe, pp. 11–15

Lapitz, Juan José 1980 *Comer en Euskalherria*. Madrid: Penthalon

—— 1983a 'La alimentación de nuestros antepasados' in *Cocina Vasca. Nuestra Cocina por nuestros mejores cocineros*. San Sebastian: Sendoa, pp. 11–14

—— 1983b 'Panorama actual de la Cocina Vasca' in *Cocina Vasca. Nuestra Cocina por nuestros mejores cocineros*. San Sebastian: Sendoa, pp. 21–32

—— 1989 *La Cocina Vasca. Sus recetas basicas*. Donostia: Txertoa

—— 1991 *La cocina de Shishito en la Belle Epoque*. San Sebastian: Cofradía Vasca de Gastronomía/Baroja

Larrea, Carmen O. de 1977 'Fundamentos sociológicos del arte culinaro guipuzcoano', *Vida Vasca LIV*, pp. 77

Larronde, J.-C. 1977 *El nacionalismo vasco. Su origen y su ideología en la obra de Sabino Arana-Goiri*. San Sebastian: Txertoa.

Laskurain Argarate, Juan Luis 1991 'El Guggenheim ¿un museo?' *El Correo Español* 26 Decembe.

Lasterra, C. 1933a 'Charlas sobra la pintura vasca', *Euzkadi* 13 July

—— 1933b 'Charlas sobre la pinture vasca', *Euzkadi* 26 July

—— 1933c 'Charlas sobre la pintura vasca', *Euzkadi* 2 August

—— 1933d 'Charlas sobre la pintura vasca', *Euzkadi* 6 August

Layton, Robert 1991 *The anthropology of art*. Second edition. Cambridge: Cambridge University Press

Leguineche, Manuel, Unzueta, Patxo and Segurola, Santiago 1998 *Athletic 100. Conversaciones en La Catedral*. Madrid: El País Aguilar

Leizaola, Fermin de 1983 'Los pastores, los quesos y otros productos lacteos de Euskalherria' in *Cocina Vasca. Nuestra Cocina por nuestros mejores cocineros*. San Sebastián: Sendoa, pp. 281–312

Letamendía, Francisco and Coulon, Christian (eds) 2000 *Cocinas del mundo. La política en la mesa*. Madrid: Fundamentos

Lévy-Bruhl, Lucien 1905 *Ethics and moral science*. London: Archibald Constable

Linde-Laursen, Anders 1993 'The nationalization of trivialities: how cleaning becomes an identity marker in the encounter of Swedes and Danes', *Ethnos*, 3–4, pp. 275–93

Linstroth, John 2002 'The Basque conflict globally speaking: material culture, media and Basque identity in the wider world', *Oxford Development Studies*, 30, no. 2, pp. 205–22

Litvak, L. 1991 *El tiempo de los trenes. El paisaje español en el arte y la literatura del realismo (1849–1918)*. Barcelona: Ediciones del Serbal

Lizundia, José María 2000 *Vasca Cultura de Altura*. Alegia, Gizpuzkoa: Hiria

Llano Gorostiza, Manuel 1977 'Regionalismo y socialismo en el arte vasco', *Guadalimar* October, pp. 31–6

—— 1986 *Clasicos de la Cocina Vasca*. Bilbao: Banco de Vizcaya

Llanos Ortiz de Landaluze, Armando 1990 'La Edad del Hierro y sus precedentes, en Àlava y Navarra', *Munibe (Antropólogia –Arkeólogia)* 42, pp. 167–79

Llobera, Josep R. 1994 *The god of modernity. The development of nationalism in western Europe*. Oxford: Berg

Llorente, Angel 1995 *Arte e ideología en el franquismo (1936–1951)*. Madrid: Visor

London, John 1995 'Competing together in fascist Europe: sport in early Francoism' in Gunter Berghaus (ed.), *Fascist theatre. Comparative studies on the politics and aesthetics of performance*. Oxford: Berg

López Aguirre, Elena 1996 *del txistu a la telecaster. Crónica del rock vasco*. Vitoria: Alanai

López del Olmo, Eduardo 1930 'El Bacalao a la Vizcaína', *Vida Vasca VII*, p. 87

López de Maturana, Jose 1904 'El pintor Diaz Olano', *La Baskonia* 20 August, pp. 514–15

Luengo Teixidor, Félix 1999 'De la taberna a la sociedad popular: ocio y sociabilidad donostiarra en la primera mitad del siglo XIX (1813–1863)' in Luis Castells (ed.) *El Rumor de lo Cotidiano. Estudios sobre el País Vasco Contemporáneo*, Bilbao: Universidad del País Vasco

—— 2001 *San Sebastián. La vida cotidiana de una ciudad. De su destrucción a la Ciudad Contemporánea*. San Sebastián: Txertoa

Maalouf, Amin 2000 *On identity*. Trans. Barbara Bray. London: Harvill

MacClancy, Jeremy 1992 *Consuming culture*. London: Chapmans

—— 1988 'The culture of radical Basque nationalism', *Anthropology Today*, October, pp. 34–8

—— 1989 'GAC: Militant Carlist activism under the ageing Franco', in W. Douglass (ed.), *Essays in Basque social anthropology and history*. Reno: University of Nevada Press, pp. 140–54

—— 1993 'At play with identity in the Basque Arena' in Sharon Macdonald (ed.) *Inside European identities*. Oxford: Berg, pp. 84–97

—— 1996a 'Bilingualism and multinationalism in the Basque Country' in A. Smith and C. Mar-Molinero (eds) *Nationalism and national identity in Iberian Peninsula: Competing and conflicting identities*. Oxford: Berg, pp. 207–20

—— (ed.) 1996b *Sport, identity and ethnicity*. Oxford: Berg

—— 1997 'The museum as a site of contest. The Bilbao Guggenheim' *Focaal*, no. 29, pp. 91–100

—— 1999 'Navarra: historical realities, present myths, future possibilities' in William A. Douglass, C. Urza, L. White and J. Zulaika (eds) *Basque Politics and Nationalism on the Eve of the Millennium*. Reno: Basque Studies Program, University of Nevada, Reno, pp. 127–54

—— 2000 *The decline of Carlism*. Basque Book Series. Reno: University of Nevada Press

—— 2002 'Taking people seriously', in J.MacClancy (ed.) *Exotic no more. Anthropology on the front lines*. Chicago: University of Chicago Press, pp. 1–14

—— 2003 'Anthropology: the latest form of evening entertainment', in David Bradshaw (ed.) *A concise companion to modernism*. Oxford: Blackwell, pp. 75–94

—— 2004 'Food, identity, identification' in H. Macbeth and J. MacClancy (eds) *Researching food habits. Methods and problems*. Oxford: Berghahn, pp. 63–74

—— 2005 'Imaging the Basques: anthropological perspectives' in S. Leone and J. MacClancy (eds) *Imaging the Basques: outsiders' views of the Basques*, Oxford Basque Series, no.1. San Sebastian: Eusko-Ikaskuntza, pp. 101–18

Macdonald, Nancy 2001 *The graffiti subculture. Youth, masculinity and identity in London and New York*. London: Palgrave

Macdonald, Sharon 1997 *Reimagining culture. Histories, identities and Gaelic Renaissance*. Oxford: Berg

MacEahern, Scott 2000 'Genes, tribes and African history', *Current Anthropology*, 41, no. 3, pp. 357–84

Macías Muñoz, Olga 2002 'Los chacolies de Bilbao a finales del siglo XIX', *Euskonews & Media* 168, http://suse00.su.ehu.es/euskonews/0168zbk. Accessed 25 May 2002

—— 2005 'Los banquetes en Bilbao, festejos y homenajes culinarios (1883–1921)', *Euskonews and Media*, *314*, http://www.euskonews.com/0314zbk/gaia/gaia31404es.html. Accessed 18 September 2005

Maeztu, Gustavo de 1915 'Arte. Opiniones', *La Tarde* 25 November

Magallón Botaya, María de los Angeles 1997 'La red viaria romana en el País Vasco', *Isturitz* 8, pp. 207–31

Mainer, José-Carlos 1993 'La invención estética de las periferias' in C. Pena (ed.) *Centro y Periferia en la Modernización de la Pintura Española (1880–1918)* Madrid: Ministerio de Cultura. pp. 26–33

Mallory, J.P. 1989 *In search of the Indo-Europeans. Language, archaeology and myth.* London: Thames and Hudson

Manco, Tristan 2004 *Street logos.* London: Thames and Hudson

Mandiola, Ramón 1969, 'Prólogo a la segunda edición' in Terrachet 1969, pp. 7–8

Manterola Armisen, Pedro 1986 'La pintura antigua y moderna de Gustavo de Maeztu', *Panorama* no. 6. Pamplona: Gobierno de Navarra, pp. 7–24

Manzano, C., Aguirre, A.I., Iriondo, M., Osaba, L., and de la Rúa, C. 1996 'Genetic polymorphisms of the Basques from Gipuzkoa: genetic heterogeneity of the Basque population', *Annals of Human Biology*, 23, 4, pp. 285–96

Manzano Basabe, C., de la Rúa Vaca, C., and Torre Barrueta, M. J. 1987 'Distribución de los grupos sanguineos ABO y Rh en una muestra de población alavesa. Estudio preliminar', *Eusko-Ikaskuntza. Sociedad de Estudios Vascos. Homenaje al Dr. José Maria Basabe. Cuadernos de sección Antropología y Etnografiia*, vol. 4, pp. 315–23

Manzanos Bilbao, César 2000 'Arqueología de la discriminación racista. Investigación aplicada a la sociedad vasca', *Zainak. Cuadernos de antropología urbana*, 19, pp. 61–96

Maraña, Félix 1999 *Jorge Oteiza, elogio del descontento.* Donosita: Bermingham

Marañon, Gregorio 1933 'Prólogo' to *La Cocina de Nicolasa* by Nicolasa Pradera. Madrid: Mayfe

Marquis, Alice Goldfarb 1991 *The art biz. The covert world of collectors, dealers, auction houses, museums and critics.* Chicago: Contemporary Books

Marks, Jonathan 2002 'Contemporary bio-anthropology. When the trailing edge of anthropology meets the cutting edge of bioethics', *Anthropology Today*, 18, 4, pp. 3–7

Martínez Gorriarán, Carlos, and Agirre Arriaga, Imanol 1995 *Estética de la diferencia. El arte vasco y el problema de la identidad 1882–1966.* Irun: Alberdania

Martínez Flamarique, Jesús 1972 'Pío Baroja y la Gastronomía', *Boletín de la Cofradia Vasca de Gastronomía VI*, pp. 58–75

Martínez Veiga, Ubaldo 2001 *El Ejido. Discriminación, exclusión social y racismo.* Madrid: Catarta

Maytia Romero, Danilo, and Fernández, Renee 2004 'Pintores vascos en Montevideo', *Euskonews and Media 271*, http://www.euskonews.com/0271lzbk/kosmo27101.html. Accessed 8 October 2004

McDonald, Maryon 1989 *'We are not French!' Language, culture and identity in Brittany.* London: Routledge

Medina, Xavier 2002 'Restaurantes y tabernas vasos en Barcelona: identidad y proyección de la cocina vasca', *Euskonews and Media* 179, http://suse00.su.ehu.es/euskonews/0179zbk. Accessed 13 September 2002

Merino, Juan Luis 1984, 'Pasado y presente de una hincha rojiblanca' in *Athletic Club 1986*, vol. 3, pp. 116–17

Mestaye de Echagüe, Maria 1935 *Platos escogidos de la Cocina Vasca.* Bilbao: Artes Graficas Grijelmo

Michelena, Mourlane 1915 'Arte. Opiniones', *La Tarde* 1 December

Mingolarra, José Antonio 1990 'Deporte e identidad cultural: el caso vasco'. Paper given in May 1990 at 'Le foot ball et l'Europe' conference, European University Institute, Florence.

Monahan, Jane 1992 'Art that sets the Basques apart', *The Times* 13 November, p. 40

Montes, Andia, L. A. 1990 *Memorias de un chico de pueblo.* Pamplona (privately published)

Morphy, Howard 1992 'Aesthetics in a cross-cultural perspective: some reflections on Native American basketry', *Journal of Anthropological Society of Oxford* 23, no.1, pp. 1–16

Moujan Otaño, Magdalena 1980 'Guta Gutarrah', in Bernard Goorden and Alfred E. van Vogt (eds) *Lo mejor de la ciencia ficción latinoamericana.* Barcelona: Martínez Roca, pp. 160–72

Moulin, Raymonde 1987 *The French art market. A sociological view.* New Brunswick: Rutgers University Press [orig. pub. 1967 as *Le marché de la peinture en France.* Paris: Minuit].

Mourant, A.E. 1948 'Basque blood groups', *Nature* 162, 27

Mourant, A.E., Kopec, A.C. and Domaniewska-Sobczak, K. 1976 *The distribution of human blood groups and other polymorphisms.* Oxford: Oxford University Press

Moya, Adelina 1982 *Nicolas de Lekuona. Obra fotografica.* Bilbao: Museo de Bellas Artes de Bilbao

—— 1986 'El arte Guipuzcoano entre la renovación y la innovación' in A. Moya, J. Sáenz de Gorbea, and J.A. Sanz Esquide (eds) *Arte y artistas vascos de los años 30.* San Sebastian: Diputación Foral de Guipuzcoa, pp. 139–250

Mugica, Jose Maria 1982, 'El Athletic: un club de leyenda' in La Caja de Ahorros de Bilbao (ed.) *Un siglo de fútbol, pelota y remo en Vizcaya.* Bilbao: La Caja de Ahorros de Bilbao

Mur Pastor, Pilar 1985 *La Asociación de Artistas Vascos.* Bilbao: Museo de Bellas Artes de Bilbao, Caja de Ahorros Vizcaina

—— 1988 *Las Artes Gráficas en Euzkadi y Cataluña (1888-1936).* Bilbao: Gobierno Vasco

—— 1990 'Coleccionismo privado y mecenazgo en el Bilbao de principios del siglo XX' in J.M. González Cembellín and A.R. Ortega Berruguete (eds) *Bilbao, arte eta historia. Bilbao, arte e historia, tomo 2.* Bilbao: Diputación Foral de Bizkaia, pp. 153–65

Nelken, Margarita 1981 'Apostillas a *La trama del Arte Vasco* de "Juan de la Encina"' in *La Trama del Arte Vasco y selección de articulos publicados en Hermes* by Juan de la Encina, edited by Enrique Lafuente Ferrari. (Orig. pub. in *Hermes* April 1921.) Madrid: Espasa-Calpe, pp. 19–23

Novo González, Javier 2006 'Ignacio Zuloaga y su utilización por el franquismo', *Ondare,* 25, pp. 233–43

OJPP (Organización Jefatura Provincial de Propaganda) 1939 *Texto programatico exposición patrocinada por La Excma. Diputación de Vizcaya y El Excmo. Ayuntamiento de Bilbao* (Reprinted in Guasch 1985 *Arte y ideología,* pp. 292–3)

O'Leary, Brendan 1998 'Ernest Gellner's diagnoses of nationalism: a critical overview, or, what is living and what is dead in Ernest Gellner's philosophy of nationalism?' in Hall 1998b, *The state of the nation,* pp. 40–88

Ortuzar, E. and E. Rodrigalvarez 1987 'Será dificil que el fútbol vasco vuelva tan arriba', *Deia. X aniversario 1977/1987.* 7 June

Oteiza, Jorge 1963 *Quousque tandem...! Ensayo de interpretación del alma vasca.* Zarautz: Aunameñdi

—— 1983 *Ejercicios espirituales en un tunel.* San Sebastian: Txertoa

Ott, Sandra 1981 *The circle of mountains: a Basque sheepherding community.* Oxford: Oxford University Press

Pablo, Santiago de 1995 *Trabajo, diversión y vida cotidiana. El País Vasco en los años treinta.* Vitoria: Papeles de Zabalanda

Pancorbo, M. M. de, Aguirre, A. L, Vicario, A., Lostao, C. M. and Mazon, L. J. 1988 'Genética y estructura de la población vizcaina', *Munibe,* Suplemento, no.6, pp. 249–59

Papadakis, Yiannis 1998 'Greek Cypriot narratives of history and collective identity: nationalism as a collective process', *American Ethnologist* 25, no. 2, pp. 149–65

Parry, John and Bloch, Maurice 1989 'Introduction: money and the morality of exchange' in Bloch and Parry (eds) *Money and the morality of exchange,* pp. 1–32

Pelay Orozco, M. 1978 *Oteiza. Su vida, su obra, su pensamiento.* Bilbao: La Gran Enciclopedia Vasca

Pena, Carmen 1993a 'Introduccion' in C. Pena (ed.) *Centro y Periferia en la Modernización de la Pintura Española (1880–1918)* Madrid: Ministerio de Cultura, pp. 18–25

—— 1993b 'La Modernización del Paisaje Realista: Castilla como Centro de la Imagen de España' in C. Pena (ed.) *Centro y Periferia en la Modernización de la Pintura Española (1880–1918)* Madrid: Ministerio de Cultura, pp. 42–8

Pena, J. A. 1986 'Marital migration and distribution of surnames in Orozco valley (Basque country)', *Antropología Portugesa* 4/5, pp. 283–9

—— 1987 'Estimación de la consanguinidad a partir de dispensas y de isonomia en el valle de Orozco (Vizcaya), 1880–1979', *Eusko-Ikaskuntza. Sociedad de Estudios Vascos. Homenaje al Dr. José Maria Basabe. Cuadernos de sección Antropología-Etnografia* 4, pp. 347–60

—— 1988 *Estructura demográfica y genética de la población del valle de Orozco (Vizcaya). Siglos XVI–XX* Memoria, Universidad del País Vasco. (Unpublished.)

Peñalver, Xabier 1999 *Sobre el origen de los vascos. Las fuentes arqueológicas.* San Sebastian: Txertoa

Pérez-Agote, Alfonso 1987 *El nacionalismo vasco a la salida del franquismo.* Madrid: Siglo XXI

Pérez Castroviejo, Pedro M. 2000 'Consumo, dieta y nutrición de grupos populares. La alimentación durante la industrialización de Vizcaya', *Zainak. Cuadernos de antropología-etnografia,* 20, pp. 211–26

Phillips, Susan A. 1999 *Wallbangin'. Graffiti and gangs in L.A.* Chicago: University of Chicago Press

Piazza, A., Cappello, N., Olivetti, E. and Rendine, S. 1988 'The Basques in Europe: A genetic analysis', *Munibe,* Suplemento, no. 6, pp. 169–77

Pilcher, Jeffrey M. 1998 *¡Que vivan los tamales! Food and the making of Mexican identity*. Albuquerque: University of New Mexico Press

Piquero Zarauz, Santiago 2000 'Alimentación, nutrición y salud en la Guipúzcoa del antiguo régimen. Unas consideraciones', *Zainak. Cuadernos de antropología-etnografía*, 20, pp. 227–41

Pisarro, Camille 1925 *Letters to His Son Lucien*, edited by John Rewald, translated by Lionel Abel. London: Kegan Paul, trench, Trübner

Plattner, Stuart 1996 *High art down home. An economic ethnography of a local art market*. Chicago: University of Chicago Press

Porres Marijuán, María Rosario 1995 'Alimentación y abastecimientos en Vitoria (siglos XVI–XVIII) in José Maria Imizcoz Beunza (ed.) *La Vida Cotidiana en Vitoria en la Edad Moderna y Contemporánea*, Donostia/San Sebastian: Txertoa, pp. 214–57

Prada, Manuel 1995 'Sagardotegi zaharrak (Viejas sidrerías)', *Boletín de la Cofradía Vasca de Gastronomía*, no. 33, Enero, pp. 85–9

Prieto, Indalecio 1991 *Pasado y futuro de Bilbao*. Barcelona: Fundación Indalecio Prieto

Quintana-Murci, Lluís, Semino, Ornella, Minch, Eric, Passarimo, Giuseppe, Brega, Agnese and Santachiara-Benerecetti, A. Silvana 1999 'Further characteristis of proto-European Y chromosomes', *European Journal of Human Genetics* 7, pp. 603–8

Rebato, Ester 1985a 'Analisis de las variaciones somatométricas entre poblaciones femininas', *Kobie (Serie Ciencias Naturales)*, XV, pp. 217–21

—— 1985b 'Comparación de cinco poblaciones masculinas para un conjunto de variables métricas cefalofaciales', *Principe de Viana. Suplemento de Ciencias VI*, no. 6, pp. 189–95

—— 1986a 'Caracteres métricos cefalofaciales en población vasca: comparaciones interprovinciales', *Boletín de la Sociedada Española de Antropología Biológica*, no. 7, pp. 59–70

—— 1986b 'Variation du mode d'attache du lobe de l'oreille chez les basques', *Bulletin et Memoires de la Société d'Anthropologie de Paris*, 3, pp. 177–80

—— 1987a 'Estudio de diversos caracteres de la region bucal en Vizcaya y Guipúzcoa', *Kobie (Serie Ciencias Naturales) XVI*, pp. 315–22

—— 1987b 'Caracteres somatométricos y fisiológicos (menarquia y menopausia) en mujeres adultas vascas', *Actas del V Congreso Español de Antropología Biológica (Léon)*, pp. 193–205

—— 1987c 'Estudios de la estatura en población vasca', *Eusko-Ikaskuntza. Sociedad de Estudios Vascos. Homenaje al Dr. José Maria Basabe. Cuadernos de sección Antropología-Etnografía*, 4, pp. 361–72

—— 1987d 'Estudio antropológico de la mujer vizcaina', *Arquivos do Museu Bocage I*, no. 7, pp. 91–9

—— 1987e 'Skin colour in the Basque population', *Anthropologischer Anzeiger* 45, pp. 49–55

—— 1987f 'Aspectos métricos y morfoscópicos de la region nasal en vascos', *Munibe (Antropología y Arqueología)* 39, pp. 29–37

—— 1988 'Ages at menarche and menopause in Basque women', *Collegium Anthropologicum* 12, no. 1, pp. 147–9

Rebato, Ester and Calderón, Rosario 1988 'Antropometria de la region cefalofacial del hombre vasco', *Munibe*, Suplemento no. 6, pp. 261–7

—— 1990 'Incidence of red-green colour blindness in the Basque population', *Anthropologischer Anzeiger*, 48, pp. 145–55

Reitlinger, Gerald 1961 *The economics of taste. The rise and fall of picture prices 1760–1960*. London: Barrie and Rockcliff

Rementería Arnaiz, Iskandar 2006 'Consideraciones sobre el arte y el espacio en la obra de Chillida y Heidegger', *Ondare* 25, pp. 367–75

Richards, Audrey 1932 *Hunger and work in a savage tribe: a functional study of nutrition among the southern Bantu*. London: Routledge

Richardson, John 1992 'Go go Guggenheim' *New York Review of Books* 16 July, pp. 18–22

Rilova Jericó, Carlos 2003a 'El pan en la antigua cocina vasca', *Euskonews and Media*, 211, 23–30 May

—— 2003b 'El plato fuerte de la antigua cocina vasca: carne, pescado y legumbres', *Euskonews and Media*, 213, 6–13 June

Rincon, Luciano 1985 *ETA (1974–1984)*. Barcelona: Plaza & Janes

Roberts, Michael 1994 *Between hopes and memories: a Spanish journey*. London: Picador

Roca, A. 1986, 'Carismático Athletic' in Athletic Club 1986, vol. 2, pp. 196–7

Rodrigalvarez, E. 1986 'Carta rojiblanca a la Cibeles' in Athletic Club, vol. 3, pp. 96–7

Rodriguez, Arantxa 2004 'Reinventing the city: miracles and images in urban revitalization in Bilbao'. Paper given at 'Learning from the Guggenheim' conference, Center for Basque Studies, University of Nevada, Reno, June.

Rodríguez Hernandorena, A. 1988 'Mating patterns and fertility in a Basque shepherding community, 1800 to 1975' Unpublished D.Phil. thesis, Oxford University

Ros, Xon de 2002 'The Guggenheim Museum Bilbao: high art and popular culture' in J.

Labanyi (ed.) *Constructing identity in contemporary Spain*. Oxford: Oxford University Press, pp. 280–93

Rosiques, Javier 2001 'Antropología biológica de la población vasca: la población actual y su futuro', *Euskonews and Media*, 119, http://www.euskonews.com/10119zbk/11901es.html Accessed 27 iv 2001

Ruíz Idarraga, Rosa 1990 'El complejo Auriñaco-Perigordiense en el País Vasco', *Munibe (Antropólogia –Arkeólogia)* 42, pp. 23–32

Ruiz Zapatero, Gonzalo 1995 'El poblamiento del primer milenio a.c. en los Pirineos' in Jaume Bertranpetit and Elisenda Vives (eds) *Muntayes I Població. El passat dels Pirineus des d'una perspective multidisciplinària*. Andorra La Vella: Centre de Trobada de la Cultures Pirinenques, pp. 85–105

Sáenz de Gorbea, Javier 1986 'Crónica de hechos y prácticas artísticas en Vizcaya 1931/1937' in A. Moya, J. Sáenz de Gorbea and J.A. Sanz Esquide (eds) *Arte y artistas vascos de los años 30* San Sebastian: Diputacion Foral de Guipuzcoa, pp. 251–26

—— 1990 'Arte en Bilbao (1945–1989). Una aproximación' in J. M. González Cembellin and A. R. Ortega Berruguete (eds) *Bilbo, Arte eta Historia. Bilbao, Arte e Historia, tomo 2*, Bilbao: Diputación Foral de Bizkaia. pp. 257–73

San Martín, Francisco Javier 2002 'Actualidad de la última pintura vasca (1995–2000)', *XV Congreso de Estudios Vascos II*. Donostia: Eusko-Ikaskuntza, pp. 903–20

Sánchez Masas, Rafael 1915 a 'La pintura de los hermanos Zubiaurre', *El Pueblo Vasco* 18 November

—— 1915b 'De Rafael Sánchez Masas al Señor X . . .', *El Pueblo Vasco* 19 November

—— 1915c 'Al Señor X', *El Pueblo Vasco* 23 November

—— 1993 *Vaga memoria de cien años y otros papeles*. Bilbao: El Tilo (*Vaga memoria de cien años* orig. pub. 1939 in *Vértice*)

Sánchez-Ostiz, Miguel 1998 *Palabras Cruzadas*. Zaragoza: Les Tres Sorores, Prames

—— 2001 *El corazón de la niebla*. Barcelona: Seix Barral

—— 2002 '*Última estación, Pamplona*'. Pamplona: Pamiela

Santona, H. 1987 'Sobre la gastronomia de Navarra', *Navarra Hoy*, 28 June, p. viii

Sarobe Pueyo, V. M. 1995 *La cocina popular navarra*. Pamplona: Caja de Ahorros de Navarra

Sarrailh de Ihartza, Fernando (pseud. of Federico Krutwig) 1955 *Vasconia. Estudio dialectico de una nacionalidad*. Buenos Aires: Norbait

Sarrionandia Gurtubay, Magdalena 1989 *Historia de los balnearios de Bizkaia*. Bilbao: Diputación Foral de Bizkaia

Savater, Fernando 2001 *Perdonen las molestias. Crónica de una batalla sin armas contra las armas*. Madrid: Ediciones El País

—— 2003 *Mira por dónde. Autobiografía razonada*. Madrid: Taurus

Schmidt, Karl 1987 'The two ancient Iberias from the linguistic point of view', *Procedimientos del IV Coloquio Lenguas Prehistoricas Hispanicas*, Veleia 2–3, pp. 105–21

Schneider, Arnd, and Wright, Christopher (eds) 2006 *Contemporary art and anthropology*. Oxford: Berg

Serrano Larráyoz, Fernando 2000 'Cocina y gastronomía en el Hostal de Blanca de Navarra a mediados del siglo XV (1433)', *Zainak. Cuadernos de antropología-etnografía 20*, pp. 243–53

Shaw, Duncan 1987 *Futbol y Franquismo*. Madrid: Alianza

Smith, Anthony D. 1991 *National identity*. Harmondsworth: Penguin,

Smith, Paul Julian 2003 *Contemporary Spanish culture. TV, fashion, art and film*. Cambridge: Polity

Sokal, Robert R., Oden, Neal L., and Thomson, Barbara A. 1999a 'A problem with synthetic maps', *Human Biology*, 71, pp. 1–13

—— 1999b 'Problems with Synthetic Maps Remain: A Reply to Rendine et al.' *Human Biology*, 71, pp. 447–53

Sota, A. de la 1918a 'Los restaurantes de Bilbao. no. 1. La Bilbaina', *Hermes*, no. 17

—— 1918b 'Los restaurantes de Bilbao. no. 2. Club Maritimo de Abra', *Hermes*, no. 18

—— 1918c 'Los restaurantes de Bilbao. no. 3. "El Suizo"', *Hermes*, no. 19, pp. 60–2

—— 1918d 'Los restaurantes de Bilbao. no. 4. Real Sporting Club', *Hermes*, no. 23, pp. 101–2

—— 1918e 'Los restaurantes de Bilbao. no. 5. Torróntegui', *Hermes*, no. 29, pp. 229–30

Sordo, Enrique 1987 *España, entre trago y bocado. Un viaje literario y gastronómico*. Barcelona: Planeta

Staniszewski, Mary Anne 1995 *Believing is seeing. Creating the culture of art*. New York: Penguin

Stocking, G. W. (ed.) 1988 *Bones, blood and behaviour. Essays on biological anthropology*, History of Anthropology, no. 5. Madison, Wisconsin: University of Wisconsin Press

Starkie, Walter 1934 *Spanish raggle-taggle. Adventures with a fiddle in North Spain*. London: Murray

Straus, Lawrence Guy 1990 'Human occupation of Euskalherria during the Last glacial maximum: the Basque solutrean', *Munibe (Antropólogia –Arkeólogia)* 42, pp. 33–40

Sullivan, J. 1988 *ETA and Basque nationalism. The fight for Euskadi 1896–1986*. London: Routledge

Sutton, David 1997 'Local names, foreign claims: family inheritance and national heritage on a Greek island', *American Ethnologist* 24, no. 2, pp. 415–37
Teague, Ken 1993 *Mr. Horniman and the tea trade.* London: Horniman Museum
Tellaeche, Julian de 'Arte. Opiniones', *La Tarde* 26 November
Tellechea Idigoras, J. Ignacio 1987 [1908] *Zuloaga y Unamuno. Glosas y unas cartas ineditas.* Zumaia, Guipuzcoa: Museo Ignacio Zuloaga
Tellitu, Alberto, Iñaki Esteban and González Carrera Antonio, José 1997 *El Milagro Guggenheim. Una Ilusión de Alto Riesgo.* Bilbao: Diario El Correo
Terol, Óscar 2005 *Todos nacemos vascos.* Madrid: Santillana
Terrachet, Enrique (1969), *Historia del Athletic de Bilbao. 'Caso único en el fútbol mundial'.* Bilbao: La Gran Enciclopedia Vasca
—— (1970), *Historia del Athletic de Bilbao. 'Caso único en el fútbol mundial'.* Edición Popular, Bilbao: La Gran Enciclopedia Vasca
Terrio, Susan J. 2000 *Crafting the culture and history of French chocolate.* Berkeley: University of California Press
Tolosana, Vidal 1915 'Arte. Opiniones', *La Tarde* 4 December
Tonkin, Elizabeth, McDonald, Maryon, and Chapman, Malcolm (eds) *History and ethnicity.* London: Tavistock
Torre, M. J., de la Rúa, C. and Basabe, J. M. 1987 'Estudio comparativo del sistema Kell en tres provincias vascas: Álava, Guipúzcoa y Vizcaya', *Eusko-Ikaskuntza. Sociedad de Estudios Vascos. Homenaje al Dr. José Maria Basabe. Cuadernos de sección Antropología-Etnografía* 4, pp. 405–15.
Torre, M. J., Manzano, C. and de la Rua, C. '1988 'Grupos sanguineos de la población autoctona de Alava', *Munibe*, Suplemento, no. 6, pp. 295–302
Torre, Quintin de 1915 'Arte. Opiniones', *La Tarde* 27 November
Tremlett, Giles 2006 *Ghosts of Spain. Travels through a country's hidden past.* London: Faber and Faber
Trubek, Amy B. 2000 *Haute cuisine. How the French invented the culinary profession.* Philadelphia: University of Pennsylvania Press
Txillida, Pedro 1999 'El arte es casi magia', *El Mundo* 24 April p. 11
Ugalde, Marcelino 2002 'What is Basque Cuisine: A Culinary History', *Journal of Basque Studies in America*, XXII, pp. 41–8
Ugalde, Martin 1975 *Hablando con Chillida, escultor vasco.* San Sebastian: Txertoa
Ugarte, Luxio 1995 *Chillida: dudas y preguntas.* Donostia/San Sebastian: Erein
—— 1996 *La reconstrucción de la identidad cultural vasca.* Madrid: Siglo Veintiuno
Ulibarrena Arellano, José 1990 *Museo etnográfico del reino de Pamplona.* Pamplona: n.p.
—— 1992 *La plastica étnica euskeriana.* Pamplona: n.p.
Untermann, J. 1990 *Monumenta Linguarum Hispanicarum*, vol. 3, pt. 1, Wiesbaden: Dr Ludwig Reichert Verlag
Unzueta, Patxo 1982 'Panizo', *El País*, 12 June
—— 1983a 'A mi el pelotón', *El País*, 24 January
—— 1983b 'Rompecascos', *El País*, 4 May
—— 1986 *A mi el peloton*, San Sebastian: Baroja
—— 1999 'Fútbol y nacionalismo vasco' in Santiago Segurola (ed.) *Fútbol y pasiones políticas.* Madrid: Temas de debate, pp. 147–67
Uría Irastorza, J. 1983 'La Sidra' in *Cocina Vasca. Nuestra Cocina por nuestros mejores cocineros.* San Sebastian: Sendoa, pp. 319–26
Uriarte, Iñaki 1996 'Guggenheim go home' *El Mundo (del País Vasco)* 17 April
Uriarte, Juan Maria (1986) 'Un equipo para un pueblo' in Athletic Club 1986, vol. 5, pp. 196–7
Urla, Jacqueline (1993) 'Contesting modernities. Language standardization and the production of an ancient/modern Basque culture', *Critique of Anthropology* 13, pp. 101–18
—— 1995 'Outlaw language. Creating alternative public spheres in Basque free radio', *Pragmatics*, 5, no. 2, pp. 245–61
—— 1999 'Basque language revival and popular culture' in W. Douglass, C. Urza, L. White and J. Zulaika (eds) *Basque Cultural Studies.* Reno: Basque Studies Program, University of Nevada, Reno, pp. 44–62
Urquijo, Javier 1998 'Jorge Oteiza y la Escuela Vasca', *El Mundo*, 21 October, p. 5
Urteaga Artigas, Mercedes 2003 'Arqueología emocional. Lección de Ingreso en la Real Sociedad Bascongada de los Amigos del País', *Boletín de la Real Sociedad Bascongada de los Amigos del País*, Suplemento 17-G, pp. 19–46
—— 2004 'Antigüedad romana en Hondarribia y en la desmbocure del Bidasoa' in José Luis Orella (ed.) *Historia de Hondarribia.* Hondarribia: Ayuntamiento de Hondarribia, pp. 23–48
Valle-Lersundi, Alvaro 1963a 'La Sociedad Vascongada de los Amigos del País en su segunda

epoca y la gastronomía', *Boletín de la Cofradia Vasca de Gastronomía I*, pp. 22–5
—— 1963b 'Menus Finiseculares', *Boletín de la Cofradia Vasca de Gastronomía I*, pp. 25–7
—— 1967 'Un desafio culinario en 1895', *Boletín de la Cofradia Vasca de Gastronomía III*, pp. 100–4
—— 1970 'Un menu donostiarra histórico', *Boletín de la Cofradia Vasca de Gastronomía IV*, pp. 80–1
Viar, Javier 2005 'Guggenheim Bilbao: partner in the arts – a view from the Fine Arts Museum of Bilbao' in Zulaika and Guasch (eds), *Learning from the Guggenheim*, pp. 97–112.
Videgain, Juan 1960 'La Cocina Vasca', *Vida Vasca*, pp. 113–19
Wade, Peter 2002 *Race, nature and culture. An anthropological perspective*. London: Pluto
Walton, John 1998 'Reconstructing crowds: the rise of Association Football as a spectator sport in San Sebastian, 1915–32', *International Journal of the History of Sport*, 15, no. 1, April, pp. 27–53
—— 2001 'Basque football rivalries in the twentieth century' in Gary Armstrong and Richard Giulianotti (eds) *Fear and loathing in world football*. Oxford: Berg, pp. 119–33
Walton, John, and Smith, Jenny 1994 'The rhetoric of community and the business of pleasure: the San Sebastián waiters' strike of 1920', *International Review of Social History*, 39, pp. 1–31
Watson, Peter 1992 *From Manet to Manhattan. The rise of the modern art market*. London: Random House
Weiner, James (ed.) 1994 *Aesthetics is a cross-cultural category*. Manchester: Group for Debates in Anthropological Theory, University of Manchester
Wilk, Richard R. 1993 'Beauty and the feast: official and visceral nationalism in Belize', *Ethnos*, 3–4, pp. 294–315
Wolfe, Tom 1970 *Radical chic and mau-mauing the flak catchers*. New York: Farrar, Straus and Giroux
'X' 1915a 'De arte una pregunta', *La Tarde* 11 November
—— 1915b 'De arte. La estética del País Vasco', *La Tarde* 19 November
—— 1915c 'De arte. Al Señor D. Rafael Sánchez Masas', *La Tarde* 22 November
—— 1916d 'De arte. Al Señor D. Rafael Sánchez Masas', *La Tarde* 24 November
Zaldua, Iban 2005 *Si Sabino viviría*. Madrid: Lengua de Trapo
Zapata, Lydia 2001 'El origen de las sociedades agrícolas en el País Vasco litoral : datos arqueológicos', in *XV Congreso de Estudios Vascos*, I, Donosti: Eusko-Ikaskuntza, pp. 153–59
Zapiain Irastorza, José 1947 'De las clasicas sidrerías con sus "Kupelas" a las modernas sociedades populares', *Vida Vasca XXIV*, pp. 102–4
Zeldin, Theodore 1980 *France 1848–1945: Taste and corruption*. Oxford: Oxford University Press
Zozaya, Antonio 1935 'Prólogo (a modo de aperitivos)' in *La Cocina Vasca (Laurak-Bat)* by Ignacio Domenech. Barcelona: Publicaciones selectas de cocina, pp.5–13
Zubialde, I. 1915a 'Hablemos de Zuloaga', *Euzkadi* 20 February
—— 1915b 'Sigamos hablando de arte', *Euzkadi* 1 March
Zubiaurre, Valentin and Ramon de 1915 'Arte. Opiniones', *La Tarde* 29 November
Zubillaga, Eliseo Gil 1990 'La Romanización en Alava, valoración arqueológica', *Munibe (Antropólogia –Arkeólogia)* 42, pp. 327–36
Zudaire Huarte, C. 1982 'Consanguinidad en Baztan, Santesteban y Cinco Villas', *Cuadernos de Etnología y Etnografía de Navarra XIV*, no. 40, pp. 723–51
—— 1984 'Consanguinidad en los valles de Roncal, Aezcoa y Salazar', *Cuadernos de Etnología y Etnografía de Navarra XVI*, no. 44, pp. 107–27
Zulaika, Joseba 1988 *Basque violence. Metaphor and sacrament*. University of Nevada Press, Reno.
—— 1991 'Prologue' in Luis de Barandiarán (ed.) *A view from the witch's cave: folktales of the Pyrenees*. Reno: University of Nevada Press, pp. xiii–xvi
—— 1996 *Del Cromañon al Carnaval*. Donostia: Erein
—— 1997 *Crónica de una Seducción. El Museo Guggenheim Bilbao*. Madrid: Nerea
—— 2003a 'Anthropologists, artists, terrorists: the Basque holiday from history', *Journal of Spanish Cultural Studies*, 4, no. 2, pp. 139–50
—— 2003b 'Introduction: Oteiza's return from the future' in Zualika, J. (ed.) *Oteiza's selected writings*. Center for Basque Studies, Occasional paper series no. 9. Reno: University of Nevada Press, pp. 9–81
—— 2005 'Desiring Bilbao: the Krensification of the museum and its discontents' in A.M. Guasch and J. Zulaika (eds) *Learning from the Guggenheim*, pp. 149–70
Zvelebil, 1988 'General and cultural diversity in Europe: a comment on Cavalli-Sforza', *Journal of Anthropological Research*, 54, pp. 411–16

Index